HowExpert Guide to Stamp Collecting

The Ultimate Handbook for Starting a Stamp Collection, Identifying Rare Stamps, and Preserving Philatelic Treasures

HowExpert

For more tips related to this topic, visit HowExpert.com/stampcollecting.

Recommended Resources

- HowExpert.com – How To Guides on All Topics from A to Z.
- HowExpert.com/free – Free HowExpert Email Newsletter.
- HowExpert.com/books – HowExpert Books
- HowExpert.com/courses – HowExpert Courses
- HowExpert.com/clothing – HowExpert Clothing
- HowExpert.com/membership – HowExpert Membership Site
- HowExpert.com/affiliates – HowExpert Affiliate Program
- HowExpert.com/jobs – HowExpert Jobs
- HowExpert.com/writers – Write About Your #1 Passion/Knowledge/Expertise & Become a HowExpert Author.
- HowExpert.com/resources – Additional HowExpert Recommended Resources
- YouTube.com/HowExpert – Subscribe to HowExpert YouTube.
- Instagram.com/HowExpert – Follow HowExpert on Instagram.
- Facebook.com/HowExpert – Follow HowExpert on Facebook.
- TikTok.com/@HowExpert – Follow HowExpert on TikTok.

Publisher's Foreword

Dear HowExpert Reader,

HowExpert publishes quick 'how to' guides on all topics from A to Z.

Our mission is to make a positive impact in the world for all topics from A to Z…one HowExpert book at a time!

We are dedicated to creating quick, easy-to-read 'how to' guides that are structured, comprehensive, and approachable, empowering our readers to effortlessly explore and learn about their passions and interests in a meaningful and enjoyable way.

We hope our HowExpert books bring you immense value and make a positive impact on your life. Every reader, including you, plays a vital role in helping us fulfill our mission of making a positive difference in the world across all areas of interest from A to Z.

If you enjoyed one of our HowExpert guides, we would greatly appreciate it if you could take a moment to share your feedback on the platform where you discovered this book.

Thank you, and I wish you success and happiness in all aspects of your life.

To your success,

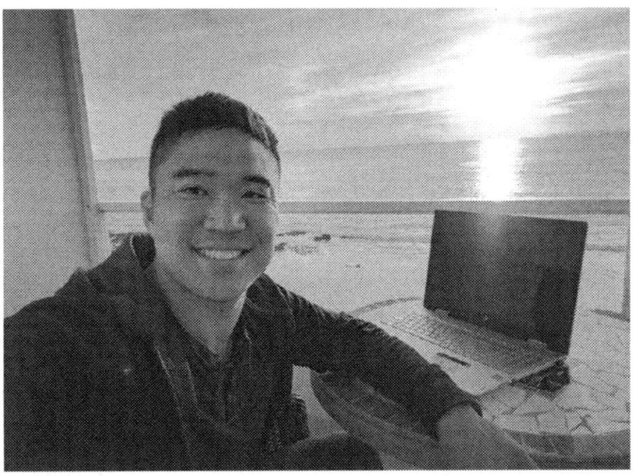

BJ Min
Founder & Publisher of HowExpert
HowExpert.com
John 14:6

HOT METHODS, INC. DBA HOWEXPERT
EMAIL: SUPPORT@HOWEXPERT.COM
WEBSITE: WWW.HOWEXPERT.COM

Table of Contents

Book Overview

HowExpert Guide to Stamp Collecting: The Ultimate Handbook for Starting a Stamp Collection, Identifying Rare Stamps, and Preserving Philatelic Treasures

If you want to start an exciting hobby, build a unique and valuable stamp collection, or uncover rare philatelic treasures, then **HowExpert Guide to Stamp Collecting** is the ultimate resource for you!

This comprehensive guide takes you step by step through the world of stamp collecting, making it accessible for beginners and invaluable for seasoned enthusiasts. Whether you're just starting out or looking to expand, preserve, and showcase your collection, this book provides everything you need to master the art of philately. From uncovering hidden gems and evaluating rarity to embracing modern trends like NFTs and digital tools, this guide has you covered.

What You'll Learn Inside This Book:

- **Chapter 1: Introduction to Stamp Collecting** – Explore the basics, history, and types of collectors to inspire your journey.
- **Chapter 2: Understanding Stamps** – Break down the anatomy, categories, and unique features that make stamps special.
- **Chapter 3: The Most Famous Stamps Ever Collected** – Discover legendary stamps, record-breaking auctions, and their stories.
- **Chapter 4: Starting Your First Stamp Collection** – Choose a focus, gather tools, and organize your collection efficiently.
- **Chapter 5: Finding Stamps** – Learn where to find stamps, from post offices and fairs to hidden gems online.
- **Chapter 6: Expanding Your Collection Like a Pro** – Use advanced strategies to grow your collection and uncover treasures.
- **Chapter 7: Evaluating and Grading Stamps** – Master valuation, grading, and authenticating rare finds to protect investments.

- **Chapter 8: Special Stamp Collecting Categories** – Explore thematic stamps, country-specific designs, and first-day covers.
- **Chapter 9: The Stories Behind Stamps** – Discover the history and cultural significance of stamps that bring collections to life.
- **Chapter 10: Protecting Your Stamp Collection** – Handle, clean, and safeguard stamps from damage and disasters.
- **Chapter 11: Displaying Your Stamps** – Create creative, professional displays for exhibitions or personal enjoyment.
- **Chapter 12: Connecting with the Stamp Collecting Community** – Join clubs, attend exhibitions, and network with collectors.
- **Chapter 13: How to Buy Stamps Smartly** – Avoid scams, find bargains, and negotiate deals like a pro.
- **Chapter 14: Selling Stamps for Profit** – Learn to time the market, create listings, and maximize profits.
- **Chapter 15: Investing in Stamps** – Build a profitable portfolio, avoid mistakes, and leverage market trends.
- **Chapter 16: Mastering Stamp Identification** – Use advanced tools to identify, evaluate, and catalog stamps effectively.
- **Chapter 17: The Future of Stamp Collecting** – Explore digital stamps, NFTs, and blockchain innovations.
- **Chapter 18: Innovative Technology for Modern Collectors** – Discover AI tools, apps, and augmented reality to enhance your collecting experience.
- **Conclusion** – Reflect on your journey, sustain your passion, and preserve your collection as a meaningful legacy.
- **Appendices** – Access glossaries, templates, trackers, and resources to simplify and enrich your collecting experience.

Take Action and Start Building Your Stamp Collection Today!

Whether you want to preserve history, invest in rare finds, or create a stunning collection, this guide will empower you to succeed. Packed with expert advice, practical tools, and inspiring stories, **HowExpert Guide to Stamp Collecting** makes learning simple, enjoyable, and rewarding.

Start today — unlock the fascinating world of stamp collecting, preserve treasures, and turn your passion into profit. Get your copy now!

HowExpert publishes quick "how to" guides on all topics from A to Z. Visit HowExpert.com to learn more.

Part 1: Foundations of Stamp Collecting

Stamp collecting is a rich and rewarding hobby with layers of history, artistry, and personal discovery. Part 1 explores the essential building blocks for beginners and seasoned enthusiasts alike. From understanding what stamp collecting entails to uncovering its historical roots and identifying the different types of collectors, this section lays the groundwork for an inspiring journey into the world of philately.

Chapter 1: Introduction to Stamp Collecting

Chapter 1 introduces the captivating world of stamp collecting, revealing its universal appeal and timeless significance. Discover how stamps transcend their practical purpose to become windows into history, culture, and art, and learn why so many people find joy and meaning in this beloved hobby.

1.1 What is Stamp Collecting?

Welcome to **HowExpert Guide to Stamp Collecting**, your ultimate resource for exploring the fascinating world of stamps. Stamp collecting, often referred to as philately, is more than just a hobby—it's a captivating journey through history, art, and culture. At its essence, stamp collecting involves gathering, organizing, and preserving postage stamps and related items such as envelopes (known as covers), postcards, and commemorative issues. But it's much more than accumulating objects; it's about uncovering stories, making connections, and exploring a world rich with discovery.

Did you know that the first adhesive postage stamp, the Penny Black, cost only one penny but is now a priceless artifact in the world of philately?

Each stamp is a miniature masterpiece, offering a window into a specific time, place, or event. They capture historical milestones, honor cultural icons, and showcase artistic achievements. Whether it's a stamp celebrating the moon landing or one featuring the intricate patterns of traditional textiles, every piece holds meaning.

What makes stamp collecting truly special is its accessibility. You don't need a fortune to get started; a handful of stamps from your local post office or an old family album is enough to begin. Your collection can grow in any direction—reflecting your personal interests, whether it's wildlife, space exploration, famous leaders, or historical events. The possibilities are as limitless as your imagination, making stamp collecting a hobby for everyone, regardless of age, budget, or location.

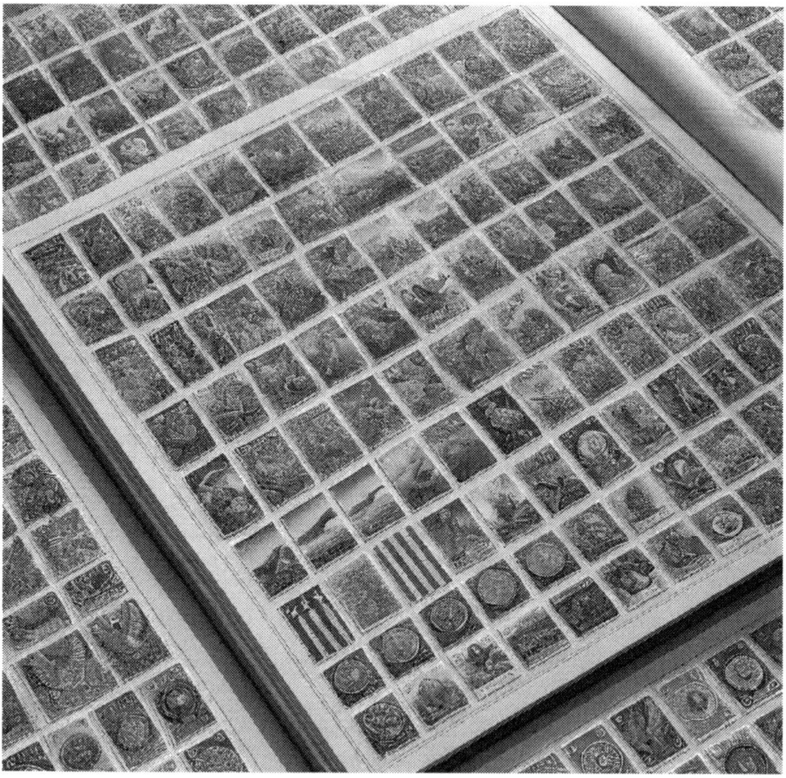

Explore the fascinating world of philately and uncover the stories behind every stamp.

1.2 A Brief History of Philately

The story of stamp collecting begins in 1840 with the introduction of the **Penny Black** in Great Britain, the world's first adhesive postage stamp. This innovation revolutionized communication by making postage affordable, reliable, and consistent. Before long, people began saving these small, beautifully designed pieces of paper, laying the foundation for a worldwide hobby.

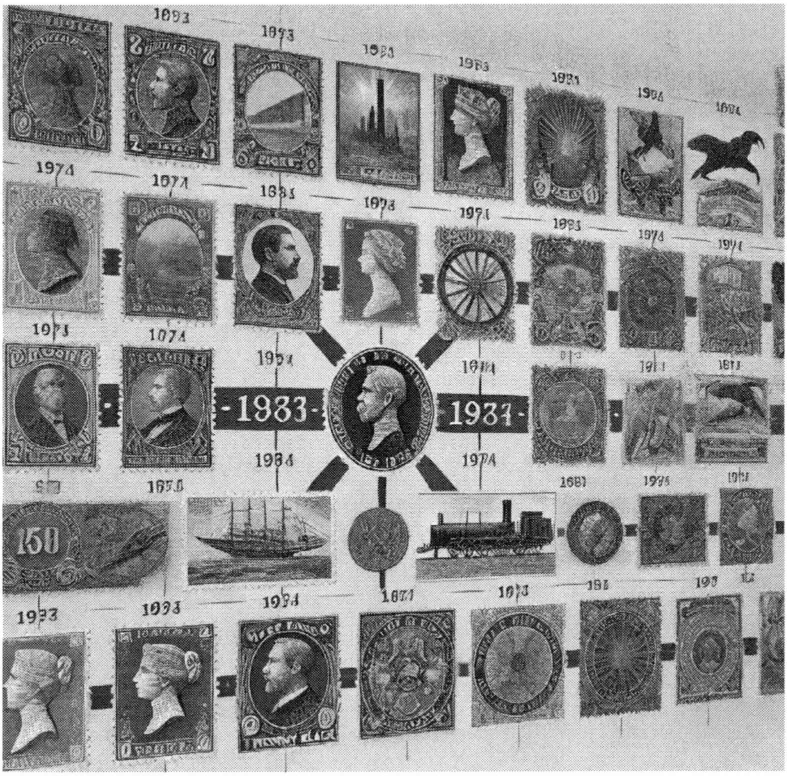

Travel through time and discover how stamp collecting has evolved over the centuries.

In the early 20th century, stamps played a key role in promoting national identities, with many countries using their designs to showcase unique cultural elements. These stamps weren't just tools for communication; they became ambassadors of a nation's history and pride.

Philately—the formal study of stamps and postal history—soon emerged as collectors sought to understand the stories behind their finds. Some key moments in the history of philately include:

- **1856:** The British Guiana 1c Magenta was issued. This unique stamp, with only one known example, would later become the most valuable stamp in the world, fetching millions at auctions.
- **1860s:** The first stamp catalogs were published, giving collectors tools to identify and organize their stamps. Around the same time, stamp societies began forming, fostering a sense of community.
- **1890s:** Commemorative stamps were introduced, celebrating historical events, famous figures, and cultural achievements. These special editions opened up new possibilities for thematic collecting.
- **20th Century:** The hobby flourished as international travel and communication made it easier to collect stamps from around the globe. Iconic stamps such as the Inverted Jenny, with its printing error, became legends in philatelic lore.

In modern times, philately has embraced technological advancements. Online marketplaces, digital tools for identification, and even blockchain for authentication have transformed how collectors interact with their collections. Yet, the heart of stamp collecting remains unchanged: the thrill of discovery and the joy of preserving history.

From its humble beginnings with the Penny Black to the digital innovations of today, stamp collecting has remained a timeless way to celebrate history and culture.

1.3 Why Collect Stamps? Hobby, Investment, and More

With this rich history in mind, it's easy to see why stamp collecting continues to captivate hobbyists and investors alike. Here's why this timeless hobby appeals to so many people:

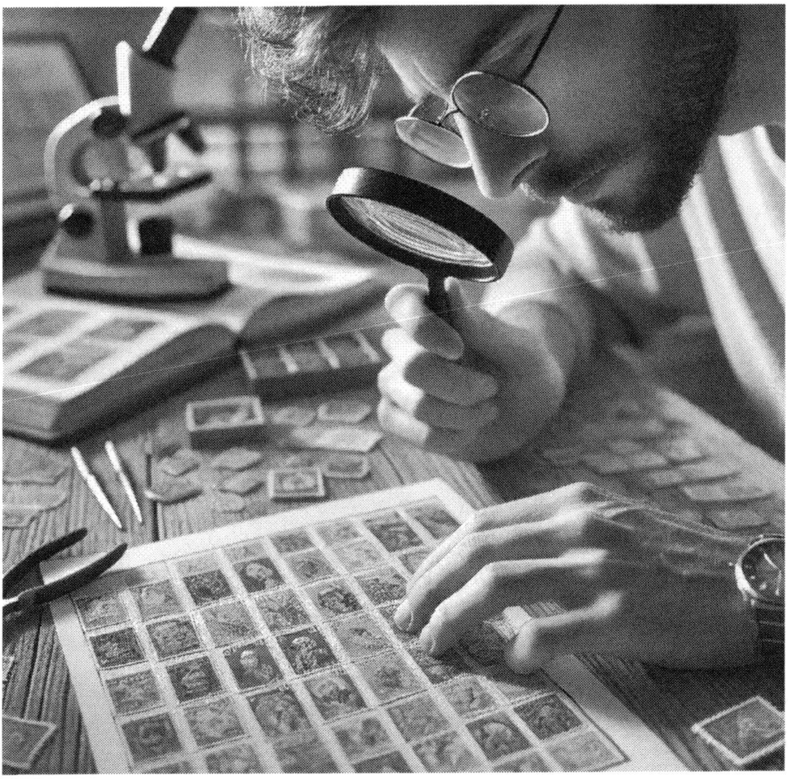

Discover the endless possibilities stamp collecting offers—as a hobby, investment, and cultural pursuit.

A. As a Hobby:

For many, stamp collecting starts as a relaxing and creative pastime. It offers a break from the demands of daily life and opens a door to exploration and self-expression. Hobbyists find joy in the diversity and artistry of stamps, which often reflect their personal interests and passions.

Each stamp tells a story. Whether it's a snapshot of a historic moment or a tribute to cultural heritage, collecting stamps allows you to hold history in the palm of your hand.

- **Relaxation and Creativity:** Sorting, organizing, and studying stamps is both calming and mentally stimulating. It's a perfect way to unwind while engaging your curiosity.

- **Educational Value:** Stamps are miniature encyclopedias, offering insights into history, geography, art, and culture. A single stamp can introduce you to the landmarks of a distant country or the milestones of scientific discovery.
- **Personal Expression:** Your collection reflects your passions. Whether you're drawn to stamps featuring famous leaders, endangered species, or Olympic Games, each stamp adds a piece of your personality to your collection.

B. As an Investment:

Stamp collecting isn't just about the fun—it can also be a smart financial move. Investors see stamps as tangible assets that appreciate in value over time. With strategic planning and market knowledge, collectors can build portfolios that combine personal passion with profit potential.

- **Financial Potential:** Rare and sought-after stamps often appreciate in value over time. A well-curated collection can be both a source of pride and a financial asset.
- **Tangible Assets:** Stamps are physical items that you can hold, display, and pass down. Unlike digital investments, they carry a tangible, personal touch.
- **Market Opportunities:** The vibrant stamp market includes auctions, dealers, and online platforms, offering plenty of opportunities to buy, sell, and trade.

C. As a Legacy:

Stamp collections often transcend generations, becoming cherished heirlooms and symbols of family history. Collectors preserve these tiny artifacts as windows into the past, ensuring that the stories they tell inspire future generations. As a legacy, stamp collecting fosters connections between people and time periods.

Imagine your grandchildren discovering your carefully preserved collection decades from now, marveling at the stories each stamp tells about your life and the world.

- **Preserving History:** Stamps are artifacts that capture moments in time. By preserving your collection, you contribute to safeguarding history.
- **Family Connections:** Stamp collections often become cherished heirlooms, sparking curiosity and sharing stories across generations.
- **Inspiring Others:** A well-curated collection can inspire others to explore the world of stamps, fostering a lifelong appreciation for philately.

1.4 Types of Stamp Collectors: Beginners, Enthusiasts, and Investors

Understanding why people collect stamps is only the beginning. Now, let's explore the different types of collectors and what sets them apart.

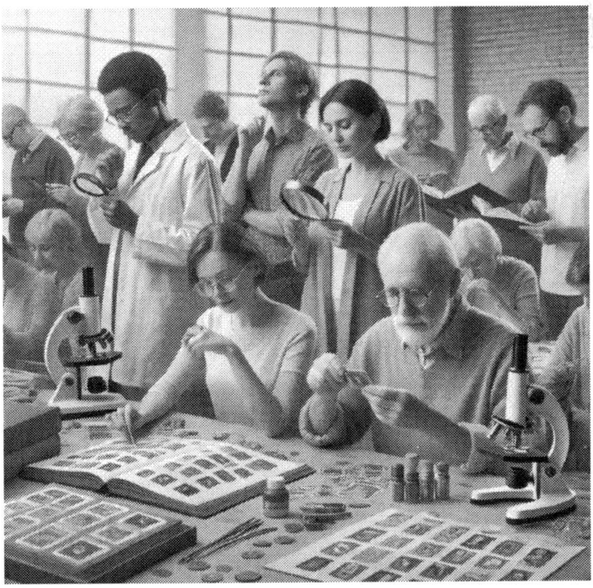

Find your place in the philatelic community, no matter your experience level.

A. Beginners:

For those who are new to stamp collecting, starting a collection can feel both exciting and slightly overwhelming. Beginners typically focus on accessible, affordable stamps and take the first steps to explore the vast world of philately.

- **Accessible Entry Points:** Many beginners start by collecting stamps from local post offices or inheriting a collection from a family member. These early experiences offer a simple way to explore the basics of philately.
- **Learning the Basics:** Beginners focus on identifying stamps, understanding their features, and organizing them in albums or binders.
- **Discovering the Hobby:** Beginners enjoy the thrill of discovery as they explore the diversity of stamps and begin building their first collection.
- **Basic Tools:** Simple tools like starter albums, magnifying glasses, and tweezers help beginners preserve and display their collections effectively.

B. Enthusiasts:

Enthusiasts are collectors who dive deeper into philately, often specializing in themes or eras. They actively participate in the broader community and continuously expand their expertise.

- **Specialized Focus:** Enthusiasts often develop thematic collections (e.g., animals, space, or art) or focus on stamps from specific regions or eras.
- **Community Engagement:** Joining clubs, attending stamp shows, and participating in forums allows enthusiasts to connect with like-minded collectors.
- **Advanced Tools:** High-quality tools like archival albums, UV lights, and perforation gauges enable enthusiasts to preserve and analyze their collections in detail.

- **Personal Pride:** Enthusiasts take pride in curating a collection that reflects their knowledge and passions.

C. Investors:

Investors approach stamp collecting with a financial perspective, combining their passion for stamps with the goal of building a profitable collection.

- **Strategic Mindset:** Investors focus on rare and high-value stamps that have significant potential for financial returns.
- **Expert Insights:** Relying on professional grading services and appraisers ensures accurate evaluations of authenticity and value.
- **Market Awareness:** Staying updated on trends and auction results helps investors identify lucrative opportunities.
- **Art and Asset:** Investors view their collections as both an art form and a financial asset, balancing passion with profit.

Whether you're a beginner finding your footing, an enthusiast refining your focus, or an investor seeking treasures, the joy of stamp collecting lies in its diversity. Every collector's journey is unique, yet all share the excitement of uncovering stories and preserving history. Together, these paths create a vibrant and inclusive philatelic community united by a shared love for stamps.

Chapter 1 Review: Introduction to Stamp Collecting

Chapter 1 immerses readers in the timeless world of stamp collecting, illustrating its appeal as a blend of history, art, and personal expression. The chapter highlights the accessibility of this hobby, its rich historical roots, and its potential to connect people with culture and legacy.

1.1 What is Stamp Collecting?

- **A Gateway to Discovery:** Stamp collecting, or philately, is more than just gathering postage—it's about exploring stories and moments in history through these miniature works of art.
- **Accessible for Everyone:** Anyone can start with a handful of stamps from local post offices, family albums, or even everyday mail, making this hobby open to all ages and budgets.
- **Endless Possibilities:** Collectors can tailor their focus to their interests, whether it's wildlife, iconic leaders, or global events, ensuring a collection that reflects personal passions.

1.2 A Brief History of Philately

- **The Birth of a Hobby:** Philately began with the Penny Black in 1840, the world's first adhesive stamp, which revolutionized communication.
- **Historic Highlights:** Iconic stamps like the British Guiana 1c Magenta and the Inverted Jenny showcase the allure and value of rare issues, captivating collectors throughout history.
- **Modern Developments:** Digital tools and online platforms have made stamp collecting more accessible, while blockchain innovations enhance authentication and trust.

1.3 Why Collect Stamps?

- **A Source of Relaxation:** Sorting and studying stamps provides a calming, creative escape while stimulating curiosity and learning.
- **Educational Value:** Stamps are windows into history, geography, and culture, making philately both engaging and informative.
- **Investment Potential:** Rare and unique stamps can appreciate in value, offering collectors both enjoyment and financial rewards.

- **Preserving Legacy:** Stamp collections often become heirlooms, linking generations and preserving moments in time for the future.

1.4 Types of Stamp Collectors

- **Beginners:** Focus on accessible and affordable options, starting with local finds and learning the basics of identification and organization.
- **Enthusiasts:** Dive deeper into specialized themes or eras, engaging with collector communities and expanding their expertise.
- **Investors:** Approach the hobby with a strategic mindset, focusing on rare and high-value stamps to build profitable collections.

This chapter sets a solid foundation for readers, blending history, practical advice, and inspiration to ignite a lifelong passion for stamp collecting. It prepares collectors for deeper exploration into the anatomy, diversity, and unique features of stamps in the chapters ahead.

Chapter 2: Understanding Stamps

To truly appreciate the art and history of stamp collecting, it's essential to understand the anatomy, variety, and creation of stamps. Chapter 2 delves into the intricate details that make each stamp unique, from their physical features to the fascinating methods of production and the stories they tell. This chapter provides foundational knowledge needed to analyze, organize, and appreciate stamps at a deeper level. Together, let's explore how these miniature masterpieces reflect the rich tapestry of global history and artistry.

2.1 Anatomy of a Stamp: Key Features Explained

Every stamp is a small yet intricate piece of art, capturing history and culture in a form that is both functional and collectible. Understanding its anatomy helps collectors evaluate authenticity, condition, and value. Let's explore the key components that make up a stamp:

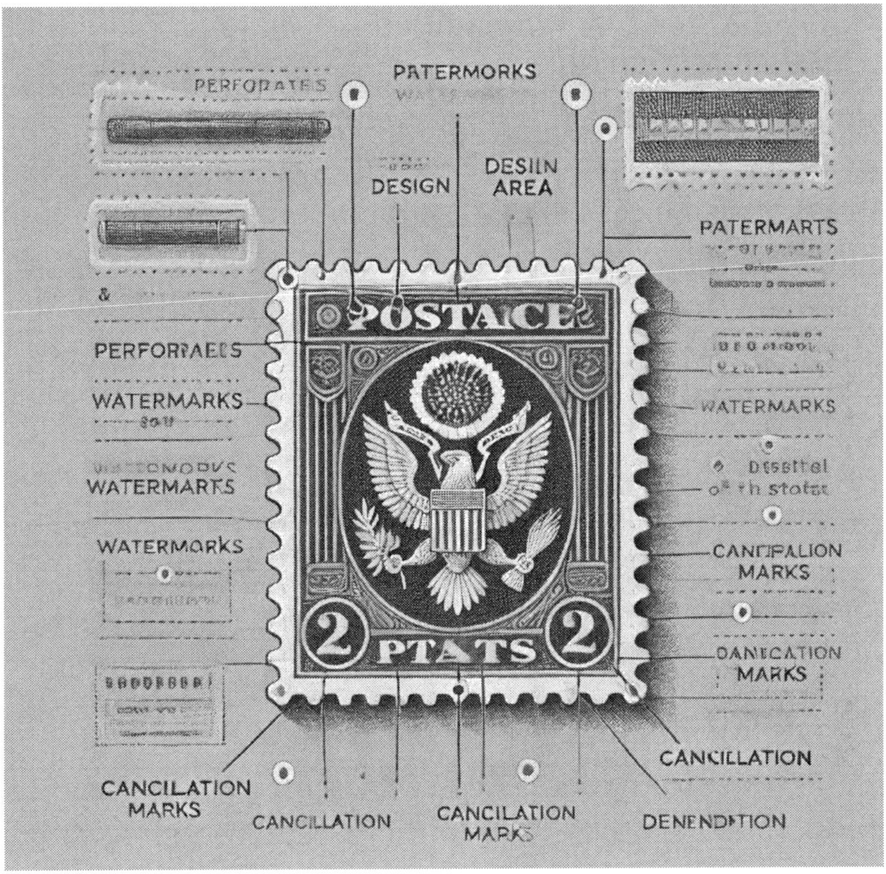

Master the anatomy of a stamp to unlock its secrets and value.

A. Design:

The design is the visual centerpiece of every stamp, showcasing historical figures, landmarks, cultural icons, or commemorative events.

- **Cultural Reflection:** Designs reflect the culture and priorities of the issuing country. For instance, the Penny Black's elegant portrait of Queen Victoria symbolizes Britain's leadership in postal innovation.

- **Artistic Appeal:** Modern stamps highlight vibrant colors, intricate patterns, and thematic elements, transforming them into captivating works of art.
- **Engaging Example:** Imagine holding a commemorative stamp celebrating the Apollo 11 moon landing—a tiny artifact encapsulating one of humanity's most inspiring achievements.

B. Perforations:

Perforations are the tiny holes or cuts along the edges of a stamp, making it easy to separate individual stamps from a sheet.

- **Measurement and Variability:** Collectors use perforation gauges to measure the number of holes per inch, which can impact rarity and value.
- **Imperforate Stamps:** Stamps without perforations are rare and highly collectible, often holding significant historical value.

C. Watermarks:

Watermarks are faint patterns embedded into the paper during production to prevent counterfeiting.

- **Detection Techniques:** Hold a stamp up to light or use watermark detection fluid to reveal hidden patterns.
- **Collector Importance:** Watermarked stamps often indicate authenticity and can increase value, especially when featuring rare designs.

D. Inscriptions:

Stamps include inscriptions that provide key information about their origin and purpose:

- **Country Name:** Identifies the issuing nation.
- **Denomination:** Indicates the stamp's postal value.
- **Special Markings:** Phrases like "Air Mail" or "Commemorative Issue" add context and significance.

Reflection: Take a moment to examine a stamp in your collection. Notice its design, perforations, or inscriptions—each feature offers a glimpse into its story. By understanding these components, collectors unlock deeper stories behind each stamp and gain a greater appreciation for the intricate craftsmanship that brings them to life.

2.2 Types of Stamps: Everyday, Special, and Limited Editions

Stamps serve a wide range of purposes and have evolved over time to fulfill practical, commemorative, and artistic roles. Each type offers unique insights into history and culture, appealing to collectors for different reasons. Here's a closer look at the main categories:

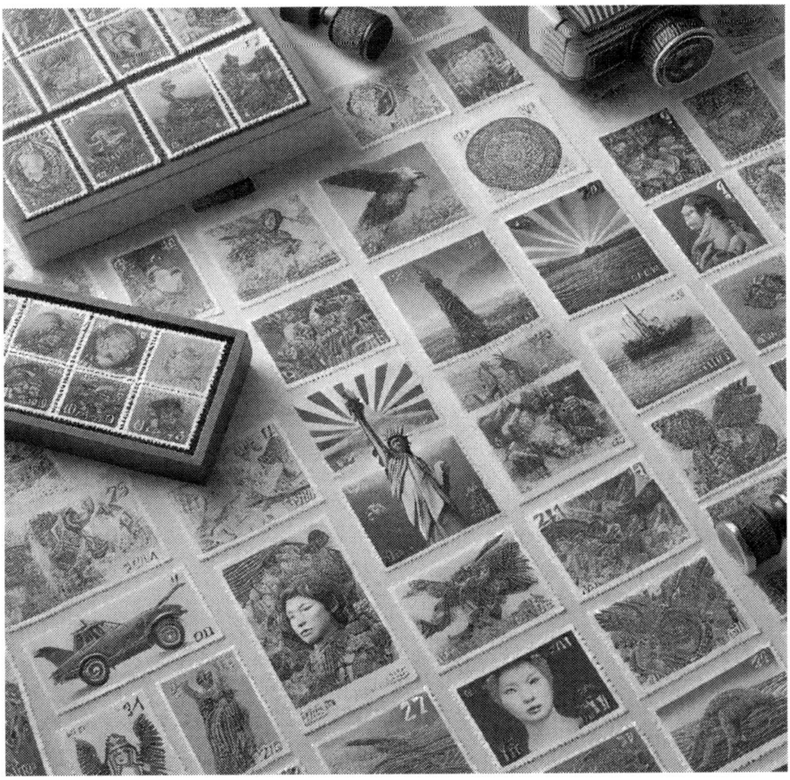

Recognize the diversity of stamps and their unique purposes in the world of collecting.

A. Definitive Stamps:

These stamps are the backbone of postal systems, issued in large quantities for everyday use.

- **Longevity:** Definitive stamps remain in circulation for years, making them a staple for both beginners and experienced collectors.
- **Simple Designs:** While less visually elaborate, definitive stamps commonly feature national symbols, leaders, or recurring motifs, ensuring widespread recognition.

B. Commemorative Stamps:

These stamps celebrate significant events, anniversaries, or notable figures, offering collectors a slice of history.

- **Limited Editions:** Printed in smaller quantities than definitive stamps, commemoratives are more exclusive and sought after.
- **Examples:** Iconic examples include stamps honoring the moon landing or major centennial celebrations, preserving moments of global importance.

C. Special Edition Stamps:

Special editions cater to specific themes or causes, often raising funds or awareness.

- **Thematic Appeal:** Popular themes include wildlife, space exploration, and sports, which resonate with diverse audiences.
- **Regional Interest:** Some focus on local culture, festivals, or achievements, appealing to niche audiences and fostering community pride.

D. Revenue Stamps:

Used to indicate tax payments, revenue stamps hold dual significance in postal and legal history.

- **Historical Relevance:** These stamps reflect governmental or economic changes, making them cherished by collectors with historical interests.
- **Crossover Appeal:** Their blend of philatelic and financial history attracts a wide audience, bridging multiple collecting niches.

Reflection: As you explore different types of stamps, think about what draws you to specific categories. Is it the historical importance, artistic beauty, or personal resonance? Exploring these categories helps collectors shape unique and meaningful collections.

2.3 How Stamps Are Made: Printing Techniques Across Time

The creation of stamps combines artistry and technology, reflecting advancements in printing and design over the centuries. Understanding these techniques provides valuable insights into the craftsmanship behind each stamp and helps collectors identify their origins.

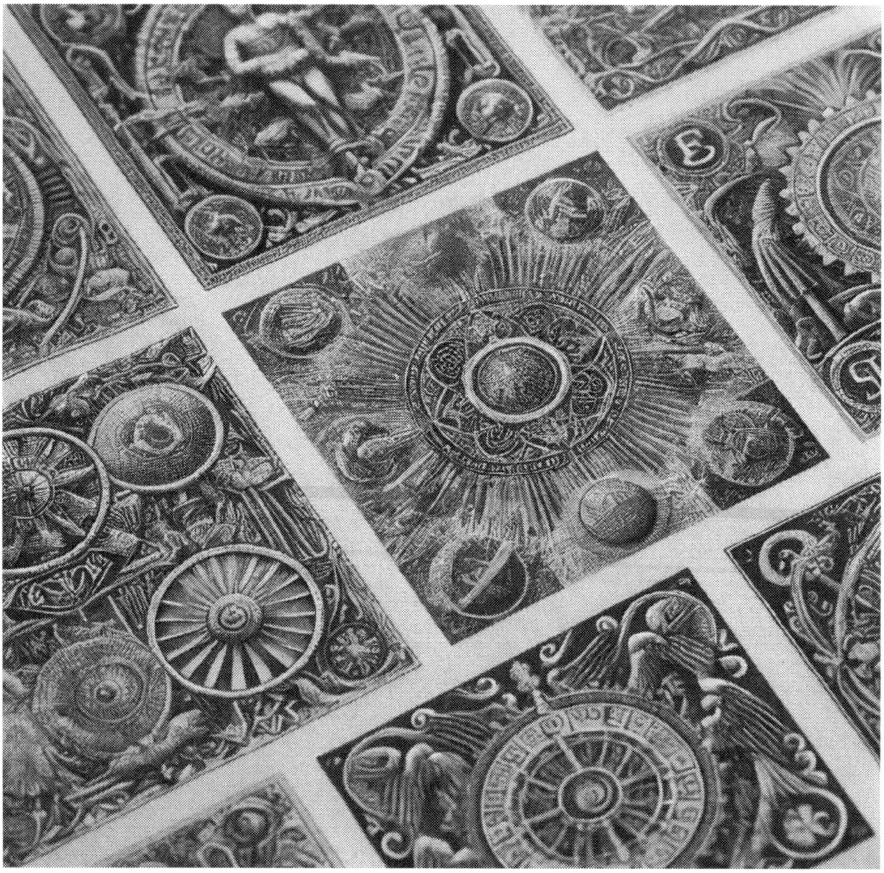

Appreciate the craftsmanship behind stamps by exploring their printing techniques.

A. Engraving:

One of the oldest and most intricate methods, engraving involves carving designs onto a metal plate.

- **Exquisite Detail:** This technique produces sharp, precise lines, as seen in early U.S. and European stamps.
- **Timeless Appeal:** Collectors treasure engraved stamps for their craftsmanship and the tactile quality of the raised designs.

B. Lithography:

Lithography uses flat printing plates to transfer designs onto paper through a chemical process.

- **Vivid Colors:** This method excels at creating bold and vibrant designs.
- **Modern Applications:** Frequently used for commemorative and thematic stamps due to its versatility.

C. Photogravure:

Combining photography and engraving, photogravure creates highly detailed images with smooth tonal gradations.

- **Mass Production:** Enables the production of large quantities while maintaining clarity and detail.
- **Visual Clarity:** Ideal for stamps featuring realistic portraits or landscapes.

D. Digital Printing:

The newest innovation in stamp production, digital printing allows for flexibility and customization.

- **Personalized Stamps:** Many postal services now offer options to create stamps featuring personal photos or designs.
- **Creative Freedom:** This method expands possibilities for unique and interactive designs, pushing the boundaries of traditional philately.

Reflection: Consider how technological advancements have influenced the look and feel of stamps in your collection. Which printing techniques do you admire most? By mastering these techniques, collectors deepen their appreciation for the artistry of stamps while honing their ability to identify and classify unique finds.

2.4 Themes, Errors, and Unique Features

Thematic stamps, production errors, and innovative design elements bring excitement and variety to stamp collecting. These unique aspects allow collectors to personalize their collections and uncover fascinating stories.

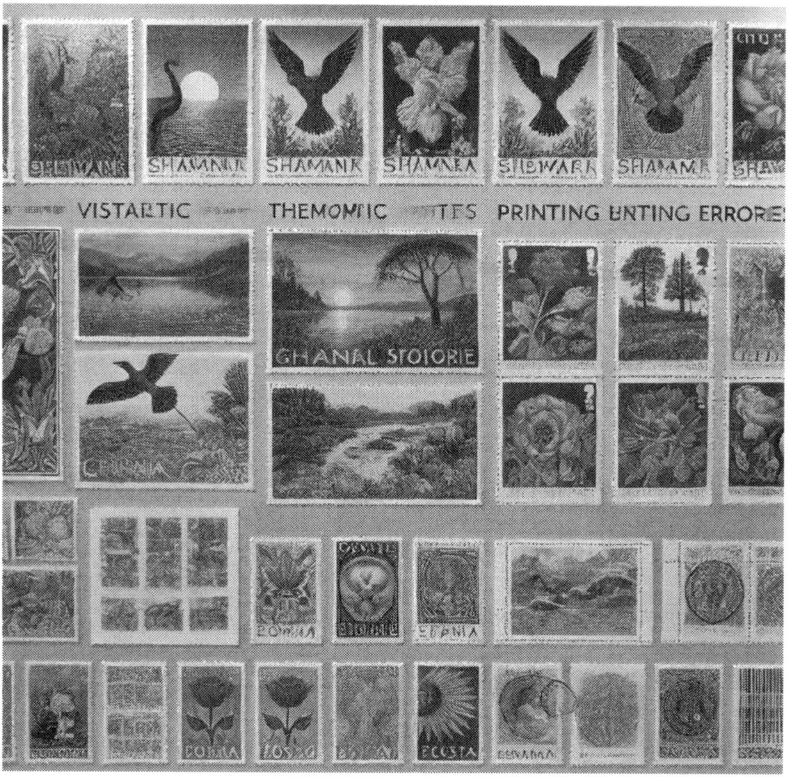

Spot themes, errors, and rare features that make collecting exciting.

A. Thematic Stamps:

Thematic stamps focus on specific topics or subjects, appealing to collectors with particular interests.

- **Popular Themes:** Animals, space exploration, art, famous people, and historical events are common themes that attract a wide range of collectors.

- **Building Collections:** Many collectors create albums dedicated to themes, such as endangered species, Olympic Games, or world landmarks, making their collections a reflection of personal passions.
- **Connection to History:** For instance, stamps commemorating World War II tell stories of resilience and global unity, bridging generations through shared history.

B. Error Stamps:

Printing errors make some stamps exceptionally rare and valuable.

- **Famous Examples:** The Inverted Jenny, featuring an upside-down airplane, is among the most famous error stamps, fetching millions at auctions.
- **Collector Fascination:** Errors such as color misprints, missing perforations, or inverted designs offer a glimpse into the complexities of stamp production.
- **Exciting Discovery:** Imagine uncovering an error stamp—a hidden treasure that transforms your collection into a conversation piece.

C. Unique Features:

Some stamps stand out due to their innovative designs or materials.

- **Unusual Materials:** Examples include stamps made from silk, wood, or even metal, which add a novelty factor to collections.
- **Interactive Elements:** Modern stamps featuring QR codes, holograms, or scented features blend traditional design with cutting-edge innovation, appealing to contemporary collectors.

Reflection: As you explore these unique aspects, think about how they add character and value to your collection. Which themes or features resonate most with your interests? These distinctive features ensure that stamp collecting remains a dynamic and ever-evolving pursuit.

Exploring these themes, errors, and unique features transforms stamp collecting into a journey of discovery, creativity, and historical preservation. Whether you're captivated by a stamp's story, its artistry, or its rarity, each addition to your collection brings a deeper connection to the past and endless possibilities for the future.

Chapter 2 Review: Understanding Stamps

Chapter 2 dives into the essential aspects of stamps, exploring their anatomy, diverse types, production methods, and unique features. It equips collectors with the foundational knowledge needed to analyze and appreciate stamps, making this chapter a key resource for understanding the artistry and history behind philately.

2.1 Anatomy of a Stamp: Key Features Explained

- **Design as the Focal Point:** Stamps showcase history and culture through designs featuring leaders, landmarks, or events. Each design reflects the artistic priorities of its issuing nation.
- **Perforations and Rarity:** Perforations enable easy separation and are critical for evaluating rarity. Imperforate stamps, for instance, are highly collectible.
- **Watermarks and Authentication:** Hidden patterns in the paper can verify authenticity and add value, while inscriptions reveal a stamp's origin and purpose.

2.2 Types of Stamps: Everyday, Special, and Limited Editions

- **Definitive Stamps:** Everyday stamps with simple designs for widespread use form the backbone of postal systems and provide an affordable entry point for collectors.
- **Commemorative Stamps:** These limited-edition issues celebrate significant events or figures, making them prized for their historical significance.

- **Revenue Stamps:** Reflecting both postal and economic history, revenue stamps bridge the gap between philatelic and financial collecting interests.

2.3 How Stamps Are Made: Printing Techniques Across Time

- **Engraving and Craftsmanship:** Early engraved stamps feature precise, tactile designs that collectors admire for their artistry.
- **Lithography and Vibrancy:** This technique excels in bold colors, making it ideal for thematic and commemorative stamps.
- **Digital Innovation:** Modern digital printing allows for customized designs and interactive elements, expanding the creative potential of stamps.

2.4 Themes, Errors, and Unique Features

- **Thematic Collections:** Popular themes like space exploration, animals, or historic events allow collectors to express personal interests while preserving history.
- **Error Stamps:** Rare production mistakes, such as the Inverted Jenny, captivate collectors for their rarity and the stories they tell.
- **Innovative Designs:** Stamps made from unique materials or featuring holograms and QR codes showcase the evolving creativity in philately.

This chapter provides readers with an in-depth understanding of stamps as functional and artistic artifacts. By exploring their anatomy, types, and production, collectors gain the skills to analyze and appreciate their collections more deeply. With this foundation, readers are prepared to discover the stories behind the world's most famous stamps in the next chapter.

Chapter 3: The Most Famous Stamps Ever Collected

Stamp collecting often revolves around iconic pieces that capture the imagination of collectors worldwide. Chapter 3 highlights some of the most famous stamps in history, explores record-breaking auctions, and delves into what makes these stamps legendary. These stories not only inspire collectors but also underscore the rich historical and cultural value of philately.

3.1 Iconic Stamps in History: The Penny Black, Inverted Jenny, and More

Some stamps stand out as milestones in philatelic history, cherished for their design, rarity, and historical significance. Let's explore a few of these iconic pieces:

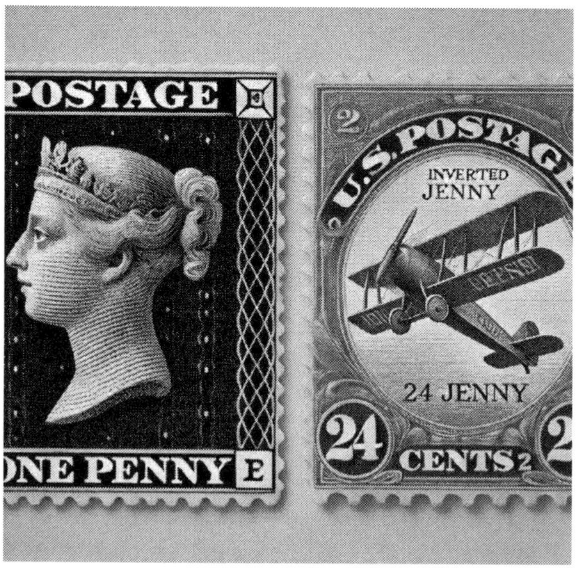

Learn about the legendary stamps that have captured the world's attention.

A. The Penny Black:

The world's first adhesive postage stamp, issued in Great Britain in 1840, revolutionized communication and marked the beginning of modern philately. Its introduction was not just a logistical innovation but a cultural milestone, reflecting the evolution of a global postal system that made communication more accessible than ever before.

- **Design and Impact:** Featuring a portrait of Queen Victoria, its elegant black engraving symbolized Britain's pioneering postal system and set the standard for postage stamps worldwide.
- **Cultural Significance:** The Penny Black democratized communication, making it accessible to all citizens regardless of social class.
- **Collectible Appeal:** While not exceedingly rare due to its large initial production, its historical significance and classic design make it a prized possession for collectors.

B. The Inverted Jenny:

This U.S. airmail stamp from 1918 gained fame for its printing error, depicting an upside-down Curtiss JN-4 airplane. It stands as a reminder that human errors can create enduring legends in the world of collectibles.

- **Error and Value:** Only 100 were accidentally printed, and its rarity has made it one of the most sought-after stamps globally.
- **Famous Sales:** A single Inverted Jenny has fetched millions of dollars at auctions, cementing its legendary status.
- **Cultural Impact:** The Inverted Jenny is a symbol of how human error can turn an ordinary object into an extraordinary artifact.

C. The British Guiana 1c Magenta:

Dubbed the "Mona Lisa of stamps," this 1856 stamp from British Guiana is unique—the only one of its kind known to exist. Its mystique lies not only in its rarity but in the remarkable stories that have surrounded its discovery and ownership.

- **Rarity and Provenance:** Printed as a temporary solution during a shortage of regular stamps, its crude design belies its immense value.
- **Record-Breaking Auction:** It has repeatedly set records for the highest price paid for a single stamp, most recently selling for nearly $9.5 million.
- **Historical Intrigue:** The stamp's ownership includes famous collectors like John du Pont, adding layers of mystique.

D. Other Notable Icons:

Beyond the legendary status of the Penny Black, Inverted Jenny, and British Guiana 1c Magenta, there are other notable stamps that capture the imagination of collectors and philatelists alike. These stamps exemplify the creativity, innovation, and occasional serendipity that make philately such a fascinating pursuit.

- **The Treskilling Yellow:** This Swedish error stamp, issued in 1855, is renowned for its accidental color variation. It stands as one of the rarest and most intriguing pieces in philatelic history, captivating collectors for over a century.
- **Basel Dove:** Issued in 1845, this Swiss stamp is celebrated for its multicolor printing and artistic beauty. Its design, featuring a dove carrying a letter, symbolizes peace and communication, making it a standout in philately.

These iconic stamps not only reflect the artistry and history of their times but also fuel the passion of collectors worldwide, serving as enduring symbols of the joy and mystery in philately.

3.2 Record-Breaking Auctions: The World's Most Expensive Stamps

The allure of rare stamps has led to jaw-dropping auction results, with some pieces selling for millions. These record-breaking sales reveal the high stakes and deep fascination within the world of philately.

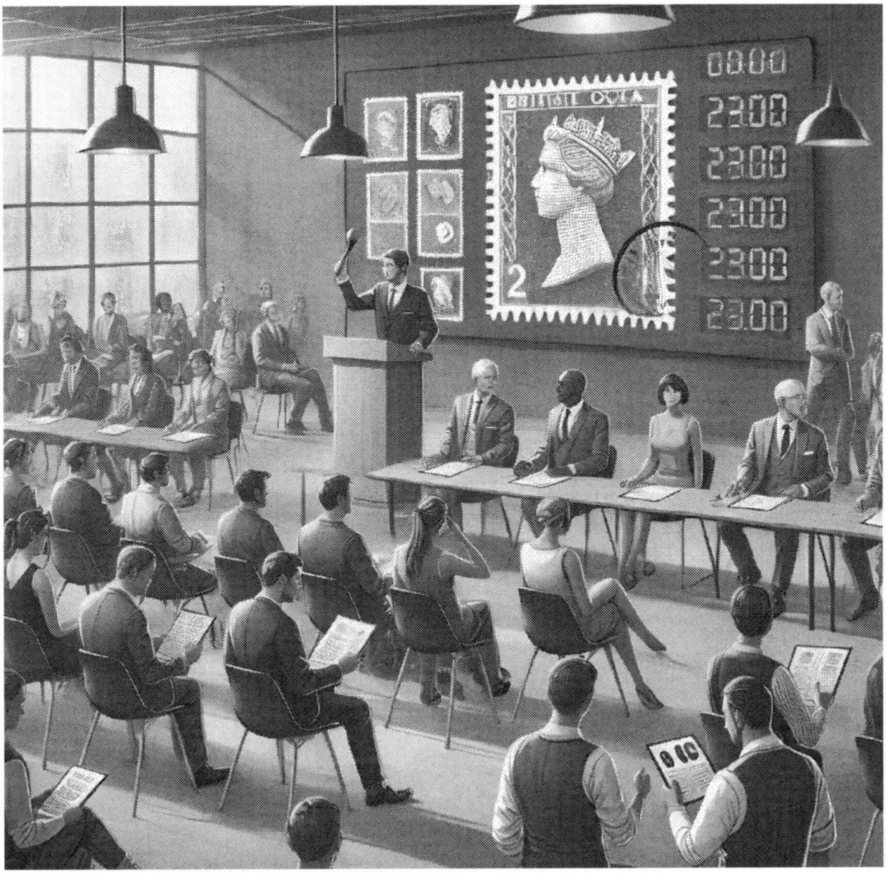

Discover the jaw-dropping auctions where stamps made history.

A. British Guiana 1c Magenta:

This stamp's auction history is a testament to its unparalleled status in the philatelic world. As the only known example of its kind, its value is driven by its uniqueness and the intrigue surrounding its provenance.

- **Auction History:** This stamp's most recent sale in 2021 for nearly $9.5 million broke its own previous records.
- **Why It's Priceless:** Its status as a one-of-a-kind artifact and its storied provenance make it a crown jewel in any collection.
- **Cultural Legacy:** Its value transcends philately, symbolizing the human desire to preserve rare and extraordinary objects.

B. The Inverted Jenny Plate Block:

The Inverted Jenny Plate Block represents one of the most coveted configurations of this legendary stamp. Its rarity and intact grouping amplify its appeal among collectors.

- **Auction Milestones:** A block of four Inverted Jenny stamps sold for $4.9 million in 2016, showcasing the amplified value of intact groupings.
- **Rarity and Significance:** The block's rarity and the famous printing error combine to create unmatched appeal for collectors and investors alike.

C. The Treskilling Yellow:

This Swedish stamp's journey through auctions has captivated collectors worldwide. Its enigmatic history and rarity make it a perennial favorite in philatelic lore.

- **Unique Auction History:** This Swedish stamp's sales have repeatedly made headlines, though its exact current ownership remains a mystery.
- **Value Estimate:** Believed to be worth over $2 million due to its rarity and intriguing backstory as an error stamp.
- **Global Fascination:** Its vibrant color and rarity have made it an enduring symbol of the excitement in philatelic discovery.

D. Modern Contributions:

The rise of international interest in rare stamps has expanded the scope of record-breaking auctions. Stamps from emerging markets now command significant attention.

- **The Whole Country Is Red:** A Chinese Cultural Revolution-era stamp depicting a map with a printing error sold for $2 million, highlighting the rise of international markets.
- **Emerging Trends:** Rare stamps from regions like China and India are increasingly dominating auction records, reflecting the global expansion of philately.

These high-profile auctions highlight the extraordinary value collectors place on rarity, history, and provenance. They also demonstrate the evolving dynamics of the stamp market, where cultural significance and international interest continue to drive prices higher.

3.3 Why These Stamps Are Legendary

What elevates certain stamps to legendary status? Beyond rarity, these iconic pieces embody unique stories, cultural significance, and artistic mastery. Let's examine the factors that make them so unforgettable:

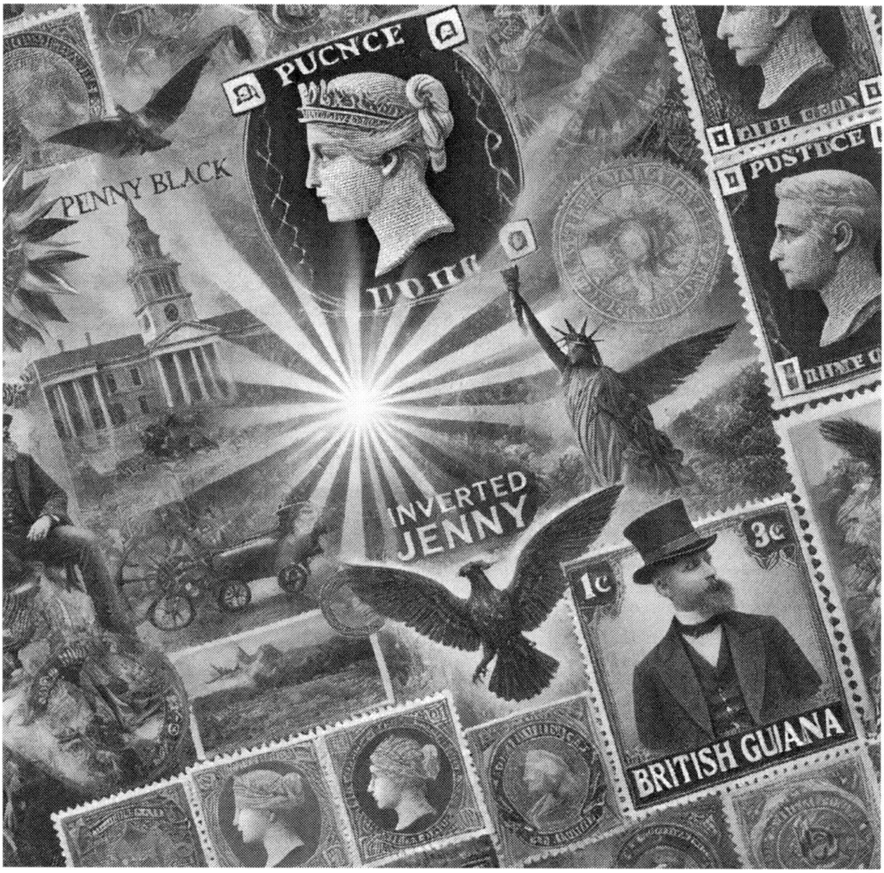

Uncover the stories and artistry that make these stamps iconic treasures.

A. Rarity:

Rarity is perhaps the most defining feature of a legendary stamp. Whether through limited production or accidental errors, rarity fuels the demand and mystique surrounding these pieces.

- **Limited Production:** Many legendary stamps were produced in small quantities or have few surviving examples, such as the British Guiana 1c Magenta.
- **Accidental Rarities:** Printing errors like the Inverted Jenny add an element of chance and intrigue, capturing the imagination of collectors.

- **Uniqueness:** The Treskilling Yellow and the 1c Magenta stand alone in their respective categories, symbolizing the pinnacle of philatelic exclusivity.

B. Historical Significance:

Stamps serve as miniature time capsules, capturing pivotal moments in history and reflecting the societal context of their creation.

- **Global Impact:** The Penny Black revolutionized communication and postal systems worldwide, creating a legacy of accessibility and efficiency.
- **Cultural Representation:** Stamps often reflect pivotal moments in history, like the "Whole Country Is Red" during China's Cultural Revolution.
- **Timeless Connection:** These stamps serve as tangible links to historical events, leaders, and societal shifts.

C. Provenance and Storytelling:

The journey of a stamp often adds to its allure. Ownership by notable figures or an intriguing backstory can elevate its status.

- **Famous Owners:** The British Guiana 1c Magenta's ownership history includes renowned collectors like John du Pont and even appearances in high-profile exhibitions.
- **Fascinating Origins:** Unique backstories, such as emergency printings or accidental errors, add layers of intrigue to these legendary pieces.

D. Artistic and Technical Mastery:

The aesthetic and technical aspects of stamps contribute significantly to their legendary status. From intricate engravings to bold design choices, artistry plays a central role.

- **Innovative Designs:** Stamps like the Basel Dove showcase pioneering techniques and aesthetic excellence that were groundbreaking for their time.

- **Errors with Beauty:** Even mistakes, such as the Inverted Jenny, captivate collectors with their charm and historical significance.

Reflection: These legendary stamps remind us that collecting is about more than monetary value—it's about preserving pieces of history, celebrating human creativity, and fostering a deep appreciation for the artistry and stories behind each piece. For collectors, owning even a replica of an iconic stamp can spark the same excitement as uncovering a treasure.

Stamp collecting thrives on the stories, rarity, and artistry of these legendary pieces. From the Penny Black to the Inverted Jenny, these stamps represent more than just collectibles—they are windows into history, culture, and human creativity. Their enduring appeal inspires collectors to explore, preserve, and celebrate the rich legacy of philately, keeping the passion for this timeless hobby alive.

Chapter 3 Review: The Most Famous Stamps Ever Collected

Chapter 3 explores the world of legendary stamps, showcasing how rare and iconic pieces captivate collectors with their history, artistry, and cultural significance. By examining some of the most famous stamps, their record-breaking auctions, and the factors behind their legendary status, this chapter inspires readers to appreciate the depth and excitement of philately.

3.1 Iconic Stamps in History: The Penny Black, Inverted Jenny, and More

- **The Penny Black:** Issued in 1840, this was the world's first adhesive postage stamp, marking a revolution in communication. Its elegant design featuring Queen Victoria and its historical importance make it a cornerstone of philately.

- **The Inverted Jenny:** Known for its famous printing error depicting an upside-down airplane, this 1918 U.S. airmail stamp is one of the most sought-after and valuable stamps in the world.
- **The British Guiana 1c Magenta:** Often called the "Mona Lisa of stamps," this unique 1856 issue is unparalleled in rarity and value, fetching record-breaking prices at auctions.
- **Other Notables:** Stamps like the Treskilling Yellow and the Basel Dove exemplify the artistry, rarity, and serendipity that make stamp collecting so fascinating.

3.2 Record-Breaking Auctions: The World's Most Expensive Stamps

- **The British Guiana 1c Magenta:** This one-of-a-kind stamp has set multiple auction records, most recently selling for $9.5 million, underscoring its unmatched status in philately.
- **The Inverted Jenny Plate Block:** A block of four stamps sold for $4.9 million in 2016, showing how configurations amplify rarity and value.
- **Emerging Markets:** Stamps like China's "The Whole Country Is Red" demonstrate how cultural significance and rising international interest are reshaping the stamp market.

3.3 Why These Stamps Are Legendary

- **Rarity and Exclusivity:** Limited production and errors, like the Inverted Jenny and Treskilling Yellow, make these stamps exceptionally desirable.
- **Historical Significance:** Stamps like the Penny Black revolutionized communication, while others commemorate pivotal events, such as China's Cultural Revolution.
- **Provenance and Stories:** Ownership by famous collectors or intriguing backstories enhances a stamp's mystique and value.

- **Artistic Excellence:** Stamps such as the Basel Dove showcase groundbreaking designs and craftsmanship that continue to inspire admiration.

This chapter highlights how legendary stamps embody history, artistry, and human ingenuity. Whether it's their rarity, their stories, or their cultural impact, these iconic pieces remind collectors of the profound joy in preserving philately's rich legacy. By understanding what makes these stamps extraordinary, readers gain deeper insight into the allure of stamp collecting.

Part 2: Starting and Growing Your Collection

Stamp collecting is an incredibly rewarding hobby that evolves as you build and refine your collection. Part 2 is dedicated to helping you take those crucial first steps and grow your collection into something meaningful and unique. Whether you're a beginner or looking to expand your expertise, this section provides practical advice and inspiration for starting and nurturing your philatelic journey.

Chapter 4: Starting Your First Stamp Collection

Building a stamp collection can be one of the most rewarding and creative hobbies to embark upon. Chapter 4 is your guide to laying the foundation for a fulfilling and exciting philatelic journey. Whether you're drawn to specific themes, countries, or historical periods, this chapter will help you identify your focus, gather essential tools, and learn how to organize your stamps effectively. Let's start your collection on the right note!

4.1 Choosing a Focus: Themes, Countries, or Time Periods

Stamp collecting is as versatile as your imagination, with endless possibilities to tailor your collection to your interests. Choosing a focus gives your collection structure and makes it uniquely yours.

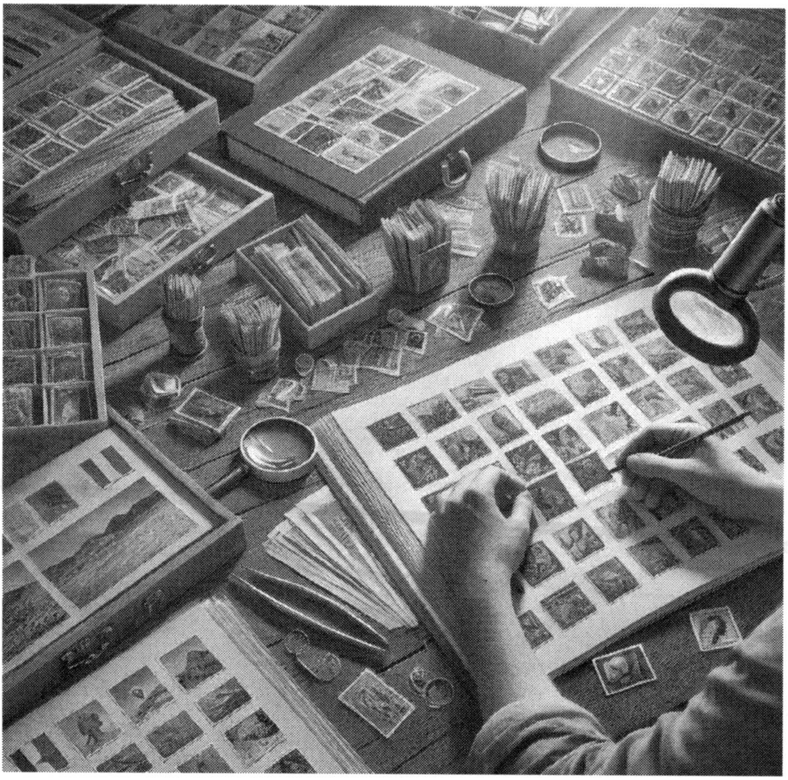

Set a focus for your collection to make it meaningful and rewarding.

A. Themes:

Thematic collecting allows you to explore your passions and interests while adding a personal touch to your collection. Themes bring a sense of excitement and creativity to stamp collecting.

- **Examples:** Wildlife, famous leaders, historical events, or even sports.
- **Why It's Rewarding:** Themes add a personal connection and make every stamp an exciting discovery.
- **Starting Tip:** Begin with a broad theme and narrow it down as your collection grows. For instance, if you're passionate about

wildlife, you might focus specifically on endangered species or birds of prey.

B. Countries:

Focusing on specific countries lets you delve into the unique history, culture, and artistry of a particular region. This approach creates a rich narrative within your collection.

- **Examples:** British stamps, U.S. airmail, or Asian designs.
- **Why It's Rewarding:** Country-specific collections highlight cultural diversity and design evolution.
- **Starting Tip:** Begin with countries that hold personal significance, such as your homeland or places you've visited.

C. Time Periods:

Collecting stamps from specific historical eras is like stepping back in time. Each stamp captures the essence of its era, making it a fascinating way to study history.

- **Examples:** Victorian-era stamps or World War II commemoratives.
- **Why It's Rewarding:** Stamps from specific times provide insights into history and societal changes.
- **Starting Tip:** Focus on periods of personal or historical interest, such as the era of space exploration or pivotal wartime years.

Choosing your focus is the first step to creating a collection that reflects your passions and tells a story. Imagine the satisfaction of curating a collection that resonates deeply with your personal interests.

4.2 Essential Tools You'll Need: Albums, Tweezers, and More

Every collector needs the right tools to preserve and showcase their collection. Having these essentials will set you up for success:

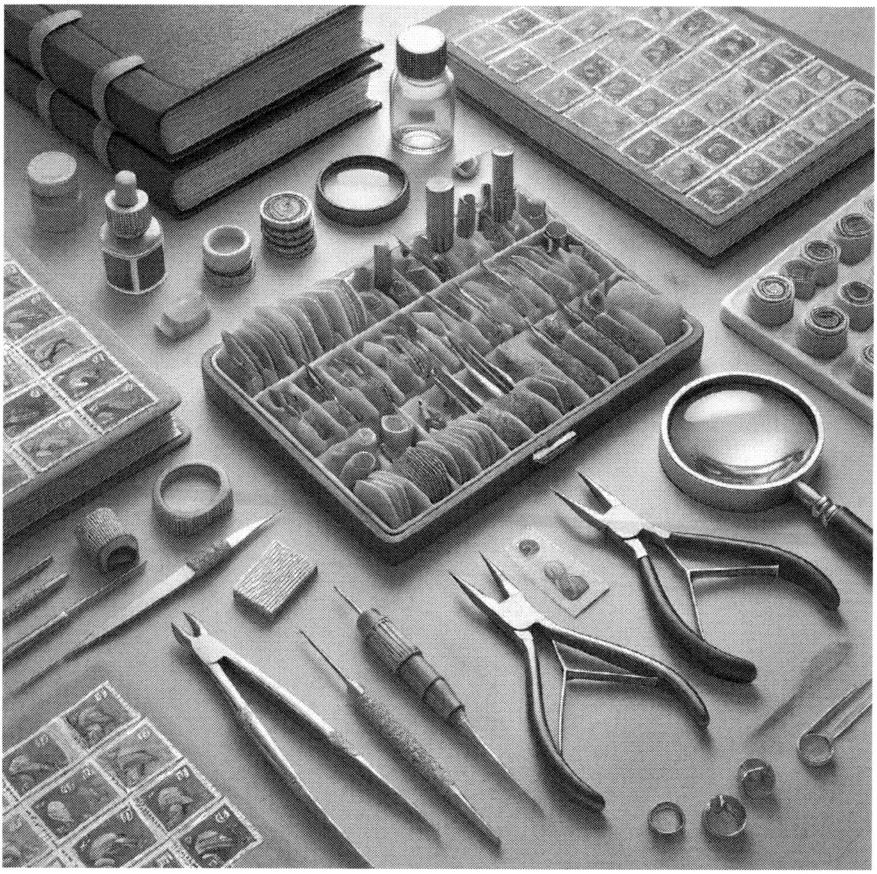

Equip yourself with the right tools to handle and preserve your stamps with care.

A. Albums and Stock Books:

Proper storage is crucial to preserving your collection. Albums and stock books offer different ways to organize and display your stamps securely.

- **Purpose:** To safely store and display your stamps.
- **Options:** Choose between albums with adhesive mounts or stock books with sleeves. Stock books are ideal for flexibility, while albums provide a polished presentation.
- **Pro Tip:** Opt for archival-quality, acid-free materials to ensure your stamps remain in pristine condition for decades.

B. Tweezers:

Handling stamps with care is essential to maintaining their condition. Tweezers are a must-have tool for every collector to avoid accidental damage.

- **Purpose:** Prevent damage from oils on your hands.
- **Tips:** Use soft-tipped tweezers designed specifically for handling stamps. These ensure precision without risking tears.
- **Pro Tip:** Keep multiple tweezers on hand, including angled ones for hard-to-reach stamps.

C. Magnifying Glass:

A magnifying glass helps uncover the fine details and unique features of your stamps. This tool is indispensable for identifying watermarks and assessing perforations.

- **Purpose:** Inspect details like perforations and watermarks.
- **Tips:** A high-quality magnifier, ideally with LED lighting, makes identification easier and more accurate.
- **Pro Tip:** Consider a loupe magnifier for advanced inspection.

D. Watermark Detector and Perforation Gauge:

For more advanced collectors, these tools provide insights into a stamp's authenticity and rarity. They are especially useful for evaluating high-value items.

- **Purpose:** Advanced tools for identifying rare or unique features.
- **Why It's Useful:** Helps verify authenticity and condition, especially for valuable pieces.
- **Pro Tip:** Test your tools on lower-value stamps first to gain confidence in their use.

By investing in these tools, you'll ensure your collection remains pristine while uncovering fascinating details about each stamp.

4.3 How to Find Your First Stamps: Simple Ways to Begin

Starting your collection doesn't have to be expensive or complicated. Here are some simple ways to gather your first stamps:

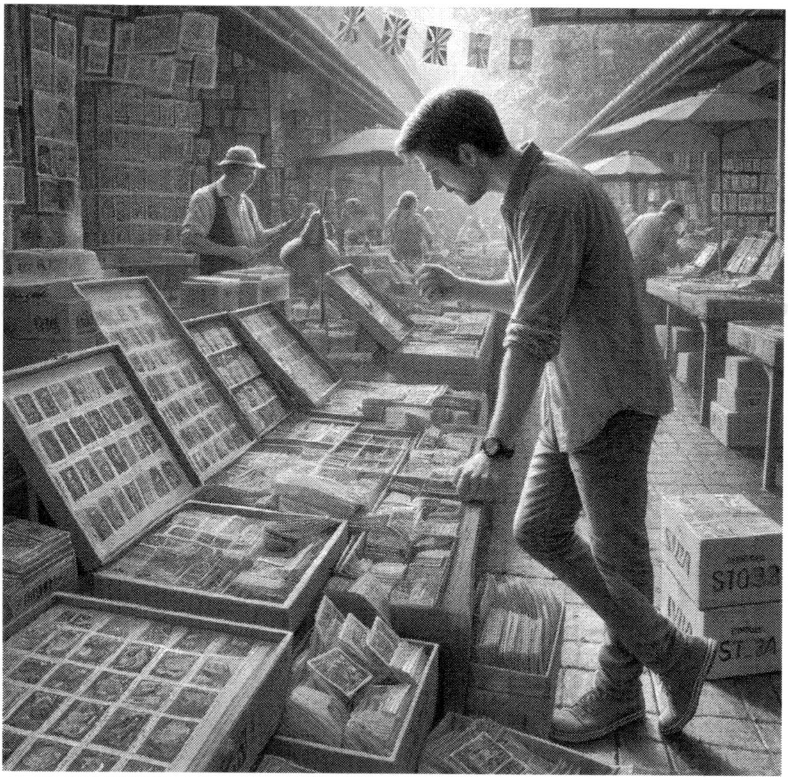

Start small and build your collection with accessible and exciting finds.

A. Check Your Mail:

One of the simplest ways to start collecting is by examining the stamps that come with everyday mail. This approach is cost-effective and often surprising.

- **Why It Works:** Everyday mail often has interesting stamps.

- **Tip:** Save envelopes from family, friends, or even international mail. Use scissors to carefully cut around the stamp and soak it off later.
- **Pro Tip:** Ask friends or family abroad to send you letters with unique stamps.

B. Visit Post Offices:

Post offices often carry commemorative and special edition stamps. Visiting your local post office is an easy way to start building a unique collection.

- **Why It Works:** Many post offices sell commemorative or special edition stamps.
- **Tip:** Ask about current issues and limited releases. They're an affordable way to start building a unique collection.
- **Pro Tip:** Subscribe to your postal service's philatelic program for regular updates on new releases.

C. Explore Online Marketplaces:

Online platforms open up a world of possibilities for collectors. These marketplaces are excellent sources for discovering diverse and affordable stamps.

- **Why It Works:** Platforms like eBay offer affordable starter packs.
- **Tip:** Look for reputable sellers with good reviews. Be cautious about authenticity for higher-value stamps.
- **Pro Tip:** Start with bulk lots to build your collection quickly and identify stamps to research further.

D. Attend Local Stamp Shows or Clubs:

Networking with fellow collectors provides inspiration and learning opportunities. Stamp shows and clubs are great places to find unique items and expert advice.

- **Why It Works:** Networking with other collectors opens doors to trades and advice.
- **Tip:** Use these opportunities to learn and find unique pieces, often at bargain prices.
- **Pro Tip:** Attend beginner workshops at shows to deepen your understanding of philately.

Exploring these sources can quickly build your collection and introduce you to the vibrant philatelic community.

4.4 Organizing and Labeling Your Collection

A well-organized collection is easier to manage and more enjoyable to explore. Here's how to organize your stamps effectively:

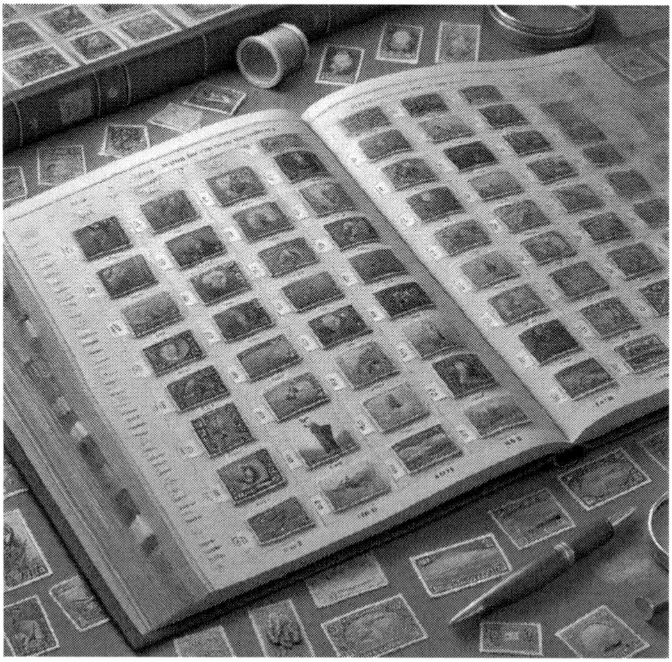

Organize and label your collection to showcase its uniqueness and value.

A. Sorting:

Organizing your stamps into categories is the first step toward creating a cohesive collection. Sorting by themes, countries, or eras ensures clarity and structure.

- **Methods:** Sort by themes, countries, or eras based on your chosen focus.
- **Tip:** Use temporary labels or folders during the sorting process to avoid confusion.
- **Pro Tip:** Revisit and refine your sorting system periodically to keep it relevant.

B. Labeling:

Labeling your stamps adds context and enhances their educational value. Clear labels make your collection more accessible and enjoyable to explore.

- **Purpose:** Add context and make your collection easier to navigate.
- **Tip:** Write descriptions about each stamp's origin or historical significance. This can be done on index cards or digital spreadsheets.
- **Pro Tip:** Include catalog numbers from trusted references like Scott or Stanley Gibbons for added precision.

C. Cataloging:

Keeping a catalog helps you track your collection and plan future acquisitions. Cataloging is especially useful for preventing duplication and monitoring growth.

- **Why It's Important:** A catalog helps you keep track of your stamps and prevents accidental duplication.
- **Tip:** Use a digital spreadsheet or a dedicated stamp-collecting app to document your collection.

- **Pro Tip:** Back up your catalog in cloud storage to prevent data loss.

D. Displaying:

Showcasing your collection highlights its beauty and significance. A well-displayed collection brings your stamps to life while protecting them from damage.

- **Purpose:** Highlight your favorite pieces while protecting them from damage.
- **Tip:** Use acid-free mounts and UV-protected frames for special stamps to maintain their condition.
- **Pro Tip:** Rotate displayed stamps periodically to avoid prolonged exposure to light.

An organized collection not only protects your stamps but also enhances the joy of exploring them. The effort you put into sorting and labeling pays off every time you admire your growing treasure trove.

Stamp collecting is a journey of discovery, and starting with a solid foundation ensures that every step is rewarding. By choosing a focus, gathering the right tools, and organizing your collection, you're setting yourself up for a lifetime of enjoyment and learning. Each stamp tells a story—now it's time to start telling yours!

Chapter 4 Review: Starting Your First Stamp Collection

Chapter 4 provides a practical and inspiring guide to launching your philatelic journey. It emphasizes the importance of building a collection that reflects your personal interests, equipping yourself with essential tools, and organizing your stamps effectively. With clear, actionable advice, this chapter sets a solid foundation for a lifetime of stamp collecting.

4.1 Choosing a Focus: Themes, Countries, or Time Periods

- **Themes for Personal Connection:** Collecting by theme allows you to reflect your passions, such as wildlife, historic events, or famous leaders, adding creativity and individuality to your collection.
- **Country-Specific Collections:** Focusing on stamps from particular nations provides insight into their history, culture, and artistic evolution.
- **Exploring Time Periods:** Collecting stamps from specific eras, such as Victorian times or World War II, offers a fascinating way to connect with history.

4.2 Essential Tools You'll Need: Albums, Tweezers, and More

- **Storage Solutions:** Albums and stock books protect stamps and display them attractively. Archival-quality materials are key to preserving condition.
- **Tweezers for Careful Handling:** Soft-tipped tweezers prevent damage from oils or pressure, ensuring your stamps stay pristine.
- **Magnifying Glasses and Advanced Tools:** Magnifiers reveal fine details, while perforation gauges and watermark detectors help identify rarity and authenticity.

4.3 How to Find Your First Stamps: Simple Ways to Begin

- **Everyday Mail as a Resource:** Start by examining stamps on incoming mail, a cost-effective way to find unique pieces.
- **Post Office Visits:** Local post offices often offer commemorative and special-edition stamps, ideal for new collectors.
- **Online Marketplaces:** Platforms like eBay provide access to bulk lots and affordable starter packs, though authenticity should be verified.

- **Stamp Shows and Clubs:** Networking with collectors at shows or clubs provides inspiration, advice, and access to rare finds.

4.4 Organizing and Labeling Your Collection

- **Sorting by Categories:** Organize stamps by themes, countries, or eras for clarity and focus.
- **Labeling for Context:** Adding details about origin, significance, or catalog numbers enriches the educational value of your collection.
- **Cataloging for Growth:** Use digital spreadsheets or apps to track your collection, monitor progress, and prevent duplication.
- **Displaying Your Collection:** Showcase favorite stamps with acid-free mounts or UV-protected frames, balancing preservation and presentation.

This chapter emphasizes the importance of starting with intention and preparation. By defining a focus, investing in tools, and organizing your collection thoughtfully, you'll create a meaningful and enjoyable collecting experience. Chapter 4 ensures readers are equipped to begin their philatelic journey with confidence and creativity.

Chapter 5: Finding Stamps: Where and How to Look

Building a robust stamp collection begins with knowing where to look and how to find unique, valuable, and fascinating stamps. Chapter 5 is your guide to discovering stamps in a variety of settings, from local post offices to bustling online marketplaces. With this chapter, you'll learn how to navigate different sources effectively, ensuring your collection grows with quality and diversity.

5.1 Local Post Offices and Commemorative Issues

Your local post office is one of the simplest and most accessible places to start your stamp-collecting journey. Post offices offer a range of stamps, from standard designs to limited-edition commemoratives.

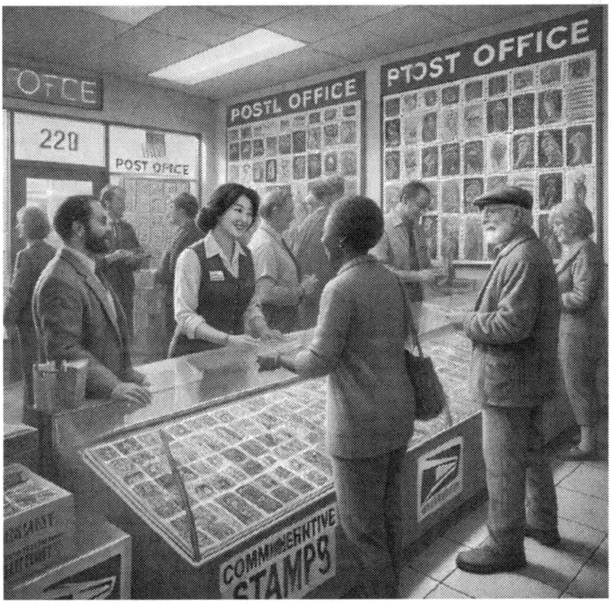

Check local post offices for commemorative issues that enrich your collection.

A. Everyday Stamps:

Visiting your local post office provides access to everyday postage stamps, often featuring national symbols, famous figures, or cultural icons. These stamps are great for new collectors and serve as a foundation for growing your collection.

- **Variety:** Everyday stamps often include national icons and cultural motifs.
- **Accessibility:** Easily available and affordable for beginners.
- **Tip:** Visit your post office regularly to check for new releases and seasonal designs.

B. Commemorative Stamps:

Commemorative stamps celebrate events, anniversaries, and notable achievements. These limited-edition pieces are often beautifully designed and highly collectible.

- **Significance:** Commemorative stamps mark historical milestones and cultural achievements.
- **Limited Editions:** Often issued in small quantities, making them highly collectible.
- **Tip:** Ask about upcoming commemorative issues and pre-order them to ensure availability.

C. First-Day Covers:

First-day covers are envelopes with stamps postmarked on their release date. These items are valuable additions for collectors who enjoy the historical significance of specific releases.

- **Historical Value:** Capture a stamp's official release with postmarked covers.
- **Thematic Appeal:** Complements themed collections.
- **Tip:** Collect first-day covers to enhance your collection's narrative.

D. Stamp Subscription Services:

Many postal services offer subscription programs that provide collectors with a steady supply of new and commemorative stamps throughout the year.

- **Consistency:** Regularly receive new issues without having to visit the post office.
- **Exclusive Access:** Some subscriptions include limited-edition releases.
- **Tip:** Subscribe to your country's philatelic program to keep your collection current.

Your local post office is more than just a source of postage—it's a gateway to discovering the artistic and cultural heritage of your nation.

5.2 Stamp Shows, Auctions, and Fairs: Best Tips for Collectors

Stamp shows, auctions, and fairs are exciting venues to explore the world of philately, meet other collectors, and find rare stamps.

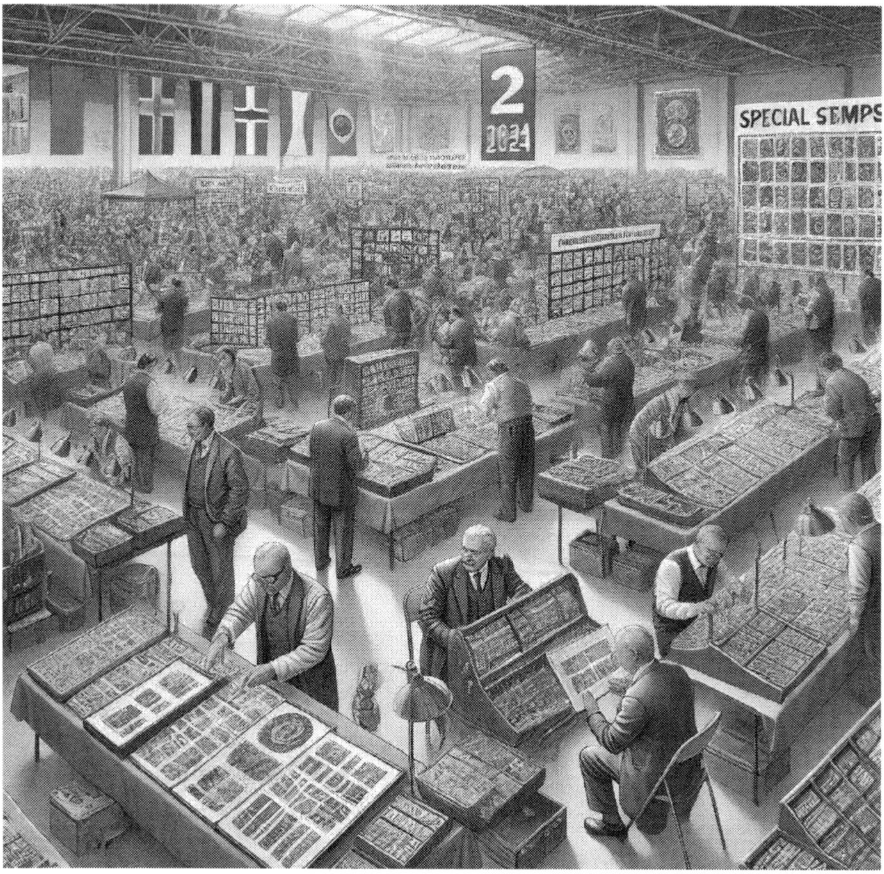

Discover rare finds and connect with fellow collectors at stamp shows and auctions.

A. Stamp Shows:

Stamp shows often feature dealers, exhibitors, and special events. These gatherings are ideal for learning and purchasing stamps in person.

- **Opportunities:** Access a wide range of stamps and expert advice.
- **Networking:** Meet dealers and other collectors to exchange insights.
- **Tip:** Attend stamp shows with a checklist of what you're looking for to stay focused.

B. Auctions:

Auctions, both live and online, provide opportunities to acquire rare and valuable stamps. However, they require careful planning and bidding strategies.

- **Rarity:** Auctions often feature unique or high-value stamps.
- **Preparation:** Research auction catalogs and set a budget beforehand.
- **Tip:** Start with smaller auctions to build confidence in bidding.

C. Fairs and Exhibitions:

Fairs and exhibitions combine the thrill of discovery with the chance to view curated collections. These events often highlight specific themes or eras.

- **Learning:** Gain insights from expert exhibitors and themed displays.
- **Exploration:** Discover stamps that fit your focus.
- **Tip:** Use fairs to network with other collectors and gain expert advice.

D. Workshops and Seminars:

Many fairs and shows include workshops where collectors can learn specialized skills like stamp grading, authentication, and thematic organization.

- **Skill Development:** Enhance your philatelic knowledge and techniques.
- **Interactive Learning:** Hands-on sessions provide practical experience.
- **Tip:** Sign up for workshops in advance to secure your spot.

Attending these events not only helps you find exceptional stamps but also immerses you in the vibrant philatelic community.

5.3 Estate Sales, Flea Markets, and Antique Shops

Sometimes, the most valuable treasures are found in unexpected places. Estate sales, flea markets, and antique shops offer unique opportunities for collectors.

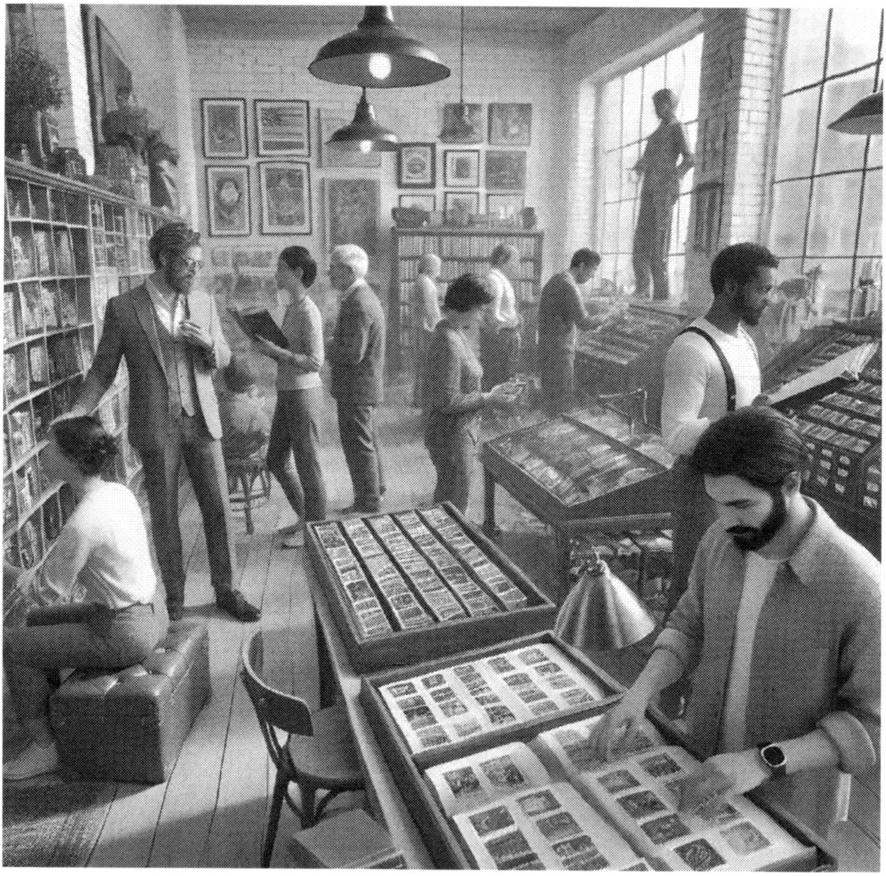

Unearth hidden treasures in unexpected places like estate sales and flea markets.

A. Estate Sales:

Estate sales often include collections from long-time enthusiasts, providing access to rare or vintage stamps.

- **Rich Selection:** Collections often feature well-preserved and historically significant stamps.

- **Cost-Effective Finds:** Potential for acquiring entire collections at reasonable prices.
- **Tip:** Arrive early to secure the best items and consider negotiating prices for larger purchases.

B. Flea Markets:

Flea markets are ideal for discovering overlooked gems among miscellaneous items.

- **Hidden Treasures:** Sellers may undervalue stamps, providing opportunities for great deals.
- **Diverse Inventory:** Includes a mix of old and new stamps.
- **Tip:** Examine items carefully to assess condition and authenticity before buying.

C. Antique Shops:

Antique shops often house stamps alongside vintage postcards and collectibles, adding historical depth to your collection.

- **Curated Selections:** Includes rare or themed items that reflect local history.
- **Expert Advice:** Shop owners may have insights into the stamps they sell.
- **Tip:** Build relationships with shop owners for early access to new arrivals.

D. Local Classifieds:

Check local classified ads or community boards for individuals selling personal collections.

- **Unadvertised Finds:** Many collections are sold privately and may not be listed online.
- **Affordable Deals:** Sellers may offer items at bargain prices to clear space.

- **Tip:** Approach sellers politely and inquire about the history of their collection.

These unconventional sources can uncover treasures that add character and uniqueness to your collection.

5.4 Online Marketplaces: Safely Buying Stamps

The internet has revolutionized stamp collecting, offering access to a global marketplace. However, a strategic approach is essential for safe and successful purchases.

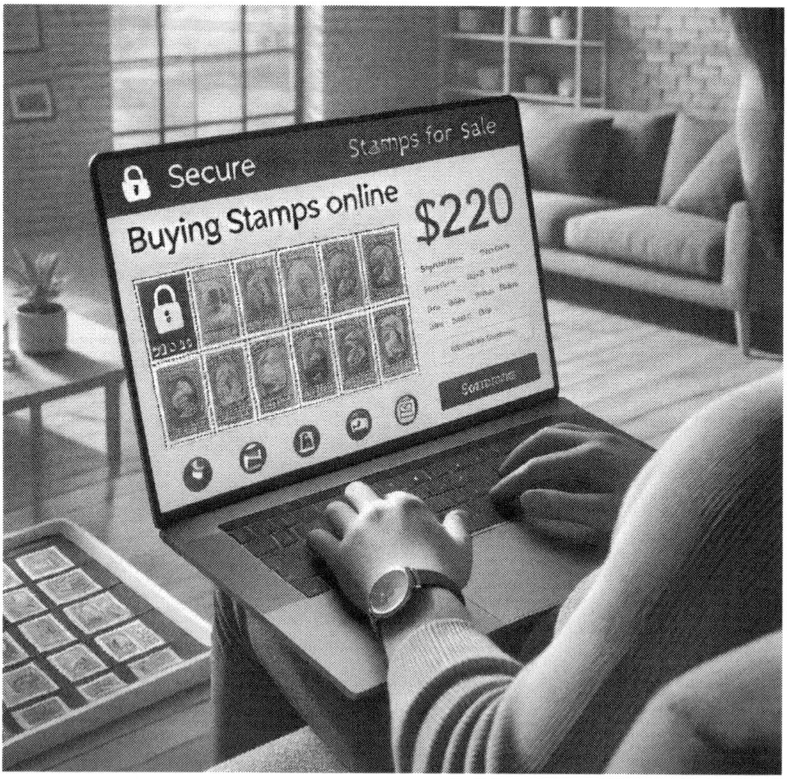

Navigate online marketplaces confidently with smart buying strategies.

A. Platforms to Explore:

Websites like eBay, Delcampe, and HipStamp connect collectors with sellers offering a vast variety of stamps.

- **Global Access:** Purchase stamps from sellers worldwide without leaving your home.
- **Search Filters:** Easily find stamps by themes, regions, or rarity.
- **Tip:** Use advanced filters to streamline your search and save time.

B. Evaluating Sellers:

Choosing reputable sellers ensures that you're purchasing authentic and quality items.

- **Reputation Matters:** Look for positive reviews and clear descriptions from sellers.
- **Photo Quality:** High-resolution images help verify the condition and details of stamps.
- **Tip:** Contact sellers with questions about authenticity or provenance before finalizing a purchase.

C. Verifying Authenticity:

For high-value stamps, authentication adds an extra layer of confidence.

- **Certification Options:** Some platforms offer third-party verification services.
- **Avoiding Scams:** Be cautious with deals that seem too good to be true.
- **Tip:** Verify details with official catalogs or authentication services for rare items.

D. Managing Costs:

Online marketplaces include auctions, fixed-price listings, and bulk lots. Budgeting and smart shopping are key to growing your collection affordably.

- **Bulk Lots:** Save money by purchasing large assortments.
- **Budget-Friendly Strategies:** Set spending limits to stay within budget.
- **Tip:** Track your purchases to monitor expenses and avoid duplications.

E. Specialized Online Communities:

Join forums or online groups dedicated to stamp collecting. These platforms often feature buy/sell threads or exclusive listings from trusted members.

- **Trustworthy Sources:** Community members are often more invested in preserving the hobby's integrity.
- **Exclusive Deals:** Access rare finds not available on larger platforms.
- **Tip:** Participate in discussions to build credibility and trust within the community.

Online platforms offer unparalleled convenience, connecting you to a global community of collectors and dealers while expanding your collection.

Stamp collecting is a dynamic and exciting hobby, and knowing where and how to look for stamps ensures your collection grows in both quality and diversity. Whether you're browsing local post offices or bidding in global auctions, each new acquisition brings you closer to building a collection that tells your story. Let the hunt begin! 🚀

Chapter 5 Review: Finding Stamps: Where and How to Look

Chapter 5 is an essential guide for collectors, detailing where and how to find stamps to build a collection rich in quality, variety, and history. From local post offices to global online marketplaces, this chapter equips readers with practical tips and strategies for navigating diverse sources.

5.1 Local Post Offices and Commemorative Issues

- **Everyday Stamps:** Accessible and affordable, these foundational pieces often feature national symbols and cultural motifs, ideal for beginners.
- **Commemorative Stamps:** Limited-edition issues celebrating events and achievements add historical and artistic value to collections.
- **First-Day Covers:** Postmarked envelopes from a stamp's release date provide unique historical significance.
- **Subscription Services:** Regularly receive new stamps, including exclusive releases, through postal programs.

5.2 Stamp Shows, Auctions, and Fairs

- **Stamp Shows:** These events offer diverse stamps, expert advice, and networking opportunities with other collectors.
- **Auctions:** Rare and valuable stamps can be found here, though preparation and budgeting are crucial.
- **Fairs and Exhibitions:** These combine education and exploration, with themed displays and workshops to enhance your skills.
- **Workshops and Seminars:** Learn specialized techniques like grading and authentication in hands-on sessions.

5.3 Estate Sales, Flea Markets, and Antique Shops

- **Estate Sales:** Often feature well-preserved collections, offering opportunities to acquire rare stamps at reasonable prices.
- **Flea Markets:** Hidden treasures can be found, but careful examination for authenticity is key.

- **Antique Shops:** Stamps paired with vintage collectibles provide historical depth and unique finds.
- **Local Classifieds:** Personal collections sold privately can yield affordable, unadvertised gems.

5.4 Online Marketplaces: Safely Buying Stamps

- **Global Access:** Platforms like eBay and Delcampe connect you to sellers worldwide, with search filters to narrow your focus.
- **Seller Reputation:** High ratings and clear descriptions ensure authenticity and quality.
- **Authentication Services:** Third-party verification provides confidence for high-value purchases.
- **Community Platforms:** Forums and specialized groups offer exclusive listings and trustworthy transactions.

Chapter 5 empowers collectors to explore both traditional and modern methods for sourcing stamps. Whether hunting for treasures at local venues or browsing international online marketplaces, the guidance provided ensures every collector can grow their collection with confidence, diversity, and quality. This chapter prepares readers to embrace the thrill of the search and expand their philatelic horizons.

Chapter 6: Expanding Your Collection Like a Pro

As you advance in stamp collecting, expanding your collection with rare and specialized stamps can take your passion to the next level. Chapter 6 delves into strategies for finding exceptional stamps, building meaningful connections with fellow collectors, and curating a collection that reflects your unique interests and expertise.

6.1 Exploring Rare and Specialized Stamps

Rare and specialized stamps offer collectors an exciting challenge and a deeper connection to history and artistry. Pursuing these stamps allows you to focus on specific themes, regions, or eras that resonate with your interests.

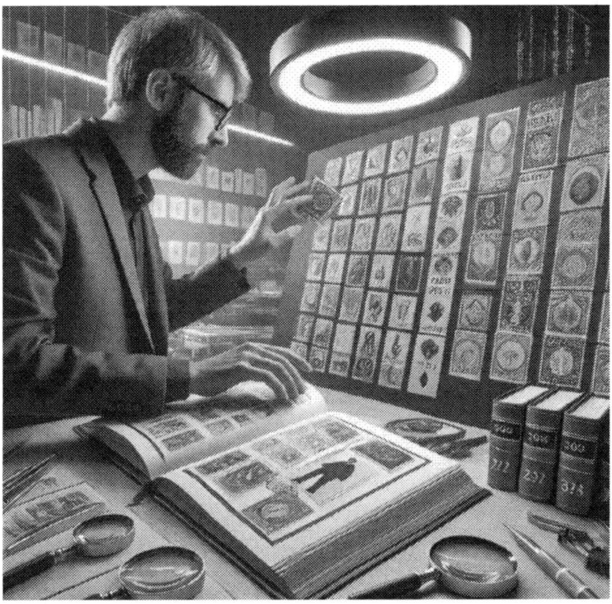

Take your collection to the next level with rare and specialized stamps.

A. Rare Stamps:

Rare stamps are often sought after due to their limited availability, unique features, or historical significance.

- **Limited Editions:** Produced in small quantities, making them highly collectible.
- **Errors and Misprints:** Stamps with printing errors, such as inverted designs, are prized for their rarity.
- **Tip:** Use stamp catalogs and expert resources to identify and prioritize rare stamps for your collection.

The thrill of finding rare stamps often lies in their stories. For instance, the discovery of the legendary Treskilling Yellow error stamp illustrates how unexpected finds can become invaluable treasures in philately.

B. Thematic Stamps:

Thematic collecting focuses on stamps related to specific topics, such as wildlife, space exploration, or famous personalities.

- **Personal Connection:** Build a collection around themes that inspire you.
- **Storytelling Potential:** Thematic collections tell compelling stories through carefully curated stamps.
- **Tip:** Explore international stamps for diverse thematic designs.

Themes like "Historic Landmarks" or "Natural Wonders" allow you to explore stamps that represent global beauty and achievements, adding layers of personal meaning to your collection.

C. Regional and Historical Stamps:

Collecting stamps from particular regions or historical periods adds depth and cultural significance to your collection.

- **Regional Focus:** Highlight the artistic styles and histories of specific countries.

- **Historical Context:** Stamps from significant time periods offer unique insights into the past.
- **Tip:** Attend exhibitions or fairs to find regionally significant stamps.

For example, stamps from colonial-era Africa or post-war Europe provide unique windows into societal changes and artistic evolution, enriching your perspective as a collector.

6.2 Connecting with Other Collectors to Trade and Learn

Building relationships with fellow collectors is an invaluable part of expanding your collection. Networking helps you access new stamps, share knowledge, and deepen your appreciation for the hobby.

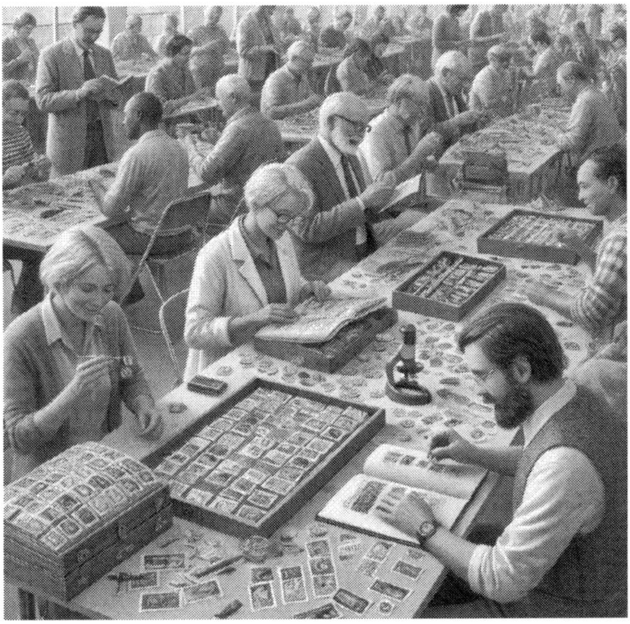

Build relationships with collectors to trade, learn, and grow your collection.

A. Joining Clubs and Societies:

Stamp-collecting clubs and societies bring enthusiasts together to share resources and foster community.

- **Networking Opportunities:** Connect with collectors who share your interests.
- **Access to Resources:** Many clubs provide exclusive access to libraries, catalogs, and expert advice.
- **Tip:** Join both local and online communities to broaden your reach.

Membership in groups like the American Philatelic Society often includes access to rare auctions and mentoring from seasoned collectors, enriching your philatelic journey.

B. Trading with Collectors:

Trading stamps is a cost-effective way to acquire new pieces and engage with the philatelic community.

- **Mutual Benefits:** Exchange duplicates for stamps you need, benefiting both parties.
- **Building Relationships:** Strengthen connections through regular trading.
- **Tip:** Clearly document the condition and authenticity of stamps when trading.

Participating in swap meets or online trading forums can create exciting opportunities to grow your collection while forging connections with fellow enthusiasts.

C. Learning from Experts:

Experienced collectors and dealers can provide valuable insights and guidance as you refine your focus.

- **Mentorship Opportunities:** Learn advanced techniques for spotting rare or undervalued stamps.

- **Shared Experiences:** Gain inspiration and practical tips from seasoned collectors.
- **Tip:** Attend workshops or webinars hosted by philatelic experts.

Engaging with experts often leads to valuable lessons, such as how to authenticate stamps or recognize unique design elements, ensuring your collection grows with knowledge and precision.

6.3 Finding Hidden Gems: How to Spot Undervalued Stamps

Unearthing undervalued stamps is one of the most rewarding aspects of philately. By developing a keen eye and leveraging research, you can identify stamps with untapped potential.

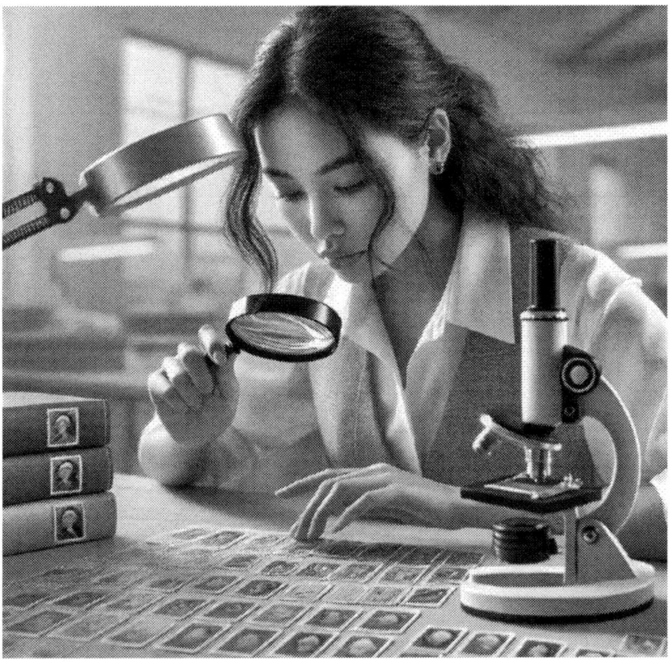

Learn how to identify undervalued stamps with potential for growth.

A. Researching Market Trends:

Understanding market trends helps you recognize stamps that may increase in value over time.

- **Auction Data:** Review past auction results to spot trends in pricing and demand.
- **Catalog Insights:** Use catalogs to identify stamps that are undervalued relative to their rarity.
- **Tip:** Stay informed about emerging themes and collector preferences.

Monitoring sales data for specific themes like "early aviation" or "colonial issues" can reveal undervalued stamps poised for future appreciation.

B. Spotting Overlooked Features:

Some stamps are undervalued due to unrecognized details or historical significance.

- **Condition Anomalies:** Look for stamps in better-than-average condition.
- **Unique Attributes:** Identify features like rare cancellations or unlisted variations.
- **Tip:** Use magnifiers and tools to analyze stamps thoroughly.

A stamp with a unique postmark or a subtle design variation might be overlooked by others but could be a treasure for your collection.

C. Patience and Persistence:

Finding hidden gems often requires time, dedication, and a willingness to explore unconventional sources.

- **Treasure Hunts:** Visit estate sales, flea markets, and lesser-known dealers.
- **Building Knowledge:** The more you know, the better you'll spot undervalued items.

- **Tip:** Keep a detailed log of your findings to track patterns and potential leads.

Collectors who approach their search methodically often discover hidden treasures that others miss, adding both value and intrigue to their collections.

6.4 Building a Collection That's Truly Yours

The ultimate goal of stamp collecting is to create a collection that reflects your personality, passions, and expertise. Curating a unique collection ensures lasting satisfaction and pride.

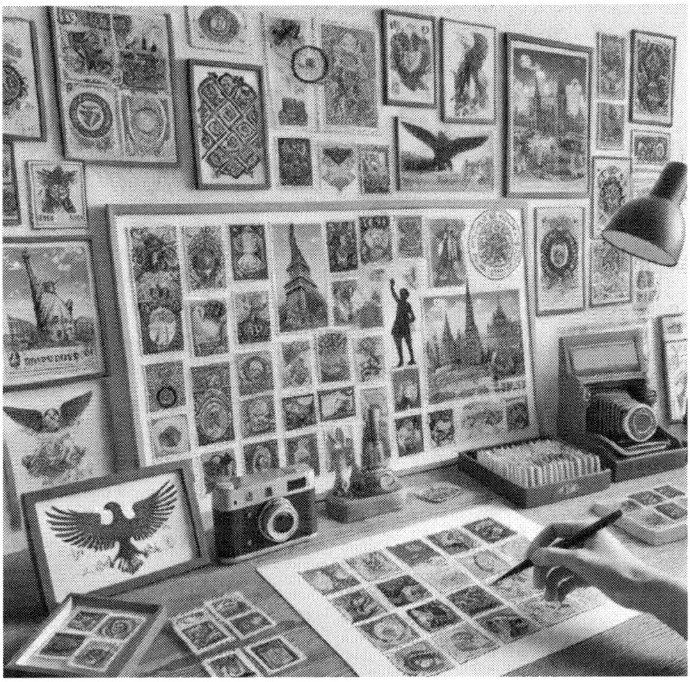

Craft a collection that reflects your personal interests and creativity.

A. Defining Your Vision:

Decide what you want your collection to represent, whether it's a specific theme, era, or cultural focus.

- **Personal Expression:** Your collection should tell a story about your interests and values.
- **Clear Focus:** A defined vision helps guide your acquisitions.
- **Tip:** Create a mission statement to stay inspired and focused.

For example, a collector with a passion for environmental conservation might focus on stamps featuring endangered species or global sustainability themes.

B. Organizing Your Collection:

A well-organized collection enhances its appeal and accessibility.

- **Categorization:** Sort stamps by themes, regions, or time periods.
- **Presentation:** Use archival-quality albums and labels for professional displays.
- **Tip:** Regularly update your organization system to accommodate new additions.

Collectors who invest time in proper organization often find greater joy in sharing and showcasing their collections.

C. Sharing Your Collection:

Sharing your collection with others adds a new dimension of enjoyment and engagement.

- **Exhibiting:** Participate in local exhibitions to showcase your work.
- **Inspiring Others:** Share your passion through presentations, blogs, or social media.
- **Tip:** Document your collection with high-quality photos and descriptions.

Sharing not only inspires others but also invites valuable feedback and connections that can enhance your philatelic journey.

Expanding your collection like a pro involves a blend of research, networking, and creativity. By exploring rare stamps, connecting with fellow enthusiasts, and curating a collection that reflects your passions, you can elevate your philatelic journey to new heights. Let every stamp you collect bring a piece of history and a touch of artistry into your life!

Chapter 6 Review: Expanding Your Collection Like a Pro

Chapter 6 guides readers through the process of elevating their stamp collections by focusing on rare finds, building connections within the philatelic community, and curating a collection that reflects their passions. With practical strategies and expert insights, this chapter encourages collectors to pursue their interests with creativity and precision.

6.1 Exploring Rare and Specialized Stamps

- **Rare Stamps:** Limited-edition stamps, errors, and misprints offer exciting opportunities for collectors to acquire highly sought-after pieces. Tools like stamp catalogs and expert resources can help prioritize these finds.
- **Thematic Stamps:** Personalize your collection by focusing on themes such as wildlife, space exploration, or historical landmarks, creating a narrative through your stamps.
- **Regional and Historical Stamps:** Delve into specific regions or eras, such as colonial Africa or post-war Europe, to gain cultural and historical insights while enriching your collection.

6.2 Connecting with Other Collectors to Trade and Learn

- **Joining Clubs and Societies:** Networking with fellow enthusiasts provides access to resources, mentorship, and exclusive opportunities like auctions and events.

- **Trading with Collectors:** Swapping duplicates for needed pieces is a cost-effective way to expand your collection while fostering relationships in the philatelic community.
- **Learning from Experts:** Workshops and advice from experienced collectors can refine your skills in areas like authentication and identifying undervalued stamps.

6.3 Finding Hidden Gems: How to Spot Undervalued Stamps

- **Researching Market Trends:** Analyze auction data and catalogs to identify stamps with growth potential or overlooked value.
- **Spotting Unique Features:** Focus on condition, rare cancellations, or unlisted variations to discover hidden treasures.
- **Patience and Persistence:** Exploring unconventional sources like estate sales or flea markets often uncovers valuable finds.

6.4 Building a Collection That's Truly Yours

- **Defining Your Vision:** Tailor your collection to reflect your personality, values, or a specific focus, such as sustainability or global history.
- **Organizing Your Collection:** Use archival-quality albums and clear categorization to enhance the presentation and accessibility of your stamps.
- **Sharing Your Collection:** Exhibiting or sharing your collection through blogs and social media inspires others while inviting valuable feedback and connections.

Chapter 6 empowers collectors to take their philatelic journey to the next level by combining research, networking, and creativity. With each new acquisition, collectors deepen their appreciation for history and artistry, creating a collection that is both meaningful and uniquely their own.

Part 3: Understanding Value, Rarity, and Special Stamps

Part 3 delves into the intricate world of evaluating, grading, and understanding the rarity of stamps. This section equips collectors with the knowledge to discern value, spot rare finds, and navigate the philatelic market with confidence. From the principles of stamp grading to mastering authentication techniques, this part empowers collectors to make informed decisions and appreciate the artistry and history behind every piece.

Chapter 7: Evaluating and Grading Stamps

Proper evaluation and grading are essential skills for every stamp collector, helping to determine the value, authenticity, and condition of a stamp. Chapter 7 delves into what makes a stamp valuable, how to use stamp catalogs and guides, the art of spotting rare finds, and the importance of authentication and certification.

7.1 What Makes a Stamp Valuable? Condition, Rarity, and Demand

Understanding the factors that influence a stamp's value is key to building a meaningful collection.

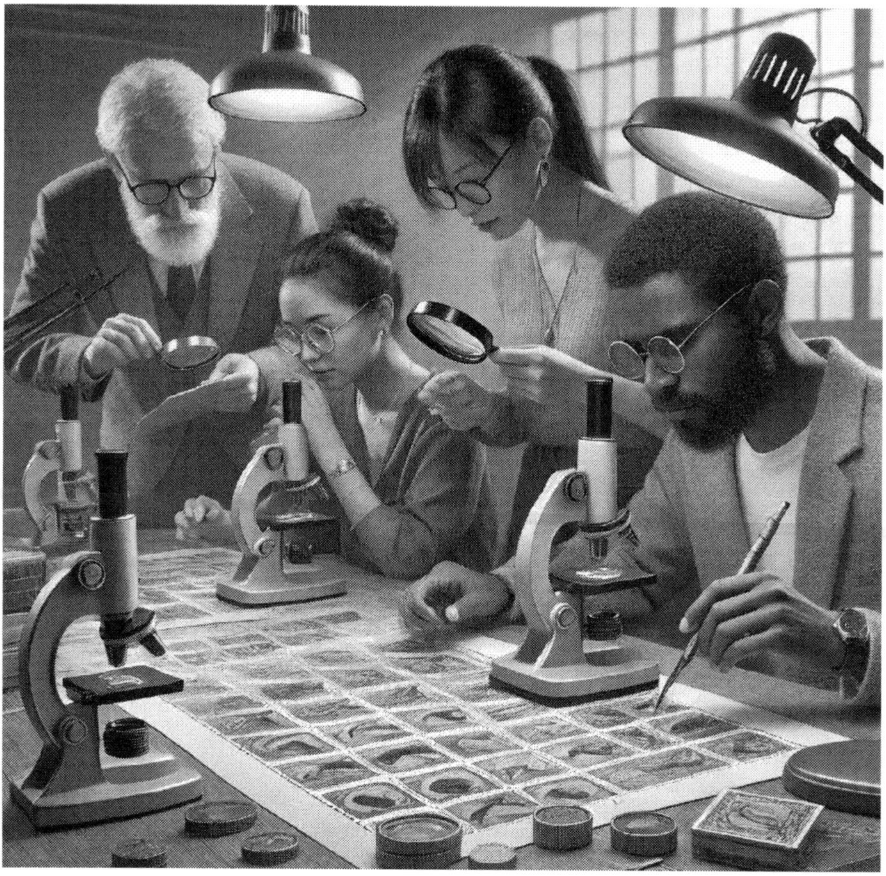

Understand the key factors that determine a stamp's value and significance.

A. Condition:

The physical state of a stamp greatly affects its value and determines its appeal among collectors.

- **Mint vs. Used:** Mint stamps—those that are unused and retain their original gum—are often more valuable because they remain in pristine condition. However, used stamps with rare cancellations or unique postal marks can also command high prices due to their historical significance.

- **Faults and Flaws:** Visible defects such as creases, tears, or fading significantly reduce a stamp's value. Even minor imperfections can affect collectability for high-grade items.
- **Centering and Perforations:** Well-centered designs with even borders and intact perforations enhance a stamp's visual appeal and are more sought after by collectors.
- **Original Gum:** For mint stamps, retaining the original adhesive gum in an undisturbed state adds considerable value.
- **Color Vibrancy:** Bright, unfaded colors indicate proper preservation and are preferred by collectors, especially for older stamps that are prone to discoloration.

B. Rarity:

Rarity often defines a stamp's desirability and market value, making it a critical factor in philately.

- **Limited Production:** Stamps with small print runs or those issued as limited editions become highly sought after, particularly if they commemorate significant events or figures.
- **Survival Rates:** Some stamps are rare not because of limited production but due to the few surviving examples, often caused by wars, natural disasters, or excessive postal use.
- **Unique Features:** Variations like inverted designs, misprints, or experimental materials make stamps stand out as rare collectibles.
- **Historical Significance:** Stamps tied to key moments in history, such as independence movements or technological breakthroughs, carry additional value.
- **Geographical Exclusivity:** Regional issues with restricted circulation often hold special appeal for collectors focusing on specific areas.

C. Demand:

The collector market plays a significant role in determining a stamp's value, driven by trends and cultural significance.

- **Trends:** Themes such as animals, space exploration, and cultural heritage influence demand, with popular motifs often attracting a wider audience.
- **Historical Interest:** Stamps linked to famous personalities, pivotal events, or national milestones draw significant attention from collectors and historians.
- **Global Appeal:** Stamps featuring universal themes, such as peace or environmental conservation, tend to resonate with collectors worldwide.
- **Cultural Significance:** Stamps showcasing unique regional traditions or historical narratives often hold a special place in the philatelic world.
- **Investment Potential:** Stamps with a consistent history of value appreciation attract investors seeking tangible, appreciating assets.

7.2 Using Stamp Catalogs and Guides: Scott and Stanley Gibbons

Stamp catalogs are indispensable tools for identifying and valuing stamps, serving as a roadmap for collectors at every level.

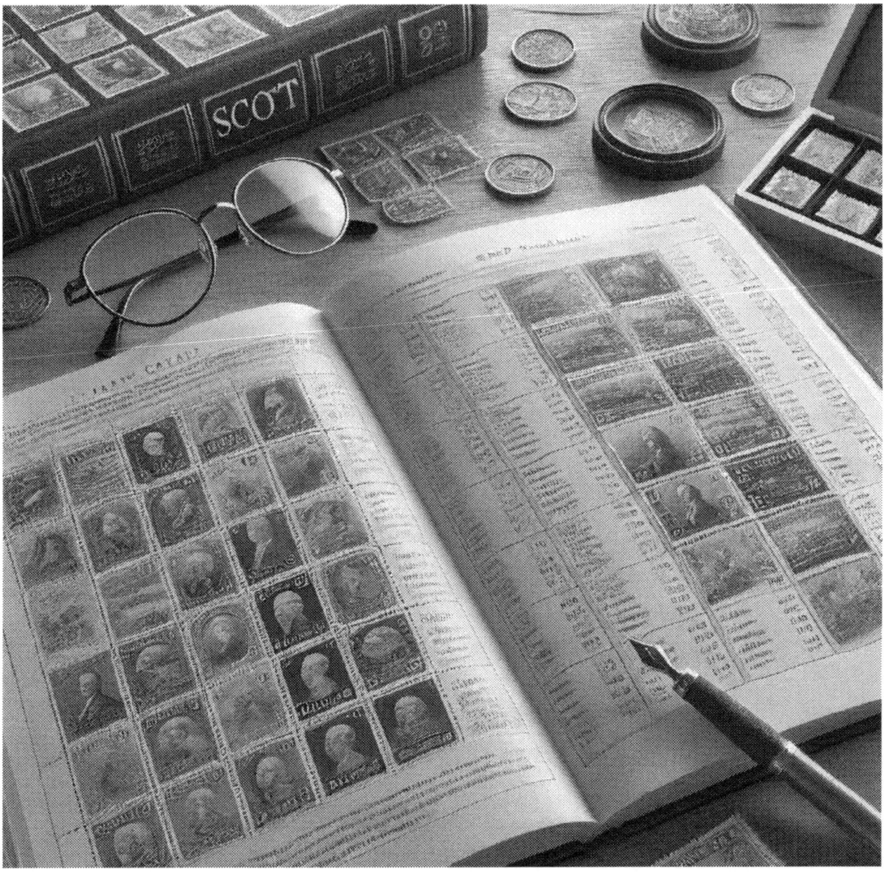

Learn how to use trusted catalogs to identify, grade, and value stamps accurately.

A. Key Features of Stamp Catalogs:

Catalogs provide comprehensive information to guide collectors in identifying and understanding their stamps.

- **Stamp Identification:** Detailed descriptions of stamp designs, issue dates, and issuing countries help collectors pinpoint specific items in their collections.
- **Market Values:** Catalogs include estimated retail prices based on rarity, condition, and demand, giving collectors a benchmark for evaluating worth.

- **Historical Context:** Many catalogs offer insights into the historical and cultural significance of stamps, enriching the collector's appreciation.
- **Catalog Numbers:** Each stamp is assigned a unique identifier to simplify organization and facilitate communication among collectors.
- **Visual References:** High-resolution images accompany listings, aiding in accurate identification and comparison.

B. Popular Catalogs:

The Scott and Stanley Gibbons catalogs are trusted resources for collectors worldwide.

- **Scott Catalog:** This comprehensive guide is known for its organized layout and global coverage, making it an essential resource for collectors of all levels.
- **Stanley Gibbons Catalog:** Renowned for its in-depth focus on British Commonwealth stamps, this catalog offers historical details and valuation insights.
- **Regional Guides:** Specialized catalogs, such as Michel (Germany) and Yvert et Tellier (France), cater to collectors with regional interests, offering localized expertise.
- **Thematic Guides:** Some catalogs focus on specific themes, such as airmail, commemorative issues, or errors.
- **Online Databases:** Many catalog publishers now offer digital versions with advanced search features and regular updates.

C. Practical Tips for Catalog Use:

To maximize the utility of stamp catalogs, consider these strategies:

- **Cross-Reference:** Use multiple catalogs to compare details and valuations, especially for rare or high-value stamps.
- **Stay Updated:** Regularly check for new editions or digital updates to keep abreast of market trends and newly discovered items.

- **Organize Your Collection:** Label your stamps with catalog numbers to streamline organization and enhance accessibility.
- **Digital Tools:** Leverage digital editions for quick searches and portable access.
- **Personal Annotations:** Make notes in your catalog to track specific acquisitions or areas of interest.

7.3 Spotting Rare Finds: Errors, Misprints, and Hidden Treasures

Uncovering rare and unique stamps is a thrilling aspect of philately, often leading to the most prized additions in a collection.

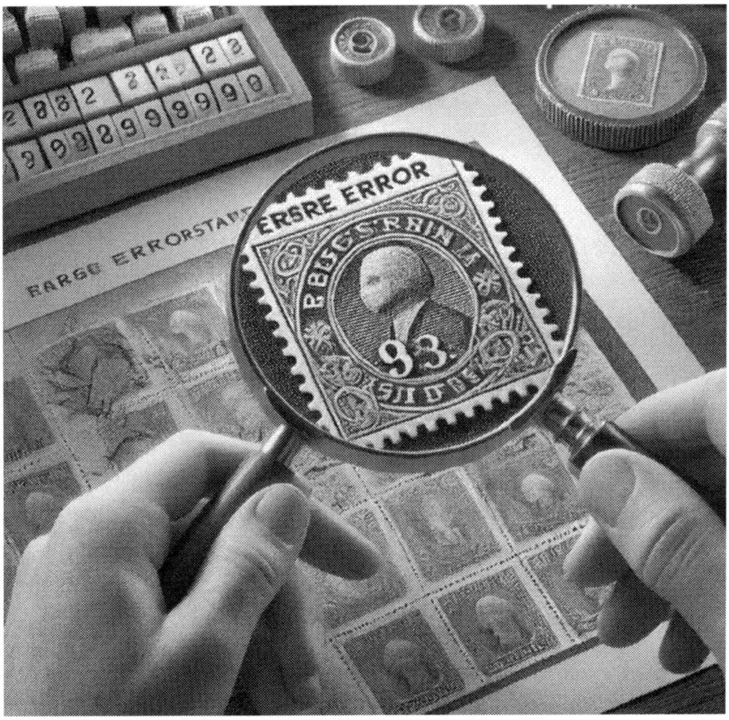

Identify errors and misprints that make stamps rare and highly collectible.

A. Printing Errors:

Mistakes during production create some of the most valuable and intriguing stamps.

- **Inverted Centers:** Iconic examples like the Inverted Jenny are highly sought after for their striking visual anomalies.
- **Color Variations:** Stamps printed in unintended or mismatched colors become instant rarities.
- **Double Prints:** Overlapping or duplicated designs offer collectors a fascinating glimpse into production errors.
- **Printing Omissions:** Stamps missing key elements, such as text or images, stand out as unique collectibles.
- **Plate Flaws:** Subtle imperfections on printing plates can result in rare and desirable variations.

B. Misprints:

Design errors add character and distinctiveness to stamps, making them attractive to collectors.

- **Missing Details:** Stamps lacking essential information, such as denominations or inscriptions, intrigue collectors.
- **Incorrect Inscriptions:** Errors in names, dates, or spellings enhance a stamp's uniqueness.
- **Unique Fonts or Layouts:** Variations caused by misaligned or experimental designs are particularly interesting.
- **Reversed Images:** Occasionally, entire designs are reversed, creating captivating rarities.
- **Shifted Prints:** Misaligned designs produce visually striking effects that collectors prize.

C. Hidden Treasures:

Rare finds often emerge from unexpected sources, rewarding diligent and resourceful collectors.

- **Inherited Collections:** Family albums may contain overlooked gems with significant value.
- **Flea Markets:** These venues can yield rare items at budget-friendly prices for eagle-eyed collectors.
- **Auction Finds:** Careful research and bidding at auctions often uncover hidden treasures.
- **Local Dealers:** Small, independent shops sometimes hold rare or unique stamps waiting to be discovered.
- **Surprise Discoveries:** Even everyday mail can occasionally contain rare and valuable stamps.

7.4 How to Authenticate and Certify Stamps

Authentication ensures the genuineness of stamps, while certification provides expert validation of their quality and value.

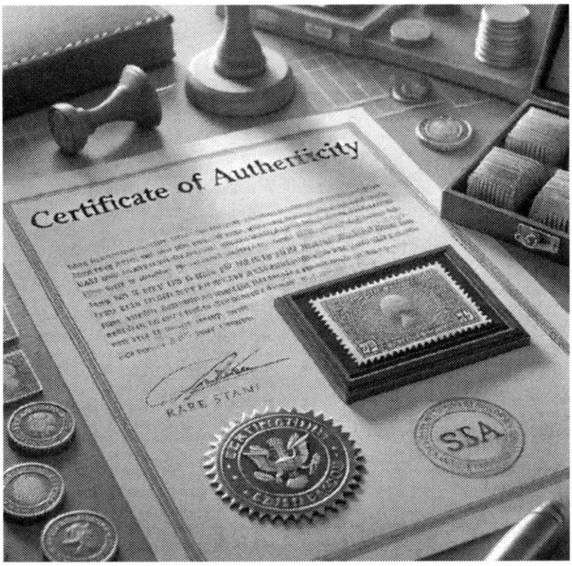

Authenticate your stamps to boost their credibility and collector appeal.

A. Importance of Authentication:

Verifying a stamp's authenticity protects collectors from counterfeits and enhances confidence in acquisitions.

- **Spotting Fakes:** Examine design details, perforations, and paper quality for inconsistencies.
- **Watermarks:** Use tools like watermark detectors to confirm authenticity and identify subtle features.
- **Expert Opinions:** Consult trusted philatelists or organizations for reliable assessments of authenticity.
- **Paper Analysis:** Authentic stamps often exhibit specific paper types or fibers unique to their era.
- **Color Consistency:** Ensure the stamp's colors match known genuine examples.

B. Certification Services:

Trusted organizations provide professional grading and certification services to validate a stamp's condition and value.

- **American Philatelic Society (APS):** Offers expert opinion services and certification.
- **Philatelic Foundation:** Provides detailed certificates for rare and high-value stamps.
- **Royal Philatelic Society London:** Known for meticulous and authoritative evaluations.
- **Professional Stamp Experts (PSE):** Specializes in precise numerical grading systems.
- **Global Stamp Experts:** Emerging services cater to international stamps and diverse markets.

C. DIY Authentication Tools:

Basic tools enable collectors to perform preliminary authentication and condition checks at home.

- **Magnifying Glasses:** Reveal fine details and potential inconsistencies in design.
- **UV Lamps:** Detect hidden markings, repairs, or alterations.
- **Perforation Gauges:** Ensure accurate alignment and count of perforations.
- **Microscopes:** Advanced magnification tools uncover subtle flaws or features.
- **Color Comparators:** Compare shades to identify potential inconsistencies or repairs.

Evaluating and grading stamps is both an art and a science, requiring attention to detail and a passion for discovery. By mastering these skills, collectors can build collections that are not only valuable but also deeply rewarding.

Chapter 7 Review: Evaluating and Grading Stamps

Chapter 7 equips collectors with the essential knowledge and skills to accurately evaluate and grade stamps, ensuring they understand a stamp's value, authenticity, and condition. This comprehensive guide highlights the factors that influence a stamp's worth, the role of catalogs, how to spot rare finds, and the importance of authentication and certification.

7.1 What Makes a Stamp Valuable? Condition, Rarity, and Demand

- **Condition Matters:** Mint stamps with original gum, vibrant colors, and intact perforations are highly desirable, while flaws such as creases or fading diminish value.
- **Rarity Defines Value:** Stamps with limited production, unique features like errors, or low survival rates command high prices. Examples include the Treskilling Yellow and Inverted Jenny.

- **Demand Drives Worth:** Themes such as famous personalities or significant historical events attract collectors, increasing value based on cultural or historical significance.

7.2 Using Stamp Catalogs and Guides

- **Key Features:** Stamp catalogs like Scott and Stanley Gibbons provide identification details, historical context, and market values to guide collectors.
- **Popular Resources:** Scott is ideal for global collections, while Stanley Gibbons specializes in British Commonwealth stamps. Regional and thematic guides cater to niche interests.
- **Practical Usage:** Cross-reference multiple catalogs, use catalog numbers for organization, and leverage digital editions for quick searches and updates.

7.3 Spotting Rare Finds: Errors, Misprints, and Hidden Treasures

- **Printing Errors:** Stamps with inverted designs, color variations, or missing elements are highly collectible due to their rarity and visual intrigue.
- **Misprints Add Uniqueness:** Design flaws such as incorrect inscriptions or reversed images create distinct collectibles prized by philatelists.
- **Uncovering Treasures:** Rare finds can emerge from everyday sources, such as inherited collections, flea markets, or even overlooked mail, rewarding resourceful collectors.

7.4 How to Authenticate and Certify Stamps

- **Authenticity Essentials:** Tools like magnifying glasses, watermark detectors, and UV lamps help identify genuine stamps and detect counterfeits.

- **Certification Services:** Organizations like the American Philatelic Society and Philatelic Foundation provide professional evaluations, ensuring confidence in high-value acquisitions.
- **DIY Tools:** Basic tools such as perforation gauges and microscopes allow collectors to perform preliminary checks before seeking expert certification.

Chapter 7 empowers collectors to approach their collections with greater confidence and precision. By mastering evaluation and grading techniques, collectors can identify valuable additions, avoid counterfeits, and appreciate the artistry and history behind every stamp. This chapter bridges the gap between amateur collecting and expert-level philately, offering a rewarding path to building a meaningful and valuable collection.

Chapter 8: Special Stamp Collecting Categories

Stamp collecting becomes even more engaging and rewarding when you delve into specialized categories. Chapter 8 explores how thematic stamps, country-specific issues, first-day covers, and unique errors can bring depth and excitement to your collection. By focusing on these categories, collectors can create vibrant, meaningful collections that tell unique stories and provide a lifetime of discovery.

8.1 Thematic Stamps: Nature, Art, History, and More

Thematic collecting focuses on stamps that share a common theme, offering collectors the chance to curate highly personalized and visually cohesive collections. Themes allow for creative exploration and provide endless possibilities for specialization.

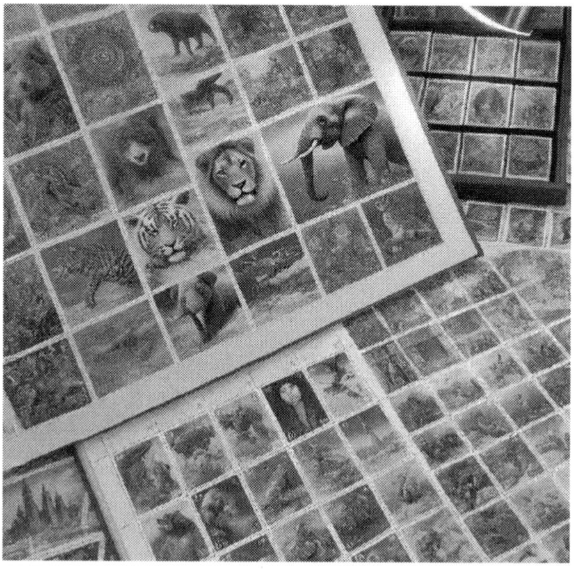

Explore the vibrant world of thematic stamps and their artistic stories.

A. Nature Themes:

Nature-themed stamps celebrate the beauty and diversity of the natural world. They highlight wildlife, flora, and environmental conservation efforts, making them perfect for collectors who love the outdoors and want to showcase the natural world in miniature form.

- **Wildlife:** Stamps featuring animals, from majestic lions and tigers to delicate butterflies and exotic birds, are among the most popular. Wildlife stamps often include beautifully detailed illustrations and vibrant colors.
- **Flora:** Botanical stamps showcase flowers, trees, and other plant species from across the globe, often tied to specific regions or cultural festivals.
- **Endangered Species:** Issues highlighting vulnerable ecosystems and endangered species bring awareness to conservation efforts. These stamps often support environmental initiatives, adding a philanthropic element to your collection.
- **Tip:** Seek out complete series like UNESCO's World Heritage flora and fauna stamps to add a curated, educational aspect to your collection.

B. Artistic Stamps:

Artistic themes bring creativity and cultural appreciation to your collection. These stamps commemorate global and regional art, featuring everything from classical masterpieces to contemporary designs.

- **Masterpieces on Stamps:** Many countries issue stamps featuring renowned artworks, such as the Mona Lisa or Van Gogh's Starry Night. These miniature reproductions are a celebration of humanity's artistic achievements.
- **Cultural Icons:** Commemorative issues often highlight famous artists, writers, and performers, reflecting their contributions to global heritage.

- **Modern Art:** Contemporary designs push philatelic aesthetics forward, showcasing innovative styles and techniques.
- **Tip:** Explore stamps issued by countries known for artistic heritage, such as Italy, France, or Japan, to find truly exceptional pieces.

C. Historical Events:

Stamps commemorating historical milestones offer a fascinating window into the past. They allow collectors to explore major events, cultural traditions, and societal changes.

- **Wars and Revolutions:** Stamps highlighting pivotal moments, such as World War II or independence movements, provide a tangible connection to history.
- **Cultural Celebrations:** Issues celebrating anniversaries, national holidays, or significant achievements often include intricate and symbolic designs.
- **Landmark Events:** Stamps that honor scientific breakthroughs, such as space exploration or medical advancements, are particularly inspiring.
- **Tip:** Research historical themes that resonate with you, such as women in history or industrial revolutions, to create a collection with personal significance.

8.2 Country-Specific Stamps: Unique Stories and Designs

Every country tells its story through stamps, making country-specific collections rich with cultural and historical significance. Collecting by country allows you to explore unique traditions, styles, and narratives.

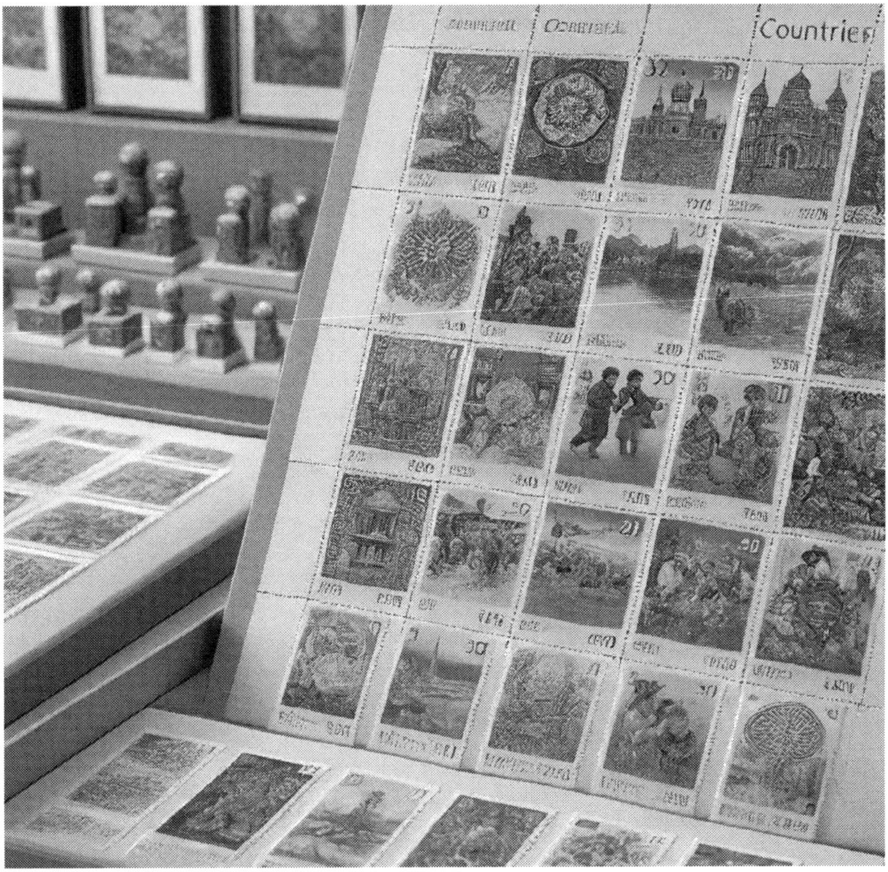

Dive into the unique designs and histories of country-specific stamps.

A. Iconic National Symbols:

National symbols on stamps often reflect a country's pride and identity. These stamps are ideal for collectors who want to celebrate the unique attributes of a particular nation.

- **Flags and Emblems:** Designs featuring national flags, seals, and other emblems symbolize heritage and unity.
- **Historical Figures:** Leaders, revolutionaries, and cultural icons depicted on stamps offer a glimpse into a nation's history.

- **Cultural Heritage:** Stamps showcasing traditional attire, festivals, and cuisines provide a vivid snapshot of a country's unique identity.
- **Tip:** Start with countries you have a personal connection to, such as your birthplace or ancestral homeland, to add deeper meaning to your collection.

B. Regional Styles:

Regional stamps highlight the diversity within nations, offering collectors a chance to explore unique traditions and landmarks.

- **Artistic Traditions:** Handcrafted patterns or motifs unique to specific areas often adorn regional issues.
- **Landscapes:** Depictions of famous natural wonders, cityscapes, and rural scenes capture the essence of a region's geography.
- **Cultural Diversity:** Stamps showcasing ethnic traditions and local folklore offer a rich tapestry of stories.
- **Tip:** Seek out stamps that highlight UNESCO World Heritage Sites or regions of ecological importance for added historical and cultural value.

C. Historical Series:

Stamps issued in historical series often provide a timeline of important events, giving collectors a deeper understanding of a nation's journey.

- **Colonial Eras:** Stamps from colonial periods often feature unique designs and geopolitical insights.
- **Independence Movements:** Commemorative issues celebrating freedom and sovereignty are particularly significant for understanding national histories.
- **Modern Achievements:** Stamps honoring technological advancements or international collaborations reflect progress and innovation.

- **Tip:** Use catalogs to identify complete series for a cohesive collection that tells a comprehensive story.

8.3 Collecting First-Day Covers, Souvenir Sheets, and Postal Stationery

Expanding beyond traditional stamps, collectors can explore first-day covers (FDCs), souvenir sheets, and postal stationery for a more diverse and engaging collection.

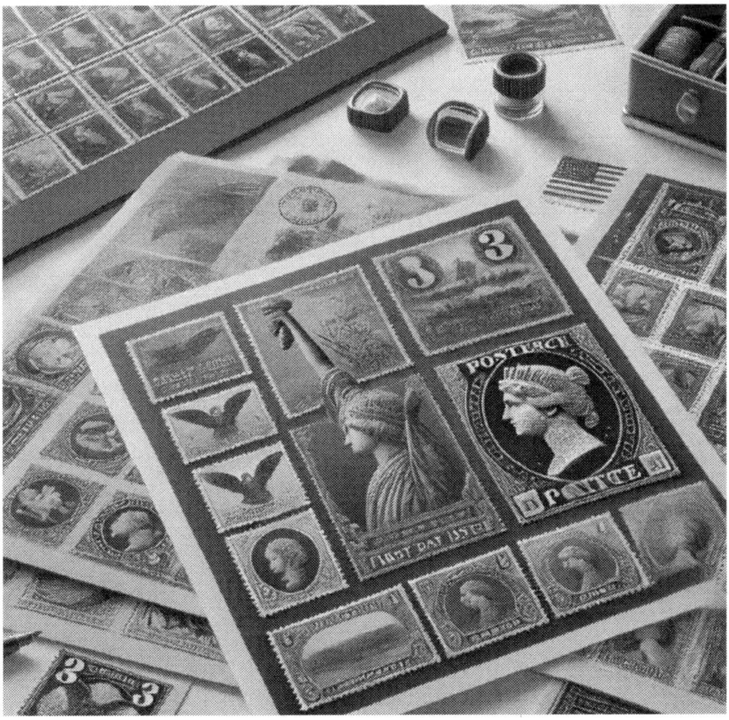

Add depth to your collection with first-day covers and exclusive postal stationery.

A. First-Day Covers (FDCs):

First-day covers mark the official release of a stamp and often include exclusive designs, making them prized items among collectors.

- **Unique Postmarks:** FDCs feature cancellations marking the date and location of a stamp's release, adding historical and regional significance.
- **Thematic Appeal:** Covers often complement the stamp's theme with related illustrations or descriptions.
- **Artistic Presentation:** Many FDCs include custom artwork, turning them into standalone collectibles.
- **Tip:** Store FDCs in archival-quality sleeves to preserve their condition and value over time.

B. Souvenir Sheets:

Souvenir sheets showcase stamps in a decorative format, offering a blend of artistry and collectibility.

- **Artistic Presentation:** These sheets often feature elaborate background designs that enhance the stamps' themes.
- **Limited Editions:** Produced in small quantities, souvenir sheets often hold higher value and appeal.
- **Commemorative Significance:** Sheets often highlight major events, anniversaries, or international collaborations.
- **Tip:** Look for souvenir sheets commemorating global events like the Olympics or World Fairs to add unique items to your collection.

C. Postal Stationery:

Postal stationery combines functionality with artistic appeal, offering a glimpse into the history of communication.

- **Functional History:** Envelopes, postcards, and letter sheets often feature pre-printed stamps, showcasing how people communicated in different eras.
- **Design Variety:** Vintage stationery frequently includes unique illustrations or embossing.

- **Historical Context:** Items like wartime postal stationery reflect the social and cultural climate of their time.
- **Tip:** Seek out vintage postal stationery with rare cancellations or regional designs for added historical value.

8.4 Errors and Oddities: Fascinating Stamp Mistakes

Error stamps and oddities bring an element of surprise and uniqueness to collections. These anomalies capture the human element of stamp production and make for intriguing additions.

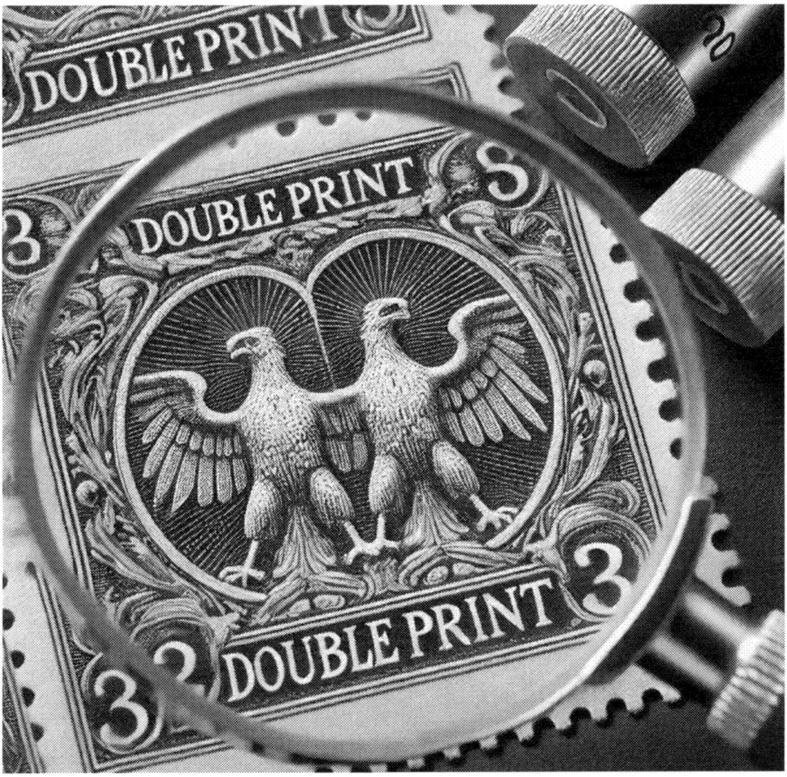

Uncover the charm of errors and oddities that intrigue philatelists worldwide.

A. Printing Errors:

Printing errors transform everyday stamps into rare and valuable treasures. Collectors often seek these mistakes for their rarity and historical significance.

- **Inverted Images:** Famous examples like the Inverted Jenny showcase the allure of accidental rarities.
- **Color Misprints:** Stamps printed in incorrect or missing colors are highly prized.
- **Misaligned Perforations:** Off-center perforations or doubled designs create fascinating visual effects.
- **Tip:** Examine stamps closely under magnification to detect subtle printing mistakes that may add value.

B. Design Oddities:

Design quirks highlight the creative and experimental aspects of philately, adding character to collections.

- **Unusual Formats:** Oddly shaped stamps, such as triangular or circular designs, stand out in collections.
- **Novelty Features:** Glow-in-the-dark ink, holograms, or scented elements on modern stamps push the boundaries of traditional design.
- **Cultural Quirks:** Stamps featuring humorous or unexpected designs often become conversation starters.
- **Tip:** Explore novelty stamps issued by international postal services for unique finds.

C. Unintended Rarities:

Some stamps become rare due to unforeseen circumstances, making them highly sought after by collectors.

- **Withdrawn Issues:** Stamps recalled shortly after release due to errors or controversies gain rarity.

- **Limited Circulation:** Issues distributed in remote locations or during short periods often hold unique appeal.
- **Unique Contexts:** Stamps associated with rare historical events or regions become coveted items.
- **Tip:** Research the stories behind these rarities to add depth and significance to your collection.

Exploring special stamp collecting categories allows you to tailor your collection to your passions and interests. Whether you focus on thematic stamps, delve into country-specific designs, or hunt for errors and oddities, each category offers endless opportunities for discovery and creativity. Let your collection tell your story while preserving the artistry and history of philately.

Chapter 8 Review: Special Stamp Collecting Categories

Chapter 8 inspires collectors to explore specialized categories of stamps, bringing depth, creativity, and personal meaning to their collections. Whether focusing on thematic stamps, country-specific designs, first-day covers, or rare errors, this chapter offers insights into how these categories can enhance the philatelic experience.

8.1 Thematic Stamps: Nature, Art, History, and More

- **Nature-Themed Stamps:** Celebrate wildlife, flora, and environmental conservation with stamps that feature detailed illustrations and vibrant colors. These collections often support awareness efforts, adding a philanthropic element.
- **Artistic Stamps:** From reproductions of masterpieces like *Starry Night* to modern art, these stamps reflect humanity's creative achievements and cultural icons.

- **Historical Events:** Commemorative stamps capture pivotal moments, such as wars, revolutions, or scientific breakthroughs, offering collectors a tangible link to the past.

8.2 Country-Specific Stamps: Unique Stories and Designs

- **National Symbols:** Stamps featuring flags, historical figures, and cultural heritage provide a vivid snapshot of a nation's identity and pride.
- **Regional Diversity:** Explore stamps showcasing local traditions, landmarks, and folklore, which add richness to your collection.
- **Historical Series:** Collecting stamps from colonial eras, independence movements, or modern achievements offers a timeline of significant events and progress.

8.3 First-Day Covers, Souvenir Sheets, and Postal Stationery

- **First-Day Covers (FDCs):** These items mark the release of stamps with unique postmarks and often include complementary designs, making them valuable additions.
- **Souvenir Sheets:** Decorative presentations featuring limited-edition stamps add artistic and commemorative value.
- **Postal Stationery:** Vintage items like pre-stamped envelopes and postcards combine functionality with historical charm.

8.4 Errors and Oddities: Fascinating Stamp Mistakes

- **Printing Errors:** Mistakes like inverted images or color misprints transform ordinary stamps into rare treasures, exemplified by icons like the Inverted Jenny.
- **Design Oddities:** Unique formats, novelty features, and experimental designs push the boundaries of traditional philately.

- **Unintended Rarities:** Withdrawn issues, limited circulation, or stamps tied to rare events create captivating stories and collectible appeal.

Chapter 8 encourages collectors to dive into these specialized categories, which bring character, variety, and personal resonance to their collections. By pursuing thematic interests, exploring unique designs, or hunting for rare errors, collectors can create vibrant collections that preserve the artistry and history of stamps while reflecting their own passions. This chapter enriches the philatelic journey, transforming it into a lifelong adventure of discovery and creativity.

Chapter 9: The Stories Behind Stamps

Stamps are more than miniature works of art—they are storytellers. Chapter 9 uncovers how stamps capture historical events, honor famous collectors, reveal hidden tales in philately, and inspire collectors to create meaningful narratives within their collections. By diving into the rich stories behind stamps, collectors can connect deeply with their collections while preserving pieces of history for future generations.

9.1 How Stamps Capture Historical Events

Stamps act as time capsules, preserving the essence of pivotal moments in history. They connect collectors to events that shaped the world and offer unique insights into global milestones.

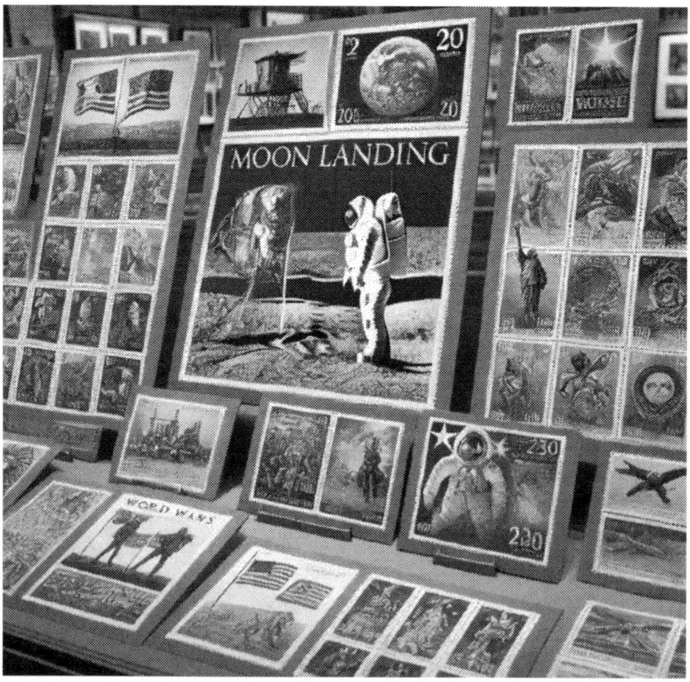

Discover how stamps chronicle and celebrate significant moments in history.

A. Commemorating Milestones:

Many stamps are issued to mark anniversaries or major achievements, encapsulating history in a tangible form. These commemorative issues highlight significant moments that have left an indelible mark on society.

- **Wars and Conflicts:** Stamps honoring peace treaties, battles, or veterans—such as World War II commemoratives—capture the sacrifices and triumphs of those eras. These stamps often feature iconic symbols like victory arches or medals of honor.
- **Scientific Breakthroughs:** Stamps celebrating achievements like the moon landing, the discovery of penicillin, or breakthroughs in renewable energy. These stamps serve as tributes to human ingenuity and perseverance.
- **Cultural Celebrations:** Stamps dedicated to festivals, heritage events, or social movements reflect the rich tapestry of traditions and progress. Examples include Diwali stamps from India or civil rights commemoratives from the United States.
- **Tip:** Research stamps related to your favorite historical topics to enrich your collection. Thematic focus adds both depth and personal significance.

B. Propaganda and Politics:

Governments often use stamps to promote national ideologies or political messages, making these designs deeply symbolic and sometimes controversial.

- **Symbolic Imagery:** Stamps featuring national heroes, flags, or slogans serve as tools of influence, reinforcing patriotism or political agendas. For instance, Soviet-era stamps often depicted workers, industrial growth, and space exploration.
- **Cold War Messaging:** During tense periods like the Cold War, stamps showcased technological superiority or political alliances. Space race-themed stamps from the U.S. and USSR illustrate this rivalry vividly.

- **Tip:** Look for stamps that reflect shifts in political landscapes for a deeper understanding of history. Political context often enhances the narrative value of these issues.

C. Honoring Heroes:

Stamps immortalize figures who have made lasting impacts, offering collectors a way to celebrate human achievement and societal progress.

- **World Leaders:** Stamps portraying presidents, monarchs, and revolutionaries—like Abraham Lincoln or Gandhi—capture their legacies.
- **Innovators and Artists:** Commemorations of inventors, writers, and cultural icons, such as Leonardo da Vinci or Maya Angelou, bring creativity and innovation to life.
- **Tip:** Build a thematic collection around stamps featuring influential individuals, creating a gallery of human achievement.

9.2 Famous Collectors Who Made History

Behind many significant philatelic achievements are passionate collectors whose stories continue to inspire.

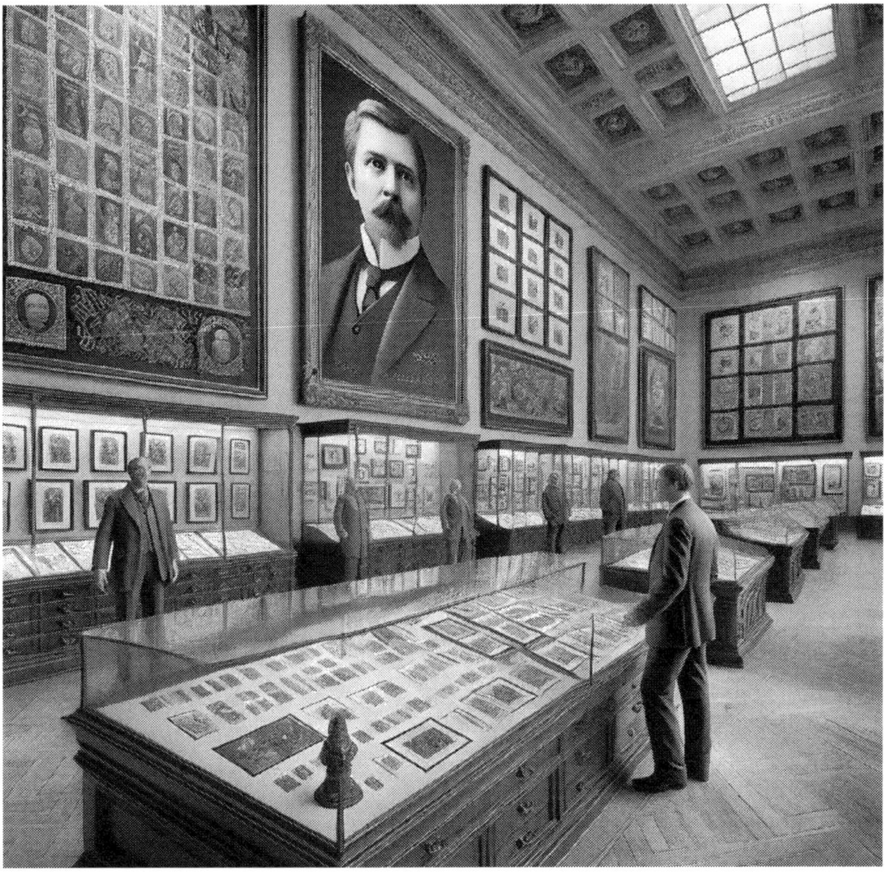

Be inspired by the collectors who shaped the history of philately.

A. Pioneers of Philately:

Early collectors laid the groundwork for modern philately, turning a hobby into a global passion that unites people across cultures and generations.

- **John Edward Gray:** Credited as one of the first stamp collectors, Gray began his collection in 1840 when the Penny Black was introduced. His passion helped spark a worldwide interest in philately.
- **Philatelic Societies:** Early enthusiasts formed clubs like the Royal Philatelic Society London, which still thrives today as a hub for collectors. These societies foster learning, networking, and preservation.

- **Tip:** Explore biographies of pioneering collectors to understand the origins of philately and gain insight into its evolution.

B. Record-Breaking Collectors:

Some individuals amassed collections that became legendary, showcasing the heights philately can achieve and inspiring others to aim high.

- **King George V:** Known as the "Philatelist King," his collection remains one of the most valuable in the world, including rare treasures like the Mauritius "Post Office" stamps.
- **Bill Gross:** The billionaire philanthropist built a renowned U.S. stamp collection and later auctioned it for charity, setting records in the process.
- **Tip:** Learn from notable collections to identify high-value stamps and themes worth pursuing.

C. Influential Women in Philately:

Women have also made significant contributions to the stamp-collecting world, often bringing unique perspectives and innovations to the hobby.

- **Princess Grace of Monaco:** Her thematic collections celebrated Monaco's history and culture, raising the profile of philately worldwide.
- **Mary Ann Owens:** An award-winning philatelist and advocate for thematic collecting, Owens championed the artistic and educational aspects of the hobby.
- **Tip:** Celebrate diversity in philately by exploring contributions from collectors of different backgrounds, enriching your appreciation of the hobby.

9.3 Hidden Stories in Philately

Stamps often hold secrets or unexpected narratives that add intrigue to their appeal.

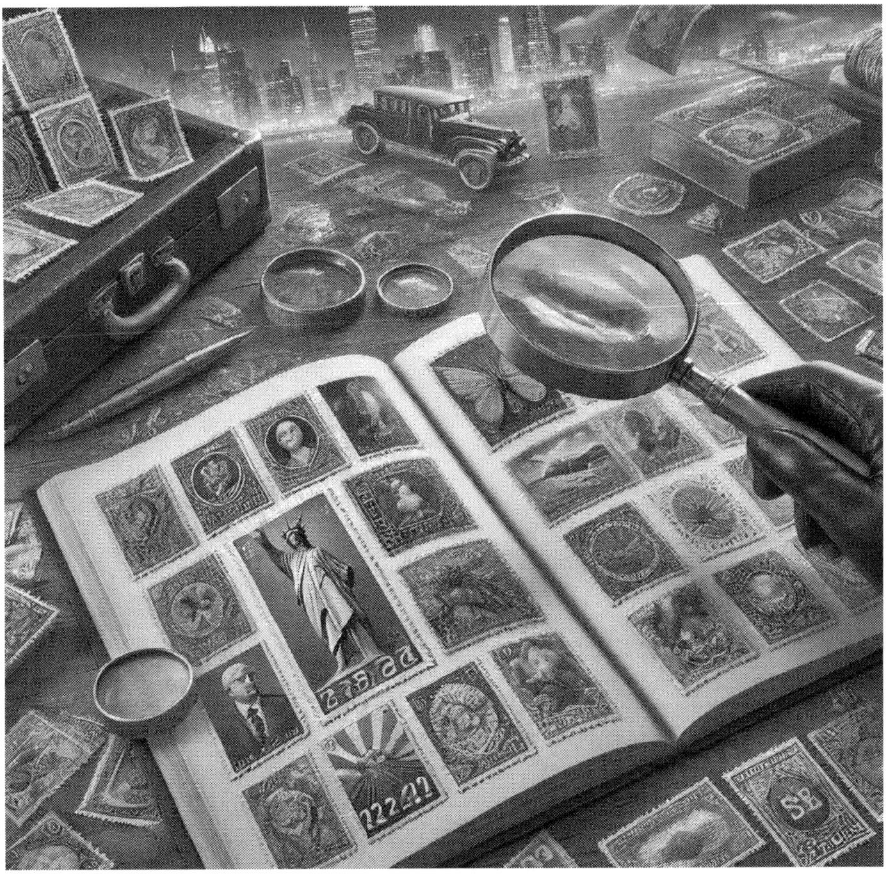

Delve into the hidden stories and secrets embedded in stamp designs.

A. Printing Errors:

Mistakes during production can tell fascinating stories, transforming ordinary stamps into rare collectibles that capture the imagination.

- **Inverted Jenny:** This iconic error—a plane printed upside down—became one of the most famous stamps in history, symbolizing the allure of philatelic rarities.
- **Color Variations:** Stamps printed in unintended colors due to production mishaps are highly prized by collectors.

- **Tip:** Investigate the history behind error stamps for a unique angle on philately, as these mistakes often have fascinating backstories.

B. Canceled to Order (CTO) Stamps:

CTO stamps reveal the intersection of commerce and collecting, offering a blend of affordability and thematic value.

- **What Are CTOs?** Stamps canceled by postal authorities for collectors rather than actual mail use, often featuring intricate designs.
- **Value Debate:** Though less valuable for postal history, CTOs remain popular among thematic collectors for their visual appeal.
- **Tip:** Include CTOs in thematic collections for affordable and visually striking additions.

C. Stamps as Hidden Messages:

In some cases, stamps have conveyed covert meanings, adding layers of intrigue and mystery.

- **Resistance Movements:** Stamps issued during wartime to signal unity or defiance, such as clandestine issues from occupied territories.
- **Subtle Symbolism:** Designs featuring hidden references to political or cultural ideas, often decipherable only to informed viewers.
- **Tip:** Research stamps from politically turbulent times to uncover their hidden messages and historical significance.

9.4 Using Stamp Stories to Inspire Your Collection

By weaving narratives into your collection, you can transform it into a storytelling masterpiece that captivates viewers and preserves history.

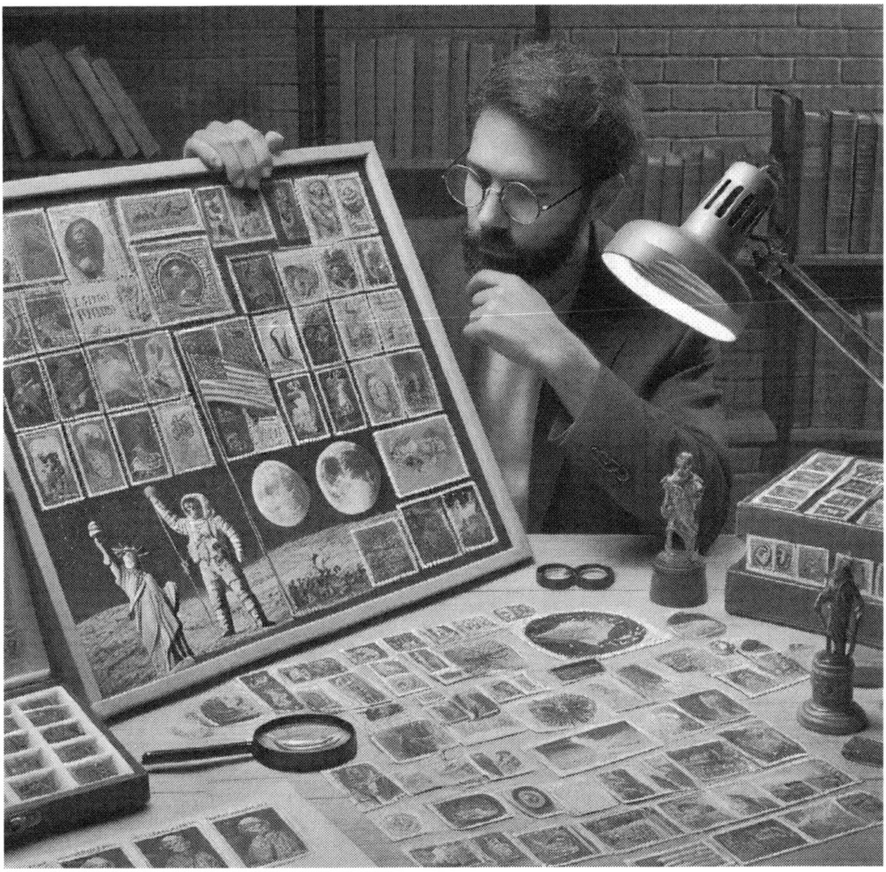

Let the stories behind stamps guide and inspire your collecting journey.

A. Thematic Storylines:

Create collections based on compelling themes, bringing history and culture to life in a cohesive and engaging way.

- **Historical Timelines:** Arrange stamps chronologically to narrate events like space exploration, civil rights milestones, or technological advancements.
- **Cultural Narratives:** Showcase stamps highlighting traditions, festivals, and artistic achievements from around the world.

- **Tip:** Use captions or write-ups to enhance the storytelling aspect of your collection, adding depth and context.

B. Personal Connections:

Incorporate stamps that resonate with your own experiences or heritage, making your collection deeply personal and meaningful.

- **Family History:** Collect stamps from your ancestors' home countries or regions that hold special significance.
- **Travel Memories:** Gather stamps from places you've visited or dream of exploring, turning your collection into a travelogue.
- **Tip:** Document your journey with notes or scrapbook-style displays to preserve the memories tied to each stamp.

C. Educational Displays:

Share the stories behind your stamps to inspire others and promote the hobby, turning your collection into a tool for learning.

- **School Exhibits:** Use stamps to teach history, geography, or art in educational settings.
- **Community Events:** Create interactive displays for local shows or libraries to engage the public.
- **Tip:** Pair stamps with supporting materials like maps, photos, or artifacts for a rich educational experience.

Stamps are powerful storytellers, capturing moments, honoring individuals, and inspiring generations of collectors. By exploring the stories behind stamps and sharing them with others, you can transform your collection into a vibrant narrative that preserves history and sparks curiosity. Let your stamps tell their tales and inspire your philatelic journey.

Chapter 9 Review: The Stories Behind Stamps

Chapter 9 unveils the storytelling power of stamps, emphasizing how these miniature artworks preserve historical events, honor famous figures, and reveal hidden narratives. Through the rich stories behind stamps, collectors can connect deeply with their collections and share captivating tales with others, enriching the philatelic experience.

9.1 How Stamps Capture Historical Events

- **Commemorating Milestones:** Stamps celebrating wars, scientific breakthroughs, and cultural traditions, such as World War II commemoratives or moon landing tributes, act as tangible links to pivotal moments.
- **Propaganda and Politics:** Designs featuring national heroes, Cold War themes, or political slogans highlight the use of stamps as tools of influence and patriotism.
- **Honoring Heroes:** Stamps immortalize world leaders, innovators, and cultural icons, like Gandhi or Leonardo da Vinci, offering collectors a gallery of human achievement.

9.2 Famous Collectors Who Made History

- **Pioneers of Philately:** Early collectors like John Edward Gray and organizations like the Royal Philatelic Society London laid the foundation for the global hobby.
- **Record-Breaking Collections:** Figures such as King George V and Bill Gross amassed legendary collections, inspiring others to pursue rare and valuable stamps.
- **Influential Women in Philately:** Collectors like Princess Grace of Monaco and Mary Ann Owens contributed significantly, showcasing the diversity and creativity within the hobby.

9.3 Hidden Stories in Philately

- **Printing Errors:** Iconic mistakes, such as the Inverted Jenny or color variations, transform ordinary stamps into rare treasures with fascinating backstories.
- **Canceled to Order (CTO) Stamps:** Though primarily for collectors, these affordable and visually appealing stamps offer thematic value and unique insights into philatelic commerce.
- **Stamps as Hidden Messages:** Issues with covert symbolism or issued during resistance movements add layers of intrigue and historical significance.

9.4 Using Stamp Stories to Inspire Your Collection

- **Thematic Storylines:** Build narratives around themes like space exploration, civil rights, or cultural traditions to create a cohesive and engaging collection.
- **Personal Connections:** Incorporate stamps tied to your heritage, travel memories, or personal milestones for a deeply meaningful collection.
- **Educational Displays:** Share your collection through exhibits or community events to inspire others while promoting the educational value of philately.

Chapter 9 highlights how stamps serve as powerful storytellers, connecting collectors to history, culture, and personal experiences. By exploring the stories behind stamps and weaving them into your collection, you can create a narrative masterpiece that preserves history, celebrates human achievement, and sparks curiosity in others. Let your stamps tell their stories and inspire your philatelic journey.

Part 4: Caring for, Displaying, and Connecting with Collectors

As you grow your stamp collection, the journey extends beyond acquisition. Part 4 focuses on essential practices for preserving the value and beauty of your stamps, showcasing them creatively, and engaging with the vibrant stamp-collecting community. Learn how to protect your treasures from damage, design compelling displays that highlight your collection's significance, and foster connections with fellow philatelists who share your passion. This section empowers collectors to transform their hobby into an enriching and enduring pursuit.

Chapter 10: Protecting Your Stamp Collection

Preserving the integrity of your stamp collection is crucial for maintaining its value and beauty. Chapter 10 provides detailed guidance on handling stamps safely, protecting them from environmental hazards, cleaning them properly, and safeguarding them from theft and disasters. By following these best practices, collectors can ensure their stamps remain in pristine condition for generations to come.

10.1 How to Handle Stamps Without Damaging Them

Proper handling is the first step in preserving the condition of your stamps. Even minor mistakes can lead to irreversible damage.

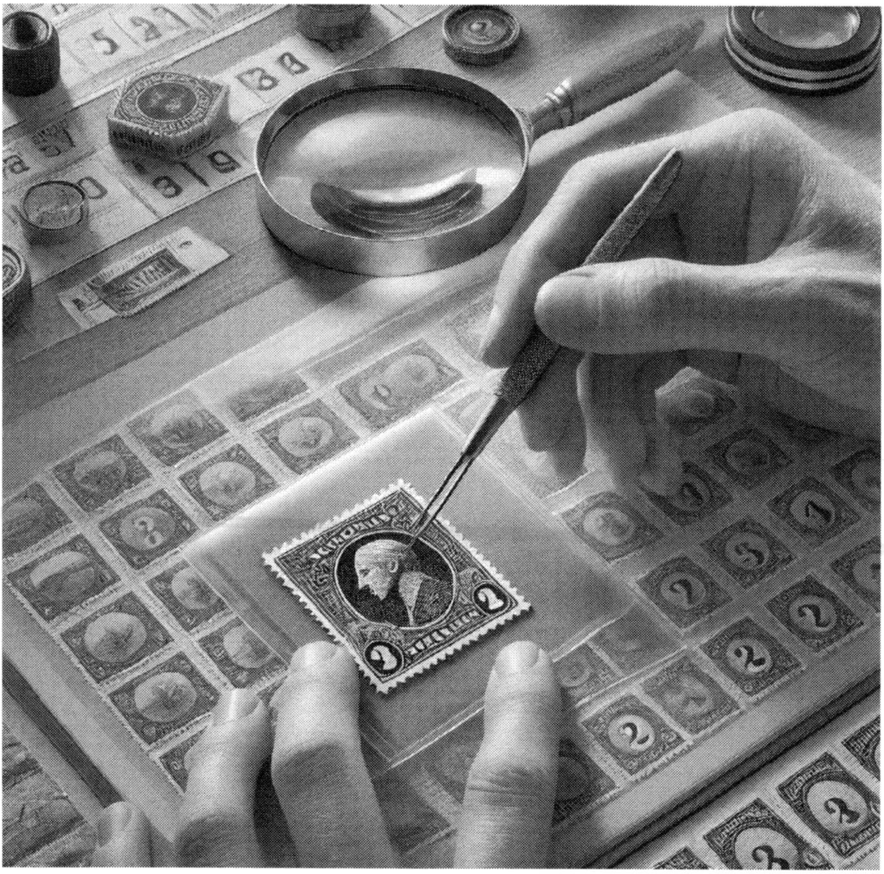

Learn safe handling techniques to preserve your stamps' integrity.

A. Use the Right Tools:

Handling stamps with appropriate tools minimizes the risk of damage and preserves their original condition.

- **Tweezers or Tongs:** Always handle stamps with soft-tip tweezers to avoid transferring oils and dirt from your fingers. Tweezers provide precision and prevent accidental folds or tears. Using tongs also reduces the risk of fingerprints that can degrade the paper or ink.
- **Gloves:** Use cotton gloves for handling rare or delicate stamps. This adds an extra layer of protection against oils, dirt, and

moisture. Gloves are especially useful when inspecting high-value items.

- **Tip:** Practice using tweezers on common stamps to develop steady handling techniques, making it easier to manage fragile or valuable items.

B. Minimize Direct Contact:

Reducing direct contact with stamps ensures their longevity and protects against wear.

- **Avoid Surface Touching:** Avoid touching the surface of stamps directly, as natural oils can cause discoloration or staining over time. The acidity in skin oils can degrade paper quality.
- **Proper Handling:** Hold stamps by their edges when using tools to prevent creasing or tearing. This ensures their structural integrity is preserved.
- **Tip:** Use a stamp mat or a clean, flat surface for examination to reduce risks of damage during handling or sorting.

C. Store Temporarily with Care:

Temporary storage can protect stamps between uses or when transitioning them to albums or displays.

- **Protective Sleeves:** Place stamps in protective sleeves or stock books immediately after handling. This minimizes exposure to harmful elements like dust and humidity.
- **Acid-Free Materials:** Use acid-free materials to prevent long-term damage, such as yellowing or brittleness. Acid-free papers and plastic sleeves are essential for archival preservation.
- **Tip:** Label temporary storage locations clearly to avoid misplacement or accidental mishandling.

10.2 Keeping Stamps Safe from Light, Humidity, and Pests

Environmental factors are a major threat to the longevity of stamp collections. Implementing proper storage conditions can significantly mitigate these risks.

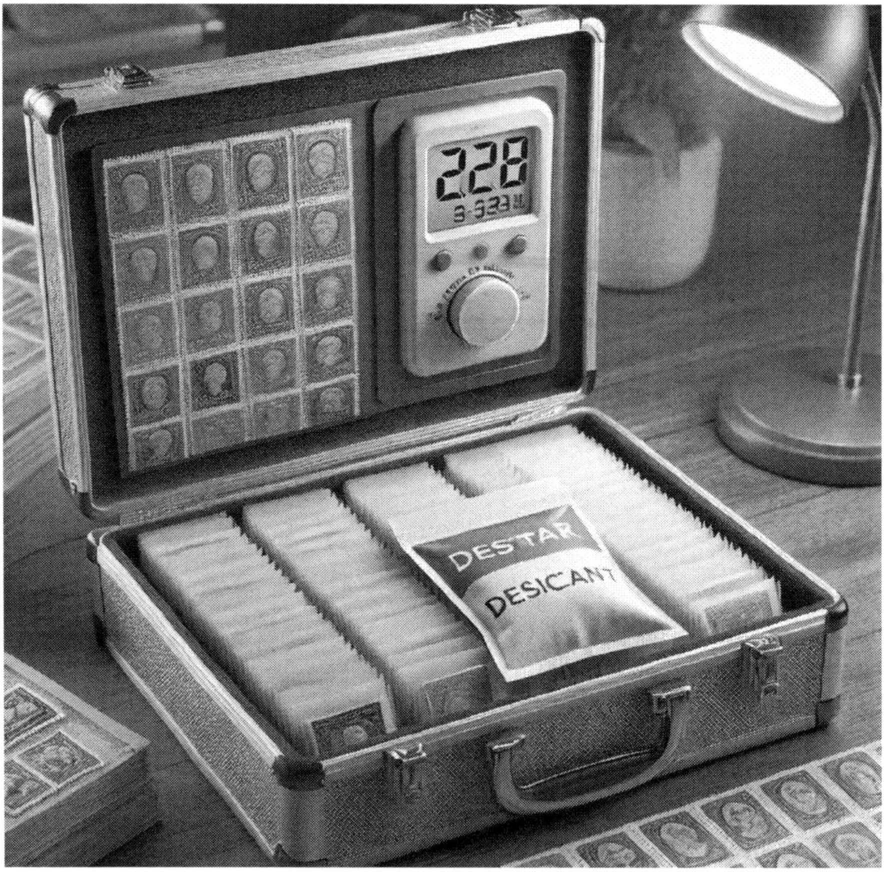

Shield your stamps from environmental threats with smart storage solutions.

A. Protecting from Light Exposure:

Light, particularly UV rays, can cause irreparable damage to stamps over time.

- **UV Damage:** Prolonged exposure to sunlight or fluorescent lighting can fade stamp colors, diminishing their visual and collectible value. UV rays are particularly harmful to older stamps with organic inks.
- **Storage Solutions:** Keep stamps in opaque albums or boxes away from direct light to preserve their original vibrancy. Opt for UV-protected materials when displaying stamps.
- **Tip:** Use UV-filtered glass for framed displays to protect stamps while showcasing their beauty.

B. Controlling Humidity:

Humidity levels play a critical role in the preservation of stamps.

- **Ideal Conditions:** Maintain a humidity level of 30% to 50% to prevent paper warping, mold growth, or adhesive degradation. Consistent conditions are key to avoiding stress on the paper.
- **Desiccants:** Use silica gel packets or dehumidifiers in storage areas to absorb excess moisture. Replace desiccants periodically to maintain effectiveness.
- **Tip:** Regularly monitor humidity levels with a hygrometer and adjust storage environments as needed.

C. Preventing Pest Infestations:

Insects and rodents can wreak havoc on stamp collections if left unchecked.

- **Common Threats:** Insects like silverfish, moths, and rodents can damage stamp collections by chewing through paper and adhesives. Even small infestations can cause significant harm.
- **Storage Practices:** Keep storage areas clean, dry, and free of food or other attractants to deter pests. Vacuum storage areas regularly and seal gaps where pests might enter.
- **Tip:** Use pest deterrents like cedar blocks or sealed storage units to protect stamps effectively.

10.3 Cleaning Stamps: What Works and What Doesn't

Cleaning stamps requires a delicate touch to preserve their original condition. Knowing what to do—and what to avoid—is essential for maintaining their value and appearance.

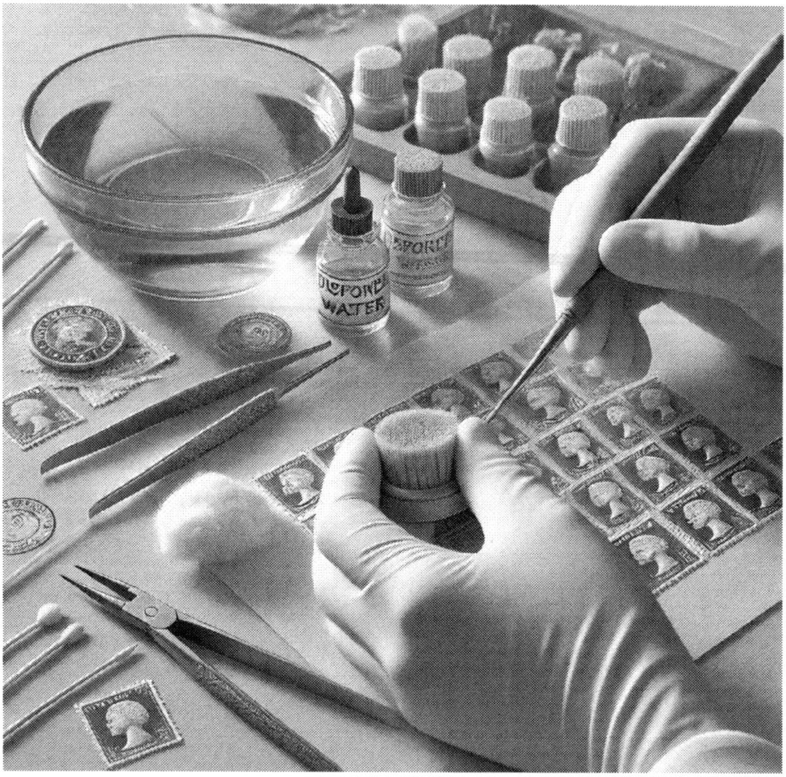

Master the do's and don'ts of cleaning stamps to avoid unintentional damage.

A. Dry Cleaning Methods:

Dry cleaning methods are the safest way to remove surface dirt and debris from stamps.

- **Soft Brush:** Gently remove surface dust with a clean, soft brush to avoid scratching or tearing the paper. A camel-hair brush is ideal for delicate cleaning.

- **Eraser Technique:** Use a specialized stamp eraser for small blemishes or stains, but avoid excessive pressure. This method works best for light smudges.
- **Tip:** Test cleaning methods on low-value stamps before applying them to rare pieces to ensure safety.

B. Avoiding Wet Cleaning:

Water and stamps don't mix well, particularly for older or delicate pieces.

- **Risks of Water Damage:** Immersing stamps in water can cause ink to run, paper to weaken, or adhesives to dissolve. Water can also create unsightly wrinkles or distortions.
- **Fragile Materials:** Never attempt to clean old or fragile stamps with water or cleaning agents, as they are highly susceptible to damage.
- **Tip:** Consult a professional for heavily soiled or valuable stamps to avoid accidental harm.

C. Removing Adhesives:

Removing adhesives must be done carefully to avoid damaging the stamp.

- **Soaking Techniques:** For modern self-adhesive stamps, use lukewarm water to gently separate them from backing paper. Avoid excessive soaking to prevent damage.
- **Avoid Harsh Chemicals:** Never use solvents, abrasive substances, or household cleaners, as these can degrade stamps irreparably.
- **Tip:** Use distilled water to prevent mineral stains or deposits during soaking.

10.4 How to Protect Your Collection from Theft and Disasters

Taking proactive measures can safeguard your collection from unforeseen events like theft or natural disasters, ensuring its safety and longevity.

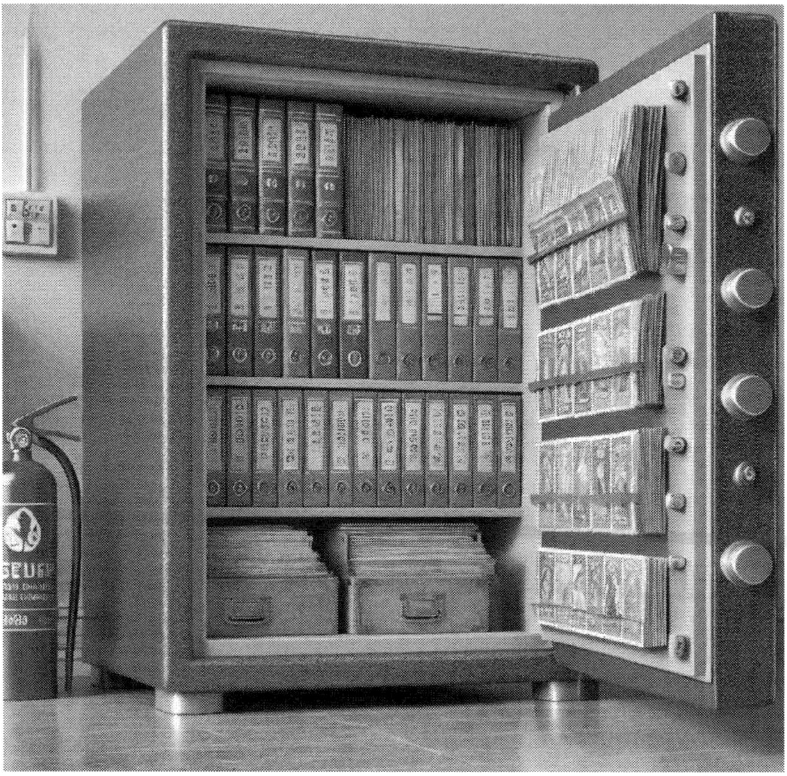

Safeguard your collection with security measures and disaster-proofing.

A. Security Measures:

Protecting your collection from theft requires strategic storage and monitoring.

- **Lockable Storage:** Use a safe or lockable cabinet to store valuable stamps, adding an extra layer of security. Safes with fireproof and waterproof capabilities provide additional protection.
- **Alarms and Surveillance:** Install security systems in your home or storage area to deter theft. Motion-activated cameras or sensors can enhance safety.
- **Tip:** Keep an inventory of high-value stamps with photographs and detailed descriptions to aid recovery if needed.

B. Disaster Preparedness:

Preparation can help mitigate the impact of natural disasters on your collection.

- **Fire Protection:** Store stamps in fireproof and waterproof containers to shield them from fire or water damage. Metal or ceramic containers provide additional durability.
- **Flood Precautions:** Avoid placing collections in basements or low-lying areas prone to flooding. Elevate storage units off the ground.
- **Tip:** Use climate-controlled storage units for optimal safety in areas with extreme temperatures or humidity.

C. Insurance and Documentation:

Proper documentation and insurance provide peace of mind and financial protection.

- **Appraisals:** Have your collection appraised regularly to determine its current value and ensure adequate insurance coverage. Appraisals should include detailed condition reports.
- **Insurance Policies:** Purchase insurance specifically designed for collectibles to cover theft, damage, or loss.
- **Tip:** Keep digital backups of all documentation, including photographs and appraisal certificates, for easy access in emergencies.

Preserving your stamp collection ensures its value, historical significance, and aesthetic appeal endure for years to come. By implementing these protective strategies, collectors can safeguard their treasures against the ravages of time, environment, and unforeseen circumstances. With careful handling and proper storage, your collection will continue to inspire and delight future generations. Let these steps guide you in creating a secure and lasting legacy for your philatelic passion.

Chapter 10 Review: Protecting Your Stamp Collection

Chapter 10 offers collectors a comprehensive guide to preserving the integrity and longevity of their stamp collections. By focusing on proper handling, environmental protection, cleaning techniques, and security measures, this chapter equips collectors with the knowledge and tools to safeguard their philatelic treasures for generations.

10.1 How to Handle Stamps Without Damaging Them

- **Use the Right Tools:** Soft-tip tweezers and cotton gloves prevent fingerprints, creases, and other damage. Practice with tools on less valuable stamps to ensure steady handling.
- **Minimize Direct Contact:** Always hold stamps by their edges to avoid transferring oils or dirt that can discolor or degrade the paper.
- **Temporary Storage:** Use acid-free protective sleeves or stock books immediately after handling to shield stamps from environmental hazards.

10.2 Keeping Stamps Safe from Light, Humidity, and Pests

- **Light Protection:** Prolonged exposure to sunlight or UV rays fades colors and degrades paper. Store stamps in opaque albums or UV-filtered frames to maintain their vibrancy.
- **Humidity Control:** Maintain a humidity level of 30%–50% with silica gel packets or dehumidifiers to prevent mold, warping, and adhesive breakdown.
- **Pest Prevention:** Keep storage areas clean and free of attractants like food. Use pest deterrents like cedar blocks and seal storage spaces to prevent infestations.

10.3 Cleaning Stamps: What Works and What Doesn't

- **Dry Cleaning:** Use a soft brush or specialized stamp eraser to gently remove surface dust and blemishes without damaging the paper.
- **Avoid Wet Cleaning:** Water can distort or damage stamps, especially older or delicate ones. Consult professionals for heavily soiled or rare items.
- **Adhesive Removal:** Carefully soak modern self-adhesive stamps in lukewarm distilled water, avoiding harsh chemicals that could degrade the material.

10.4 How to Protect Your Collection from Theft and Disasters

- **Security Measures:** Lockable safes and surveillance systems provide strong deterrents against theft. Maintain an inventory with detailed descriptions and photographs for recovery if needed.
- **Disaster Preparedness:** Use fireproof and waterproof storage containers and avoid placing collections in flood-prone areas. Climate-controlled units offer additional protection in extreme environments.
- **Insurance and Documentation:** Regular appraisals and collectible-specific insurance policies ensure financial protection. Back up documentation digitally for easy access during emergencies.

Chapter 10 emphasizes that preserving your collection is as important as acquiring it. By adopting these best practices, collectors can protect their stamps from damage, environmental hazards, and unforeseen events while maintaining their beauty and value. These strategies ensure your collection remains an enduring legacy that inspires and educates future generations.

Chapter 11: Displaying Your Stamps

Displaying your stamp collection is not just about aesthetics—it's about preserving your stamps, showcasing your passion, and sharing your story with others. Whether you're organizing a personal album or preparing a competitive display for a stamp show, Chapter 11 provides actionable advice on how to protect and present your stamps in ways that enhance their appeal and accessibility. Let's dive into the art and science of displaying your collection.

11.1 Choosing the Best Albums, Stock Books, and Mounts

Selecting the right storage solutions is essential for both preserving and presenting your stamps. High-quality albums, stock books, and mounts protect your collection from damage while showcasing its beauty. Here's how to choose the best options for your needs:

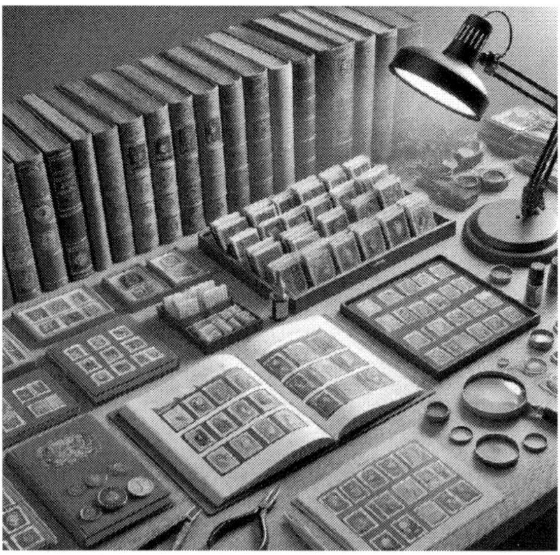

Select the best tools to protect and showcase your valuable stamps.

A. Albums:

Albums are a cornerstone for any stamp collector, offering a structured and visually appealing way to organize and display stamps.

- **Pre-Printed Albums:** These albums include placeholders for specific stamps, making them perfect for themed or country-specific collections. For instance, Lighthouse and Lindner offer albums with pre-designed pages for worldwide or regional collections. Their archival-grade materials protect stamps from yellowing and deterioration.
- **Blank Albums:** For collectors who prefer customization, blank albums allow creative freedom to design layouts that suit unique collections. They're ideal for advanced collectors aiming to showcase stamps in innovative and personalized ways.
- **Archival Quality:** Ensure the albums you choose are acid-free and made with archival-grade materials. This feature is crucial for preserving the colors and integrity of stamps over time, especially for older or rare items.

B. Stock Books:

Stock books provide an easy and versatile solution for storing and organizing stamps without adhesives.

- **Flexibility:** Stock books come with sliding pockets that allow you to rearrange or swap stamps effortlessly, making them ideal for dynamic collections. Beginners often find stock books helpful for experimenting with layouts.
- **Variety of Sizes:** Choose compact books for travel or larger ones for comprehensive storage. Stanley Gibbons and Davo stock books are popular for their quality and durability.
- **Durability:** Opt for stock books with rigid covers and thick, high-quality pages to prevent warping or tearing. Some stock books also feature interleaved glassine sheets for added protection against smudges and dust.

C. Mounts:

Mounts are essential for protecting individual stamps while keeping them visible and secure.

- **Hingeless Mounts:** These mounts secure stamps without adhesives, preserving their condition. Showgard and Lighthouse are trusted brands that offer mounts in various sizes to suit different stamp dimensions.
- **Custom Sizes:** Choose mounts tailored to fit your stamps precisely, preventing them from shifting or bending. Custom sizes are especially useful for irregular or oversized stamps.
- **Transparent Options:** Clear mounts ensure that every detail of the stamp's design, perforations, and inscriptions is visible while providing a protective barrier against environmental factors like humidity and dust.

Reflection: Investing in the right storage solutions protects your collection and enhances its presentation. Consider your collection's scale, focus, and purpose when choosing between albums, stock books, and mounts.

11.2 Creative Ideas for Showing Off Your Collection

Displaying your stamps creatively allows you to share your passion and tell a story through your collection. Here are some innovative ways to showcase your stamps:

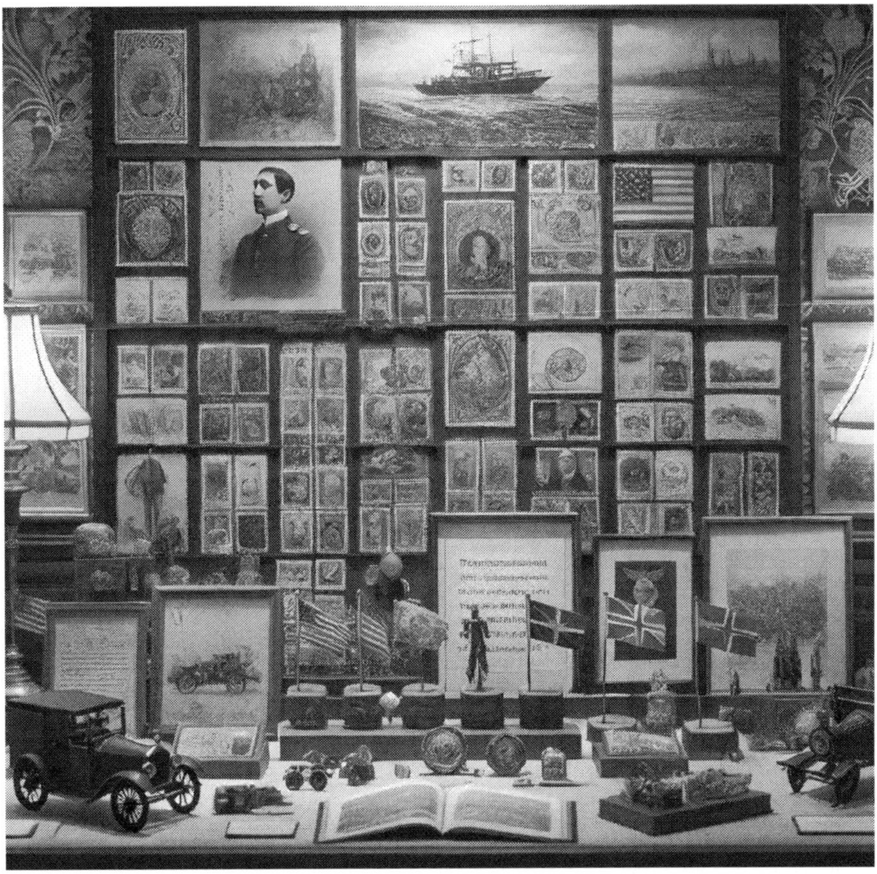

Turn your collection into a captivating showcase of art and history.

A. Thematic Displays:

Organizing stamps around themes adds depth and coherence to your collection.

- **Examples:** Create a display centered on topics like wildlife, space exploration, or historical milestones. For instance, a collection on wildlife could feature stamps of endangered species alongside conservation facts.
- **Storytelling:** Arrange stamps chronologically or by event to weave a compelling visual timeline. A historical collection might

highlight key moments like World War II or the Apollo moon landing.

- **Interactive Elements:** Add captions, QR codes, or even videos that provide viewers with additional context about each stamp. These elements create a more engaging and educational experience for viewers.

B. Shadow Boxes and Frames:

Framed displays are ideal for showcasing prized stamps while protecting them from damage.

- **Layered Effects:** Combine stamps with complementary artifacts like coins, postcards, or miniature flags to add visual interest and context.
- **UV Protection:** Use UV-resistant glass and acid-free backing materials to prevent fading and damage caused by light exposure.
- **Decorative Appeal:** A framed collection can double as unique home decor. For example, a set of maritime-themed stamps could be displayed in a nautical frame for a cohesive look.

C. Digital Displays:

Technology offers new ways to share and explore your collection.

- **Virtual Albums:** Use apps or software to create digital photo albums that showcase high-resolution images of your stamps. Tools like Adobe Lightroom allow you to organize and edit images for a polished presentation.
- **Social Media:** Platforms like Instagram and Pinterest are excellent for sharing your collection with a global audience and connecting with fellow enthusiasts.
- **Augmented Reality (AR):** Leverage AR technology to create interactive 3D displays. Imagine viewers being able to virtually "hold" your stamps and explore their details up close.

Reflection: Creative displays not only enhance the visual appeal of your collection but also engage and inspire others. Experiment with these ideas to find the best way to share your passion.

11.3 Portable Displays for Stamp Shows and Competitions

When attending stamp shows or competitions, a portable yet professional display can make a lasting impression. Here's how to prepare:

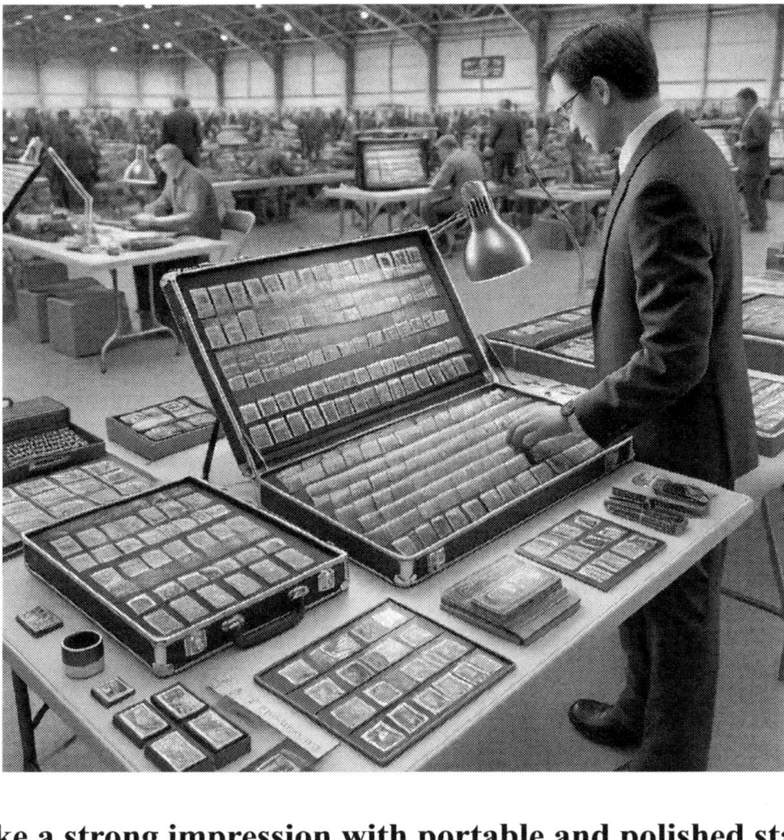

Make a strong impression with portable and polished stamp displays.

A. Presentation Cases:

Choose secure, lightweight cases designed for portability and protection.

- **Hard-Shell Cases:** Aluminum or reinforced plastic cases provide excellent durability and protection during transit.
- **Foam-Lined Interiors:** Cushioning prevents stamps from shifting or getting damaged.
- **Compact Solutions:** Briefcase-style cases with adjustable compartments are perfect for organizing and transporting your collection efficiently.

B. Display Panels:

For competitive settings, invest in professional-grade panels.

- **Exhibition Frames:** High-quality frames ensure your collection is presented in a polished and professional manner. These frames are often available for rent at major stamp shows.
- **Organized Layouts:** Arrange stamps logically, such as by chronology or theme, to guide viewers through your collection.
- **Informative Labels:** Include concise descriptions that highlight the significance of each stamp, enhancing viewer understanding and appreciation.

C. Travel Preparation:

Ensure your collection remains safe during transit.

- **Protective Layers:** Use acid-free sheets and sturdy folders to prevent scratches or damage.
- **Climate Control:** Avoid exposing your stamps to extreme temperatures or humidity. Consider using silica gel packs to maintain a dry environment.
- **Essentials Checklist:** Pack tools like tweezers, magnifying glasses, and backup materials to handle any unexpected situations.

Reflection: Portable displays protect your collection while showcasing it professionally. Thoughtful preparation ensures your collection stands out at any event.

11.4 Organizing and Labeling for Easy Access

A well-organized collection is easier to manage, share, and expand. Here's how to keep your stamps accessible:

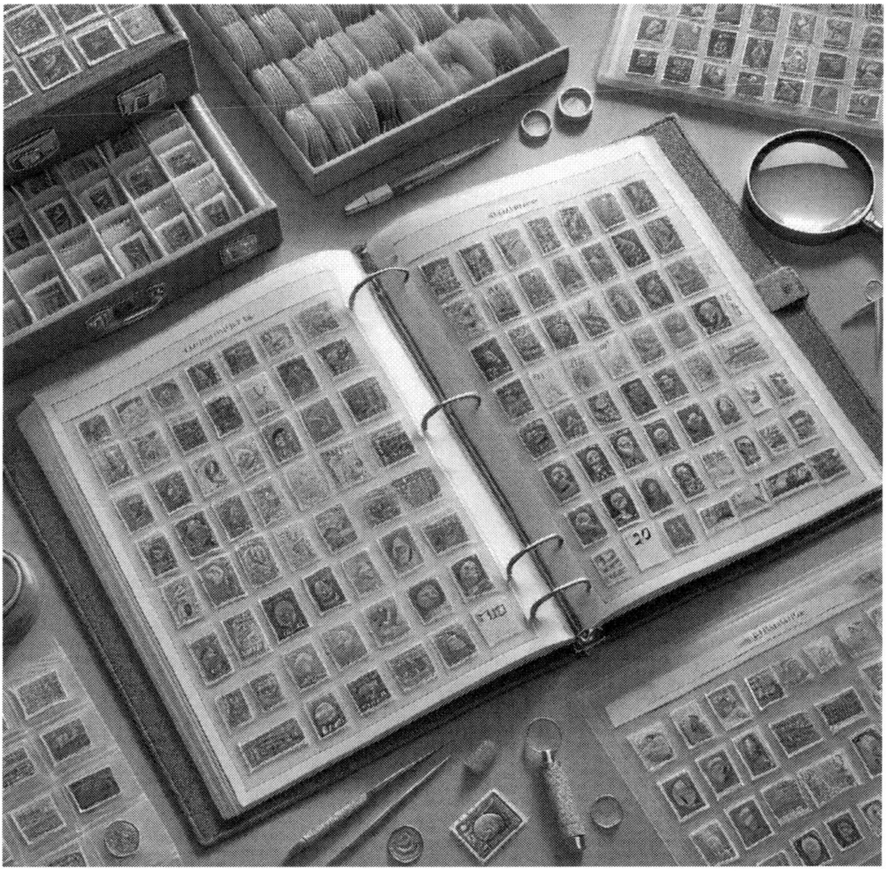

Streamline your collection with efficient organization and clear labeling.

A. Sorting by Theme or Country:

Effective sorting highlights the diversity and uniqueness of your collection.

- **Thematic Grouping:** Organize stamps by topics like nature, architecture, or cultural icons. For example, a collection on architecture could feature stamps of famous landmarks.
- **Geographical Sorting:** Arrange stamps by country to explore regional histories and design styles.
- **Chronological Order:** Sorting stamps by date allows you to trace historical trends and events.

B. Labeling Systems:

Clear labeling adds context and makes your collection easier to navigate.

- **Catalog Numbers:** Use standardized catalog numbers, such as Scott or Stanley Gibbons, for identification and valuation.
- **Custom Descriptions:** Include handwritten or printed notes detailing each stamp's history, origin, and condition.
- **Color Coding:** Employ colored labels or dividers to differentiate themes, regions, or eras, making retrieval simple and efficient.

C. Digital Cataloging:

Leverage technology to create a comprehensive inventory.

- **Inventory Software:** Tools like Stamp Mate or EZStamp help you track and manage your collection digitally, complete with high-resolution images and detailed descriptions.
- **High-Resolution Images:** Photograph your stamps to document their condition and features. Use these images for insurance or sharing purposes.
- **Cloud Storage:** Back up your inventory online to ensure it's secure and accessible from anywhere.

Reflection: Organized collections are not only more enjoyable to manage but also easier to share with others. Take advantage of modern tools and techniques to keep your stamps accessible and well-documented.

Displaying your stamps is both a practical and creative endeavor. By choosing the right tools, experimenting with unique displays, and organizing your collection effectively, you can celebrate and share the beauty of philately. Let your collection tell its story and inspire others to join the fascinating world of stamp collecting.

Chapter 11 Review: Displaying Your Stamps

Chapter 11 emphasizes that displaying your stamp collection is an art that combines preservation, presentation, and storytelling. With practical advice and creative ideas, this chapter guides collectors in showcasing their passion while protecting the integrity of their treasures.

11.1 Choosing the Best Albums, Stock Books, and Mounts

- **Albums:** Pre-printed albums are perfect for themed or country-specific collections, while blank albums offer customization for unique displays. Always opt for archival-quality, acid-free materials to ensure longevity.
- **Stock Books:** Flexible and durable, stock books with sliding pockets allow easy rearrangement and are ideal for dynamic collections. Interleaved glassine sheets add extra protection.
- **Mounts:** Hingeless and transparent mounts securely protect stamps while keeping designs visible. Custom-sized mounts prevent shifting and damage.

11.2 Creative Ideas for Showing Off Your Collection

- **Thematic Displays:** Organize stamps around themes like wildlife or space exploration to create visually compelling and educational presentations. Enhance displays with captions or interactive elements like QR codes.

- **Shadow Boxes and Frames:** Combine stamps with related artifacts for layered, artistic presentations. Use UV-protected materials to safeguard stamps from light damage.
- **Digital Displays:** Create virtual albums, share on social media, or use augmented reality for interactive, global engagement with your collection.

11.3 Portable Displays for Stamp Shows and Competitions

- **Presentation Cases:** Lightweight, hard-shell cases with foam-lined interiors ensure safe and organized transportation of stamps.
- **Display Panels:** Professional-grade exhibition frames enhance visual appeal and organization. Include descriptive labels to educate and engage viewers.
- **Travel Preparation:** Protect stamps with acid-free sheets, avoid extreme climates, and pack essential tools for emergencies during transit.

11.4 Organizing and Labeling for Easy Access

- **Sorting Systems:** Group stamps by theme, country, or chronological order to highlight diversity and historical context.
- **Labeling:** Use catalog numbers, custom descriptions, or color coding to make navigation intuitive.
- **Digital Cataloging:** Inventory software and cloud storage provide efficient management and secure backups, ensuring your collection is well-documented and accessible.

Chapter 11 inspires collectors to elevate their displays, blending creativity and practicality. By focusing on thoughtful organization and innovative presentation, collectors can protect their stamps while sharing the beauty and history of philately with others. Let your collection become a story that captivates and inspires!

Chapter 12: Connecting with the Stamp Collecting Community

Stamp collecting is more than a solitary pursuit; it's a global community united by a shared passion for philately. By engaging with clubs, attending exhibitions, and forging friendships, you can enrich your experience and deepen your knowledge. Chapter 12 explores how to connect with fellow collectors, make the most of competitive opportunities, and build meaningful relationships through your hobby. Let's discover how to thrive in the vibrant world of the stamp-collecting community.

12.1 Joining Clubs and Online Communities

One of the best ways to enhance your stamp collecting journey is by joining clubs and participating in online communities. These platforms provide opportunities to learn, trade, and share your passion with others.

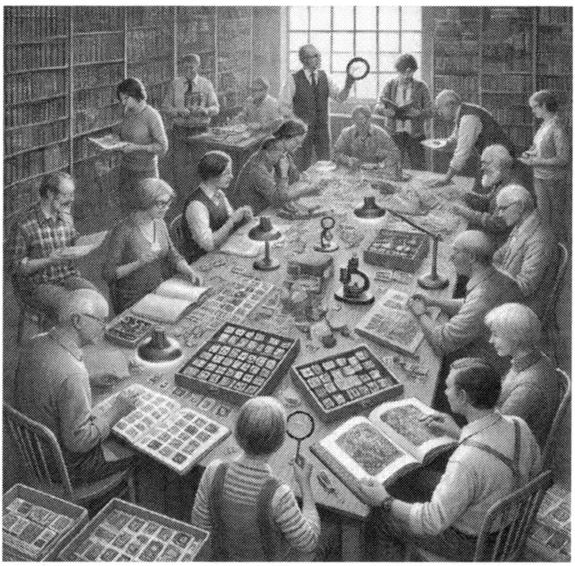

Expand your philatelic network by connecting with like-minded enthusiasts.

A. Local Stamp Clubs:

Local clubs are a great starting point for connecting with fellow collectors in your area.

- **Benefits:** Access exclusive events, auctions, and workshops tailored to your interests. Many clubs host regular meetings where you can share your collection and gain insights from others.
- **Networking:** Meet experienced collectors who can provide valuable tips, mentorship, and potentially rare trading opportunities.
- **Resources:** Clubs often have lending libraries, catalogs, and specialized tools that are otherwise difficult to find.
- **Example:** The Chicago Philatelic Society is one of the oldest stamp clubs in the U.S., offering both history and modern resources for collectors.

B. National and International Organizations:

Expand your network by joining prestigious philatelic societies.

- **Examples:** The American Philatelic Society (APS) provides a wealth of resources, including an expertizing service and a vast reference library. The Royal Philatelic Society London (RPSL) offers exclusive access to exhibitions and academic studies.
- **Membership Perks:** Gain access to rare exhibits, research publications, and member-only events.
- **Global Connections:** Connect with collectors worldwide, participating in events like the International Philatelic Exhibition (IPEX).

C. Online Communities and Forums:

The digital age has revolutionized stamp collecting, providing platforms to connect with enthusiasts worldwide.

- **Social Media Groups:** Join Facebook groups like "World Stamp Collectors" or Instagram hashtags like #StampCollector to share your collection and gather inspiration.
- **Dedicated Forums:** Websites like Stamp Community Forum and Postcrossing offer spaces for in-depth discussions, trade opportunities, and expert advice.
- **Virtual Events:** Participate in webinars, online stamp shows, and live auctions to stay updated on the latest trends and discoveries.

Reflection: By joining clubs and online communities, you can expand your knowledge, discover new opportunities, and share your passion with a supportive network. These connections make the world of philately even more rewarding.

12.2 How to Shine at Exhibitions and Competitions

Exhibitions and competitions are exciting avenues to showcase your collection, gain recognition, and learn from others. Here's how to stand out:

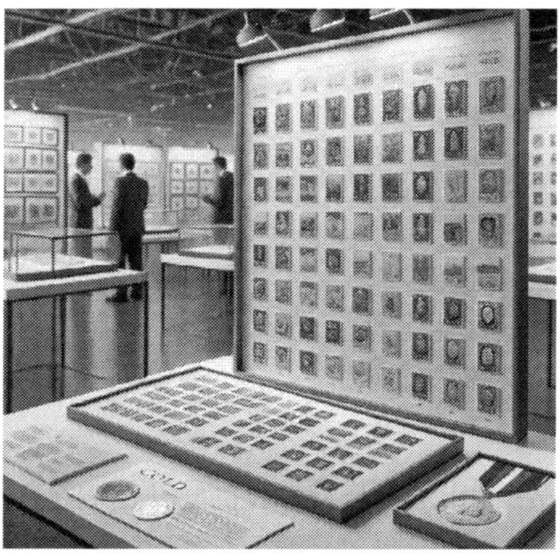

Stand out at exhibitions with well-curated and informative displays.

A. Preparing Your Display:

A well-organized display is key to making a strong impression.

- **Theme Selection:** Choose a compelling theme that tells a story or highlights a unique aspect of philately. For instance, a collection on aviation history could feature stamps depicting early aircraft and significant milestones in flight.
- **Presentation Quality:** Use archival-grade materials, clear mounts, and professional-grade frames to enhance your display. Ensure your stamps are clean, centered, and protected against environmental damage.
- **Concise Labels:** Include informative descriptions that explain the significance, history, and rarity of each stamp or set.

B. Understanding Judging Criteria:

Familiarize yourself with the standards used in competitive exhibitions.

- **Key Factors:** Judges often evaluate rarity, condition, completeness, originality, and presentation quality.
- **Authenticity:** Ensure your stamps are properly authenticated with certificates or provenance records. Forged or uncertified items can impact your credibility.
- **Innovative Approaches:** Stand out by showcasing unique themes, creative layouts, or innovative presentation techniques that captivate judges and viewers.

C. Engaging with Fellow Exhibitors:

Exhibitions are excellent opportunities to learn and network.

- **Conversations:** Discuss your collection with visitors and fellow exhibitors to exchange ideas and insights. You may gain inspiration from other displays.
- **Feedback:** Seek constructive feedback from judges and experienced participants to refine your display.

- **Networking:** Build relationships that can lead to future collaborations, mentorship, or invitations to exclusive events.

Reflection: Exhibitions and competitions offer more than accolades—they're a chance to grow as a collector, share your passion, and connect with a wider audience. Each experience is a stepping stone to refining your craft and building recognition.

12.3 Inspiring Stories of Collectors from Around the World

Stamp collecting has touched the lives of countless individuals, inspiring stories of passion, perseverance, and discovery. Here are a few examples:

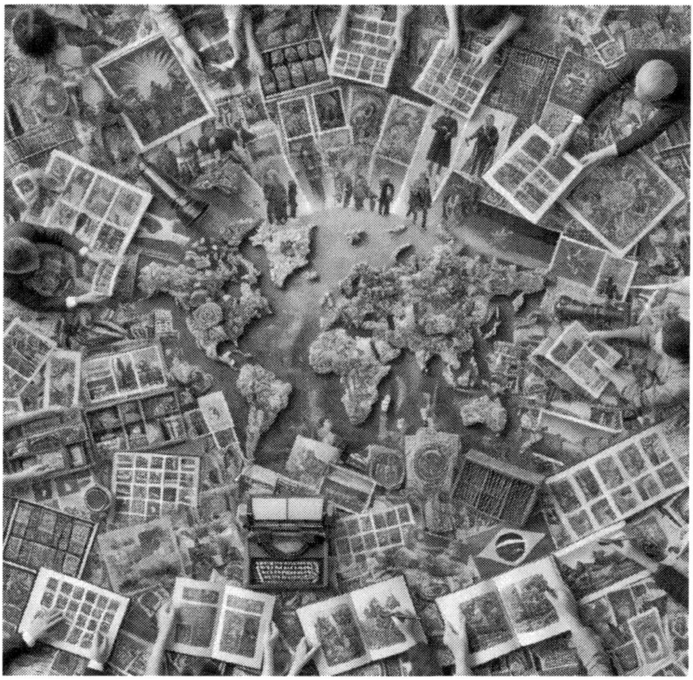

Be inspired by the stories and successes of global philatelists.

A. The Accidental Collector:

Many collectors begin their journey serendipitously.

- **Example:** A traveler discovers rare stamps while exploring a flea market abroad, sparking a lifelong fascination with philately. One collector found a misprinted stamp in an inherited collection, leading to a quest for more hidden treasures.
- **Lesson:** Inspiration can strike anywhere, turning a casual discovery into a rewarding hobby.

B. The Competitive Enthusiast:

Some collectors thrive on the thrill of competition.

- **Example:** A young philatelist entered a national exhibition and won accolades for a thematic display on space exploration, using creative layouts and rare stamps.
- **Lesson:** Dedication, research, and innovation can lead to recognition and personal growth.

C. The Legacy Builder:

For others, stamp collecting is a way to create a lasting legacy.

- **Example:** A collector spent decades curating a collection on world wars, donating it to a museum where it's now part of an educational exhibit.
- **Lesson:** Philately can leave a meaningful impact, preserving history and inspiring future generations.

Reflection: Stories of collectors worldwide highlight the diverse ways in which philately enriches lives. These accounts inspire newcomers to embark on their own journeys, showing the power of passion and perseverance.

12.4 Building Friendships Through Your Hobby

Stamp collecting is a social hobby that fosters friendships and connections across cultures and generations. Here's how to cultivate meaningful relationships through philately:

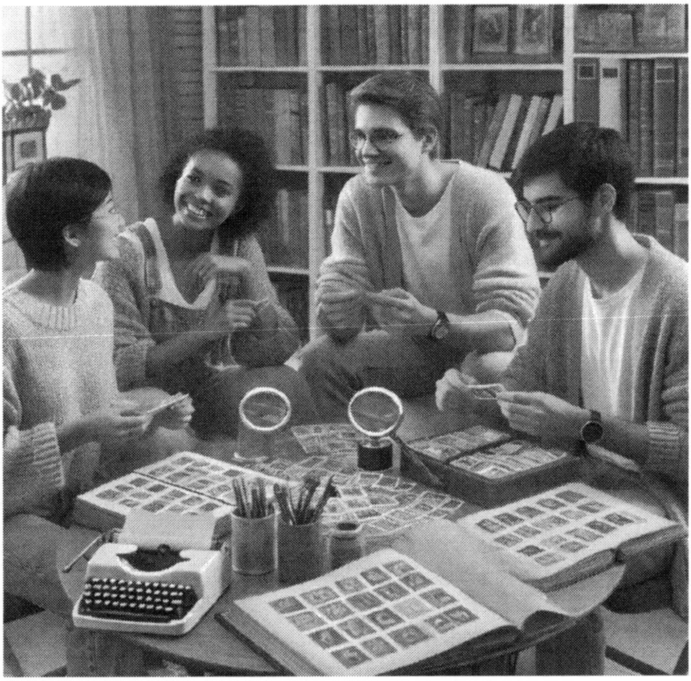

Forge lasting friendships through your shared love of stamps.

A. Sharing Your Passion:

Openly sharing your interest can lead to unexpected connections.

- **Local Events:** Attend stamp fairs, workshops, or meetups to meet like-minded individuals. Many collectors form lasting friendships through shared interests.
- **Storytelling:** Share the stories behind your favorite stamps to spark conversations and build rapport. Your unique perspectives might inspire others.
- **Mentorship:** Offer guidance to beginners, creating bonds through shared learning experiences. Mentoring can be a mutually enriching experience.

B. Pen Pals and Exchanges:

Traditional pen pal programs and stamp exchanges remain popular among collectors.

- **Cultural Exchange:** Swap stamps with collectors from different countries to learn about their cultures and histories. Each exchange adds depth to your collection and friendships.
- **Platforms:** Use services like Postcrossing to send and receive postcards and stamps worldwide, fostering global connections.
- **Building Relationships:** Long-term exchanges often evolve into lifelong friendships, rooted in a shared passion.

C. Philatelic Events and Tours:

Group activities bring collectors together in unique and memorable ways.

- **Travel Groups:** Join organized tours to international stamp exhibitions, museums, or historical postal sites. These experiences create shared memories and connections.
- **Workshops and Seminars:** Participate in educational events to deepen your knowledge while bonding with others.
- **Community Projects:** Collaborate on initiatives such as creating exhibits for schools or public events, combining social impact with camaraderie.

Reflection: The friendships formed through stamp collecting often extend far beyond the hobby, creating lasting connections rooted in shared interests and mutual appreciation. These bonds enrich the experience of collecting and make it a truly rewarding pursuit.

Connecting with the stamp collecting community enhances your journey by providing opportunities to learn, grow, and share your passion. Whether through local clubs, international exhibitions, or personal exchanges, the relationships you build will add immeasurable value to your experience as a collector. Let your love of philately bring people together and inspire new connections.

Chapter 12 Review: Connecting with the Stamp Collecting Community

Chapter 12 highlights the profound benefits of engaging with the vibrant stamp-collecting community. From local clubs to global exhibitions, this chapter emphasizes how relationships, shared knowledge, and mutual inspiration elevate the hobby, making it more fulfilling and dynamic.

12.1 Joining Clubs and Online Communities

- **Local Clubs:** Local stamp clubs provide opportunities to meet experienced collectors, participate in exclusive events, and access resources like lending libraries and auctions. Clubs like the Chicago Philatelic Society offer invaluable networking and learning experiences.
- **National and International Organizations:** Organizations such as the American Philatelic Society (APS) and the Royal Philatelic Society London (RPSL) provide access to rare exhibits, publications, and expert resources, connecting collectors globally.
- **Online Communities:** Social media groups, forums, and virtual events foster worldwide connections. Platforms like Stamp Community Forum and Postcrossing allow collectors to trade, discuss, and collaborate.

12.2 How to Shine at Exhibitions and Competitions

- **Display Preparation:** Select compelling themes, use archival-quality materials, and include informative labels to craft professional and engaging presentations.
- **Judging Criteria:** Understand what judges value, such as rarity, condition, and innovative layouts, to improve your competitive displays.

- **Networking:** Exhibitions are perfect venues for building relationships, gaining feedback, and exchanging ideas with fellow collectors and experts.

12.3 Inspiring Stories of Collectors from Around the World

- **The Accidental Collector:** Serendipitous discoveries often spark lifelong passions, turning casual interest into dedicated philately.
- **The Competitive Enthusiast:** Collectors thrive on innovation and research, earning recognition through creative and thematic displays.
- **The Legacy Builder:** Collections can become powerful educational tools or lasting contributions to museums, inspiring future generations.

12.4 Building Friendships Through Your Hobby

- **Sharing Your Passion:** Participating in local events, mentoring beginners, and sharing stories behind your stamps foster meaningful connections.
- **Pen Pals and Exchanges:** Traditional exchanges and platforms like Postcrossing help collectors swap stamps and cultural insights, creating global friendships.
- **Philatelic Events and Tours:** Group travel to exhibitions, workshops, or postal landmarks builds camaraderie and shared memories.

Chapter 12 reminds collectors that philately is not just about stamps but also about the friendships and shared experiences that make the hobby enriching. By connecting with others, collectors can deepen their knowledge, expand their collections, and create bonds that last a lifetime. Let the world of philately bring you closer to a global community of enthusiasts!

Chapter 13: How to Buy Stamps Smartly

Buying stamps is an exciting part of the philatelic journey, but it requires knowledge and strategy to ensure a rewarding experience. Whether you're a beginner or an experienced collector, purchasing stamps smartly can help you avoid pitfalls, uncover hidden gems, and grow your collection wisely. Chapter 13 provides actionable advice on identifying authentic stamps, working with reputable dealers, navigating online platforms, and using tools to assess value. Let's explore how to make informed and confident purchasing decisions.

13.1 Avoiding Fakes and Common Scams

One of the biggest challenges in stamp collecting is distinguishing genuine stamps from counterfeits. By staying vigilant and informed, you can protect yourself from common scams and ensure the authenticity of your purchases.

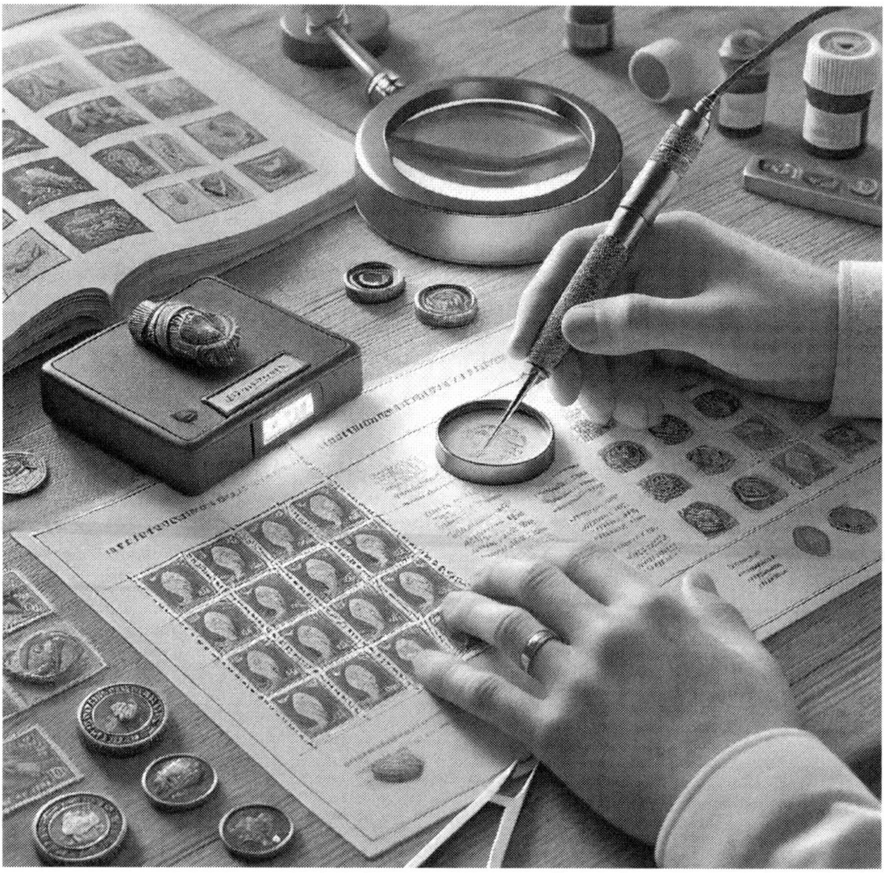

Protect your collection by learning how to spot fakes and avoid scams.

A. Recognizing Common Scams:

Understanding common scams can help you spot red flags.

- **Too Good to Be True:** Be wary of rare stamps sold at unusually low prices. Scammers often exploit a collector's desire for bargains, offering counterfeit or altered items.
- **Fake Provenance:** Some sellers fabricate stories or documents about a stamp's history to inflate its value, making it appear more prestigious.

- **Tampered Stamps:** Watch for altered stamps, such as those with forged overprints, regummed backs, or repainted details to mask damage or increase apparent rarity.

B. Authentication Techniques:

Use these methods to verify a stamp's authenticity.

- **UV Light Tests:** Ultraviolet lights can reveal hidden alterations, reprints, or added markings that aren't visible to the naked eye.
- **Watermark Detection:** Specialized fluids or detectors make it easier to identify watermarks, an essential feature for verifying older stamps.
- **Magnification Tools:** High-powered magnifiers can expose inconsistencies in printing, perforations, or edges that indicate a forgery.
- **Color Comparison:** Compare the stamp's colors to cataloged images to spot faded or tampered items.

C. Trusted Resources:

Rely on reputable sources to build your confidence.

- **Certification Services:** Organizations like the American Philatelic Society (APS) and Philatelic Foundation provide expert authentication and certification services.
- **Reputable Sellers:** Purchase from well-known dealers or auction houses that offer guarantees of authenticity and transparent return policies.
- **Educational Materials:** Use guides, catalogs, and online databases to familiarize yourself with genuine stamps, common forgeries, and pricing trends.

Reflection: Avoiding fakes and scams is crucial for building a collection you can be proud of. Invest time in research, rely on trusted resources, and never rush into a purchase without verification.

13.2 Working with Dealers and Navigating Auctions

Reputable dealers and auction houses are valuable allies in your stamp-collecting journey. Learning how to work with them effectively can open doors to incredible finds and long-term connections.

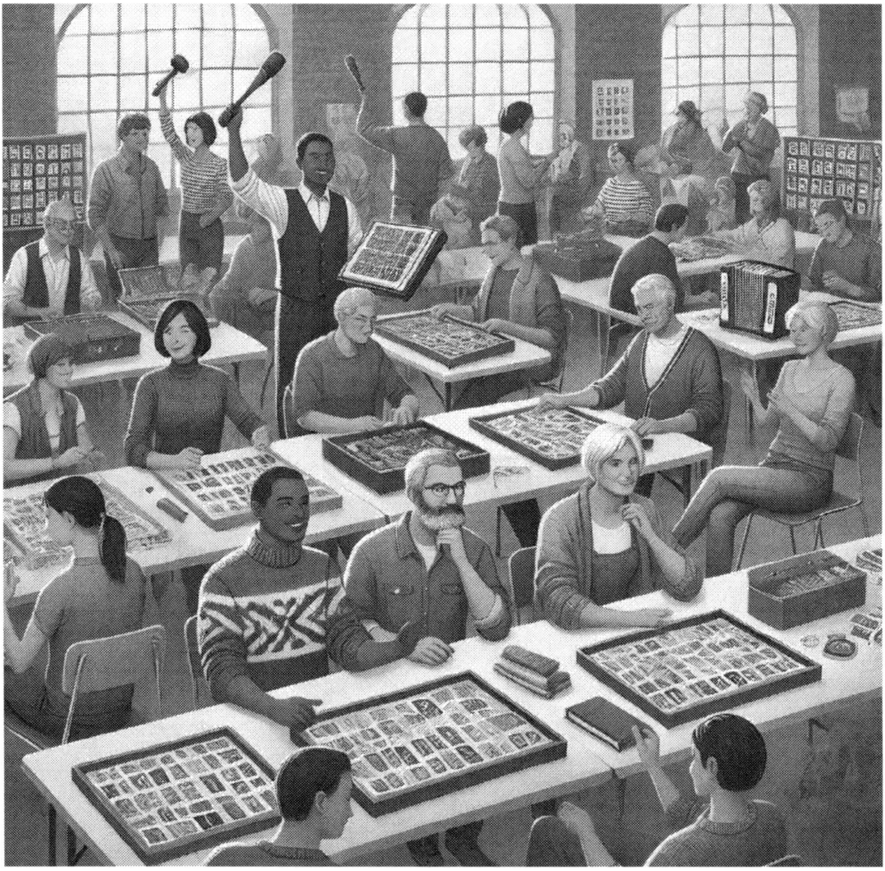

Build strong relationships with dealers and navigate auctions confidently.

A. Building Relationships with Dealers:

Establishing trust with dealers can lead to better opportunities and exclusive access.

- **Communication:** Clearly outline your collecting goals, whether it's thematic stamps, rare items, or investment-grade pieces. Dealers can offer personalized recommendations.
- **Frequent Visits:** Regular interactions with local or online dealers foster rapport and may result in insider tips or early access to new inventory.
- **Negotiation:** Most dealers are open to reasonable offers, especially from loyal customers. Always approach negotiations respectfully and know market prices beforehand.
- **Exclusive Opportunities:** Some dealers provide private previews of rare collections or auction lots to trusted buyers.

B. Navigating Auctions:

Auctions are excellent for acquiring rare or valuable stamps, but they require preparation.

- **Research Before Bidding:** Study the auction catalog thoroughly, paying close attention to descriptions, provenance, and estimated values.
- **Set a Budget:** Determine your maximum bid before the auction begins to avoid overspending in the heat of the moment.
- **Understand Terms:** Familiarize yourself with policies like buyer's premiums, payment deadlines, and return rules to avoid surprises.
- **Bid Strategically:** Start with a competitive bid to show interest but avoid escalating too quickly. Monitor other bidders and know when to step back.

C. Red Flags to Avoid:

Protect yourself from unscrupulous dealers or auction practices.

- **Lack of Documentation:** Be cautious of sellers who cannot provide clear details about a stamp's history, condition, or provenance.

- **High-Pressure Tactics:** Avoid dealers who rush you to make decisions without thorough evaluation.
- **Poor Feedback:** Online sellers or auction platforms with consistent negative reviews are red flags. Always check reputations before committing.

Reflection: Working with reputable dealers and navigating auctions skillfully can help you find high-quality stamps while staying within your budget. Strong relationships and informed strategies are the foundation of successful acquisitions.

13.3 Bargain Hunting Online: Best Practices

Online platforms have revolutionized stamp collecting, offering access to global markets and diverse inventories. However, shopping online requires caution and strategy.

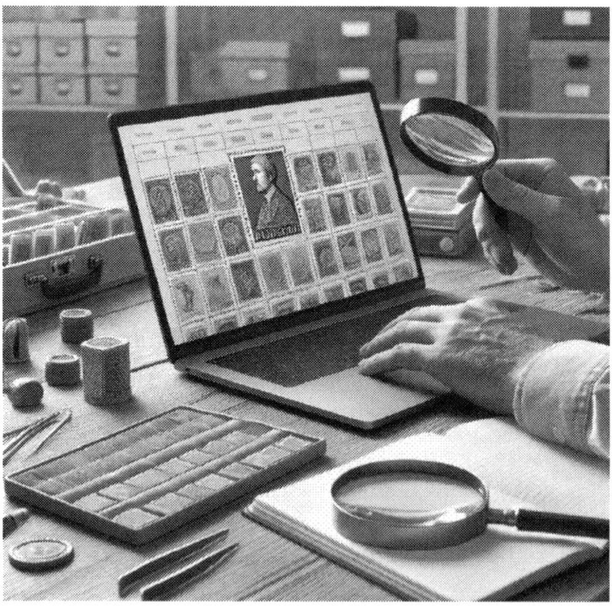

Find great deals online while staying safe and informed as a buyer.

A. Popular Platforms:

Explore reputable online marketplaces for stamps.

- **eBay:** A popular platform with a wide variety of stamps, from common to rare. Vet sellers carefully by examining reviews and descriptions.
- **Delcampe:** Known for its philatelic focus, this platform fosters a community of stamp enthusiasts with specialized listings.
- **HipStamp:** Tailored for collectors, it offers advanced filters for searching by theme, era, or country and includes buyer protection.

B. Evaluating Sellers:

Protect yourself by researching online sellers thoroughly.

- **Feedback and Ratings:** Examine reviews, ratings, and transaction histories to gauge a seller's credibility.
- **Detailed Listings:** Trust sellers who provide clear, high-resolution images and comprehensive descriptions, including condition, provenance, and catalog references.
- **Direct Communication:** Reach out to sellers with questions to assess their expertise and responsiveness.

C. Tips for Safe Transactions:

Ensure secure and satisfying purchases online.

- **Use Secure Payment Methods:** Opt for platforms offering buyer protection, such as PayPal, to safeguard your transaction.
- **Set Alerts:** Many platforms allow you to track specific auctions or keywords, ensuring you never miss a desired item.
- **Start Small:** Test the waters with lower-value purchases to evaluate a seller's reliability before committing to high-value transactions.

Reflection: Online marketplaces offer unparalleled convenience, but due diligence is crucial. With careful research and safe purchasing practices, you can uncover great deals and grow your collection confidently.

13.4 Tools to Help You Value Stamps Before Buying

Understanding a stamp's value is essential for making informed purchases. Several tools and resources can help you evaluate worth and avoid overpaying.

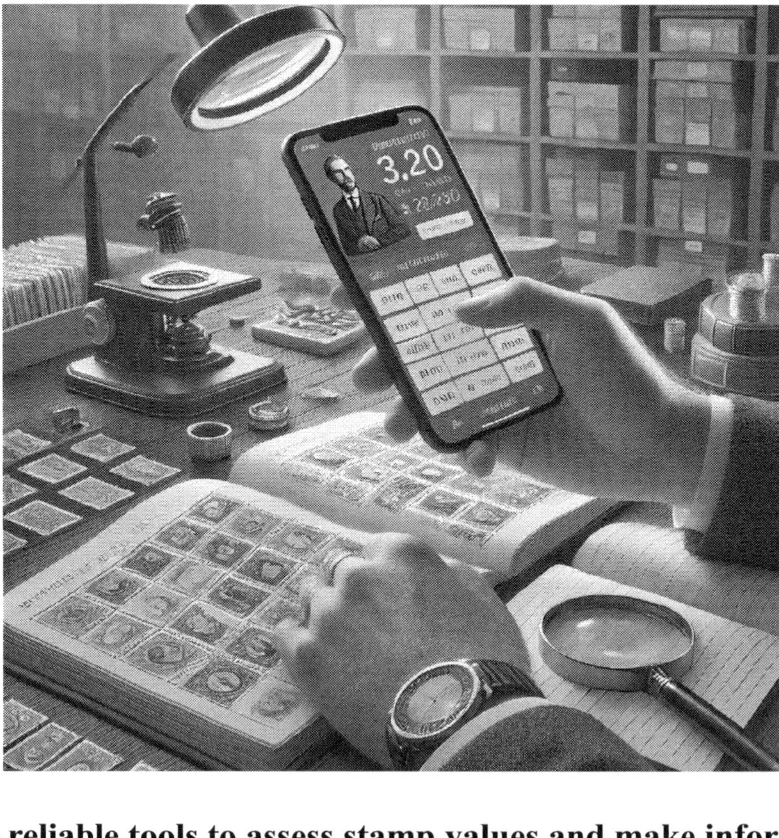

Use reliable tools to assess stamp values and make informed purchases.

A. Stamp Catalogs:

Catalogs are indispensable references for collectors.

- **Scott Catalog:** The industry standard in the U.S., it provides detailed pricing, descriptions, and identification tools.
- **Stanley Gibbons Catalogue:** Renowned internationally, it covers global stamps with expert valuation insights.
- **Michel Catalogue:** A go-to resource for European collectors, offering in-depth coverage of regional and global issues.
- **Specialized Catalogs:** For niche collections, explore resources dedicated to specific themes, eras, or countries.

B. Online Valuation Tools:

Digital platforms offer quick and convenient valuation insights.

- **Colnect:** A comprehensive database that allows collectors to compare prices, share knowledge, and track inventories.
- **StampWorld:** A user-friendly resource with global stamp listings and valuation guides.
- **Specialized Apps:** Tools like Stamp Mate provide mobile cataloging and valuation features, making it easy to research on the go.

C. Professional Appraisals:

For high-value or rare stamps, consider expert evaluations.

- **Certified Appraisers:** Seek professionals accredited by organizations like APS or major auction houses for trusted appraisals.
- **Auction Previews:** Many auction houses offer free or low-cost appraisals during events, helping you gauge value before bidding.
- **Local Experts:** Visit reputable dealers or philatelic societies to gain insights into specific stamps.

Reflection: Using the right tools to assess a stamp's value ensures you make educated purchases. Whether consulting catalogs, leveraging digital platforms, or seeking professional appraisals, accurate valuation is the cornerstone of a successful collection.

Buying stamps smartly combines research, strategy, and attention to detail. By avoiding scams, building strong relationships with dealers, navigating auctions carefully, and using valuation tools, you can enhance your collection while staying within your budget. Let every purchase be a step toward a more informed and rewarding philatelic journey.

Chapter 13 Review: How to Buy Stamps Smartly

Chapter 13 equips stamp collectors with essential knowledge and strategies for making informed purchases. From avoiding counterfeits to leveraging valuation tools, this chapter emphasizes the importance of diligence, preparation, and trustworthy resources in acquiring stamps that add value and meaning to your collection.

13.1 Avoiding Fakes and Common Scams

- **Recognize Scams:** Watch for deals that seem too good to be true, fake provenance claims, and tampered stamps, such as regummed or altered designs.
- **Authenticate Stamps:** Use tools like UV lights, watermark detectors, and magnifiers to verify authenticity and condition.
- **Rely on Experts:** Trusted organizations like the American Philatelic Society (APS) and reputable dealers offer reliable authentication and certification services.

13.2 Working with Dealers and Navigating Auctions

- **Build Dealer Relationships:** Communicate your collecting goals and maintain regular interactions for access to exclusive opportunities.

- **Navigate Auctions Smartly:** Research auction catalogs, set clear budgets, and understand terms like buyer's premiums to avoid surprises.
- **Avoid Red Flags:** Beware of sellers lacking documentation or employing high-pressure tactics. Opt for those with strong reputations and transparent policies.

13.3 Bargain Hunting Online: Best Practices

- **Explore Reputable Platforms:** Websites like eBay, Delcampe, and HipStamp provide global access to diverse inventories. Evaluate sellers based on reviews, descriptions, and images.
- **Use Secure Payments:** Platforms offering buyer protection, such as PayPal, help safeguard transactions.
- **Start Small:** Test sellers with lower-value purchases before committing to expensive items.

13.4 Tools to Help You Value Stamps Before Buying

- **Consult Stamp Catalogs:** Trusted resources like Scott Catalog and Stanley Gibbons Catalogue provide detailed pricing and identification tools.
- **Leverage Online Tools:** Platforms such as Colnect and StampWorld offer accessible, real-time valuation insights.
- **Seek Professional Appraisals:** Accredited appraisers and auction houses can accurately assess high-value or rare stamps.

Chapter 13 emphasizes that smart stamp buying hinges on research, strategy, and caution. Whether working with dealers, bidding at auctions, or shopping online, collectors are encouraged to rely on trusted resources, tools, and communities to make informed decisions. By mastering these skills, every purchase can become a step toward building a rewarding and valuable philatelic collection.

Chapter 14: Selling Stamps for Profit

Selling stamps can be both a rewarding and profitable endeavor when approached strategically. Whether you're a seasoned collector looking to refine your collection or a hobbyist ready to monetize your efforts, understanding the market and employing effective techniques can make all the difference. Chapter 14 provides actionable advice on timing sales, crafting compelling listings, working with industry professionals, and using pricing strategies to maximize profits. Let's explore how to turn your philatelic passion into a successful venture.

14.1 Timing the Market: When and Where to Sell

Knowing when and where to sell your stamps can significantly impact your profits. Strategic timing and choosing the right platforms or venues will help you reach the right buyers and secure the best prices.

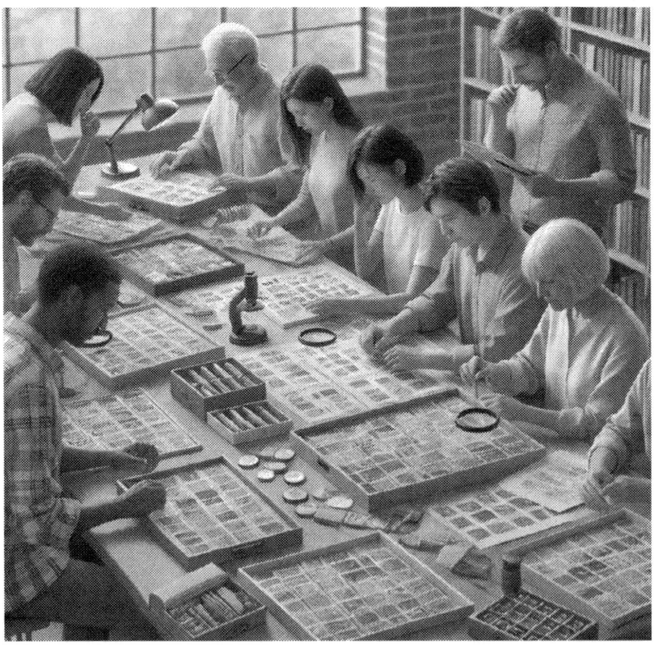

Maximize profits by timing your sales with market trends.

A. Market Trends:

Understanding the ebb and flow of the philatelic market is crucial.

- **Seasonal Patterns:** Stamp markets often see heightened activity during major philatelic events, conventions, or holiday seasons when collectors are actively seeking additions to their collections. Planning sales around these periods can yield higher profits.
- **Economic Factors:** Broader economic trends, such as disposable income levels or inflation rates, can affect the demand for collectibles. Monitor these factors to identify favorable selling windows.
- **Event-Driven Opportunities:** Milestone anniversaries, historical events, or significant auctions can spur interest in related stamps. For example, a surge in demand for moon landing stamps occurred during the 50th anniversary of the Apollo 11 mission.

B. Choosing the Right Platform:

Select the venue that aligns with your selling goals and the value of your stamps.

- **Online Marketplaces:** Platforms like eBay, Delcampe, and HipStamp provide access to a global audience. These are ideal for mid-range items or thematic collections that appeal to a broad demographic.
- **Stamp Shows:** Local or national stamp shows offer opportunities to connect with serious collectors. These in-person venues are particularly useful for showcasing high-quality items that benefit from direct inspection.
- **Specialized Auctions:** Auction houses that focus on philately, such as Cherrystone, Spink, or Sandafayre, are excellent for high-value or rare stamps. These venues often attract competitive bidding and collectors seeking premium items.

C. Timing for Maximum Profit:

Patience and planning can lead to better outcomes for your sales.

- **Wait for Demand Peaks:** Hold onto items that align with upcoming anniversaries, exhibitions, or collector trends likely to boost interest and demand.
- **Avoid Saturation:** Avoid selling during market floods when similar stamps are overly abundant. Timing your sale during periods of lower supply can result in higher bids or offers.
- **Track Market Prices:** Use resources like auction results, catalog updates, and dealer insights to stay informed about market fluctuations and identify the best time to sell.

Reflection: Timing and venue selection are critical to maximizing profits. By staying informed about market trends and carefully selecting the right selling platforms, you can achieve the best results for your collection.

14.2 How to Create Listings That Attract Buyers

A well-crafted listing can make your stamps stand out and attract serious buyers. Highlighting key details, providing clear images, and writing compelling descriptions are essential to selling successfully online or in-person.

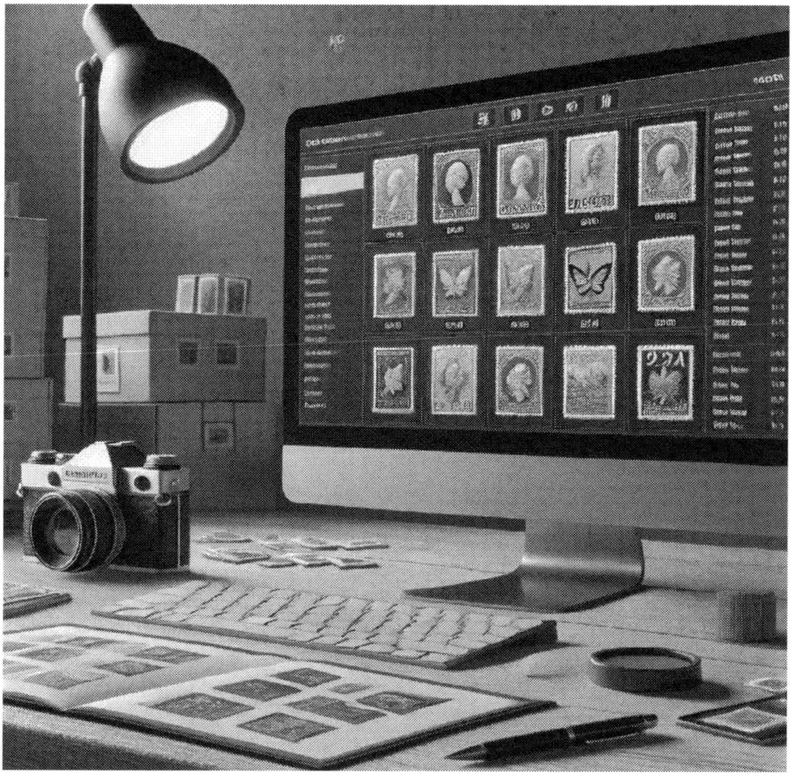

Craft compelling listings to attract serious buyers.

A. High-Quality Images:

Clear, detailed photographs are vital for online sales.

- **Focus on Details:** Use a high-resolution camera to capture close-ups of designs, perforations, watermarks, and any unique features. This level of detail assures buyers of the stamp's quality and authenticity.
- **Neutral Backgrounds:** Use plain, well-lit backdrops to eliminate distractions and make the stamp's features stand out. Natural daylight or a lightbox can help achieve professional results.
- **Multiple Angles:** Include photos of both the front and back of the stamp. If applicable, also provide images of certification documents, mounts, or accompanying materials.

B. Accurate Descriptions:

Write detailed and honest descriptions to build trust with potential buyers.

- **Key Information:** Include specifics such as catalog numbers, year of issue, country, and condition. For example, "Scott #292, 1898 $1 Trans-Mississippi Exposition Issue, Mint Hinged."
- **Historical Context:** Highlight any interesting facts, rarity, or cultural significance associated with the stamp. This adds value and engages collectors who appreciate the story behind their purchases.
- **Transparency:** Clearly disclose any flaws or repairs. Honesty about creases, stains, or perforation issues ensures buyer confidence and minimizes disputes.

C. Competitive Pricing:

Set prices that reflect market value while attracting buyers.

- **Comparable Listings:** Research similar items on platforms like HipStamp or Delcampe to gauge current market rates and set competitive prices.
- **Auction Starting Bids:** For auctions, begin with a reasonable starting bid to generate interest and competitive bidding.
- **Buy-It-Now Options:** Offer fixed-price listings for collectors who prefer straightforward transactions without the uncertainty of bidding.

Reflection: A compelling listing not only attracts buyers but also builds credibility. By presenting your stamps professionally and honestly, you'll foster trust and drive successful sales.

14.3 Working with Professionals: Appraisers and Auction Houses

Professional services can add credibility and help you navigate the complexities of selling rare or valuable stamps. Leveraging their expertise ensures you get the best value for your collection.

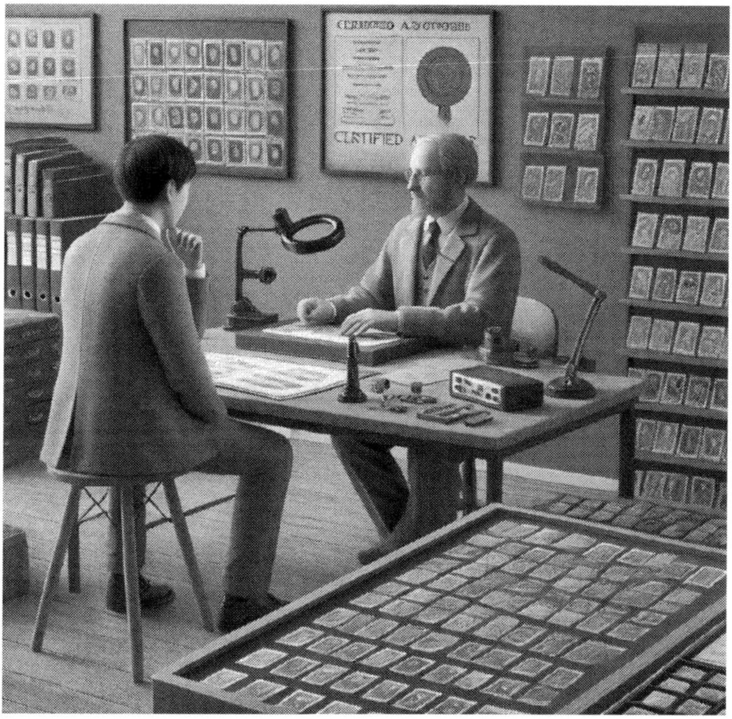

Leverage professional expertise to enhance credibility and value.

A. Appraisal Services:

An appraisal provides an accurate valuation and establishes trust with buyers.

- **Certified Appraisers:** Seek professionals accredited by organizations like the American Philatelic Society (APS) or other recognized entities. Their evaluations carry weight in the philatelic community.

- **Itemized Valuations:** Request detailed appraisals that outline the value of individual stamps or sets. This is especially useful when selling high-value collections.
- **Cost vs. Benefit:** While appraisals may involve fees, they can significantly boost buyer confidence and justify higher selling prices.

B. Choosing an Auction House:

Auction houses are ideal for high-value or rare stamps that attract competitive bidding.

- **Reputation Matters:** Work with auction houses known for their philatelic expertise and successful sales records, such as Heritage Auctions or Robert A. Siegel.
- **Marketing Support:** Many auction houses promote high-value lots through catalogs, online listings, and previews to attract serious collectors.
- **Negotiating Terms:** Understand the commission rates, reserve prices, and additional fees before consigning your collection. Negotiate terms to ensure you're comfortable with the agreement.

C. Leveraging Dealer Networks:

Reputable dealers can offer quick sales or help broker private transactions.

- **Consignment Options:** Some dealers sell stamps on your behalf, taking a commission upon sale.
- **Instant Offers:** Dealers may provide immediate cash offers for your stamps, though these offers are typically below market value.
- **Building Relationships:** Regular interactions with dealers can lead to exclusive selling opportunities and insider insights.

Reflection: Collaborating with professionals ensures that your stamps are valued accurately and marketed effectively. Their expertise can simplify the selling process and maximize your profits.

14.4 Pricing Strategies to Maximize Profits

Setting the right price is both an art and a science. Thoughtful pricing strategies can attract buyers while ensuring you get fair value for your stamps.

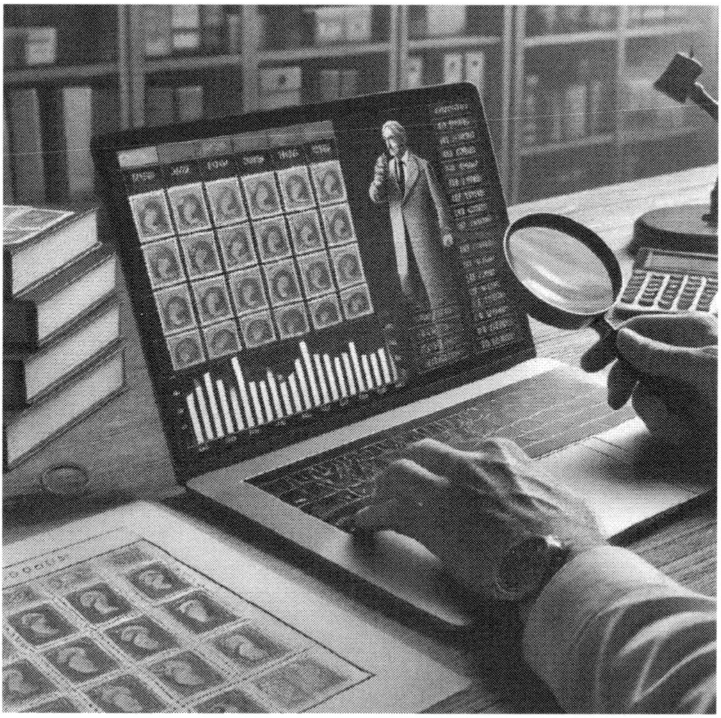

Use smart pricing strategies to ensure competitive and profitable sales.

A. Research and Benchmarking:

Know the market value of your stamps before listing them.

- **Catalog Prices:** Use resources like Scott, Stanley Gibbons, or Michel catalogs to establish a baseline for pricing.
- **Auction Results:** Study recent sales data from major auction houses to identify current demand and pricing trends.
- **Online Listings:** Analyze similar items on platforms like eBay or HipStamp to understand what buyers are paying in real-time.

B. Dynamic Pricing:

Adjust pricing strategies based on the selling platform or situation.

- **Premium for Rare Items:** Rare or in-demand stamps can command higher prices, especially on specialized platforms or during auctions.
- **Volume Discounts:** Offer discounts for bulk purchases to encourage buyers to make larger transactions.
- **Timed Promotions:** Run limited-time discounts, free shipping offers, or bonus items to incentivize purchases.

C. Psychological Pricing:

Subtle pricing techniques can make listings more appealing.

- **Odd Pricing:** Prices ending in .99 (e.g., $9.99) often appear more attractive to buyers.
- **Anchor Pricing:** Display a higher "original" price alongside a discounted one to highlight perceived value.
- **Free Add-Ons:** Include extras like protective sleeves, starter catalogs, or collector guides to enhance the buyer's experience.

Reflection: Strategic pricing can make your listings stand out and maximize profits. By staying informed and adapting to market conditions, you can achieve the best possible returns on your sales.

Selling stamps for profit combines skill, strategy, and an understanding of the market. By timing your sales wisely, crafting professional listings, working with trusted professionals, and employing effective pricing strategies, you can ensure success in the philatelic marketplace. Let your collection's story shine and watch your efforts turn into rewarding outcomes.

Chapter 14 Review: Selling Stamps for Profit

Chapter 14 equips collectors with actionable strategies to sell their stamps effectively, maximize profits, and navigate the philatelic marketplace with confidence. By emphasizing timing, professional presentation, and collaboration with industry experts, this chapter provides a comprehensive roadmap for successful sales.

14.1 Timing the Market: When and Where to Sell

- **Market Trends:** Selling during philatelic events, anniversaries, or periods of high demand can yield greater profits. Avoid oversaturated markets to capitalize on rarity.
- **Platforms:** Online marketplaces like eBay or HipStamp cater to a global audience, while stamp shows and specialized auctions are ideal for high-value or rare items.
- **Timing Tips:** Monitor economic and collector trends to identify favorable selling opportunities, and consider holding onto valuable items until demand peaks.

14.2 How to Create Listings That Attract Buyers

- **High-Quality Images:** Use high-resolution photos that clearly show designs, perforations, and watermarks. Neutral backgrounds and multiple angles build buyer trust.
- **Accurate Descriptions:** Include details like catalog numbers, historical context, and any flaws or repairs. Transparency ensures credibility and reduces disputes.
- **Competitive Pricing:** Research similar items to set fair prices. Use auction-style listings for competitive bids or fixed-price options for straightforward transactions.

14.3 Working with Professionals: Appraisers and Auction Houses

- **Appraisals:** Certified appraisers provide accurate valuations and enhance buyer confidence. Detailed itemized valuations can justify higher selling prices.
- **Auction Houses:** Trusted firms like Heritage Auctions and Spink attract serious collectors, offering marketing and competitive bidding opportunities.
- **Dealer Networks:** Reputable dealers can assist with consignment sales or direct transactions, offering quick solutions for selling bulk or valuable items.

14.4 Pricing Strategies to Maximize Profits

- **Research Tools:** Catalogs, auction results, and online platforms provide benchmarks for setting competitive prices.
- **Dynamic Pricing:** Offer discounts for bulk purchases or promotions for limited periods to attract more buyers.
- **Psychological Tactics:** Strategies like odd pricing (e.g., $9.99) or including free add-ons make listings more appealing and encourage sales.

Chapter 14 emphasizes the importance of preparation, professionalism, and market awareness in selling stamps for profit. By leveraging trusted resources, crafting compelling listings, and employing strategic pricing, collectors can achieve financial success while sharing their passion with buyers worldwide. Let your philatelic expertise shine through every sale!

Chapter 15: Investing in Stamps

Stamp collecting isn't just a hobby—it's also a fascinating and potentially lucrative investment opportunity. With a history rooted in global commerce and a tangible connection to art and culture, stamps represent a unique asset class. Chapter 15 explores the current trends in stamp investing, strategies for building a profitable portfolio, how to avoid common pitfalls, and achieving balance between short- and long-term goals. Let's dive into the art and science of turning your passion for philately into a rewarding financial venture.

15.1 Current Trends in Stamp Investing

Understanding the latest trends in the stamp market is essential for making informed investment decisions. The stamp market evolves based on collector preferences, global events, and technological advancements.

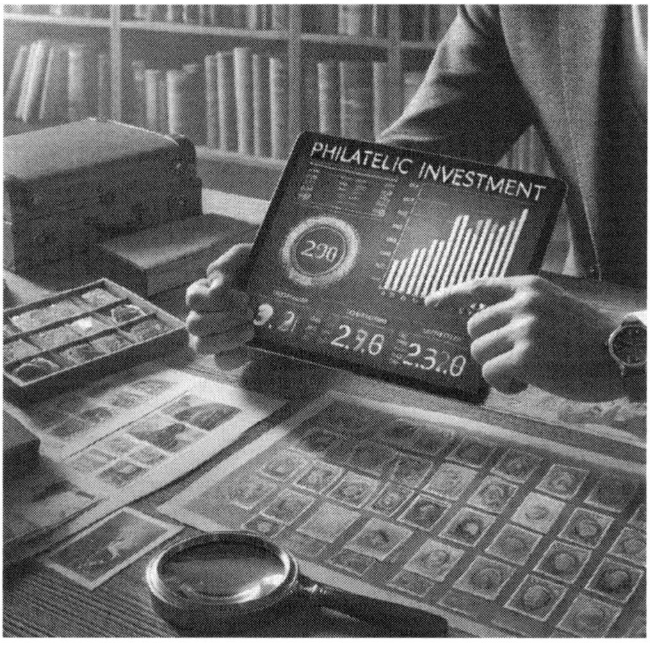

Stay ahead of the curve by tracking trends in stamp investing.

A. Increased Demand for Rare and Historical Stamps

Rare and historical stamps remain at the pinnacle of the philatelic investment world. Collectors and investors alike are drawn to pieces with storied pasts, which combine beauty, scarcity, and historical significance.

- **Historical Significance:** Stamps tied to iconic events or figures, such as the British Guiana 1c Magenta or the Penny Black, continue to command high prices at auctions. These items serve as tangible connections to pivotal moments in history.
- **Cultural Value:** Collectors increasingly value stamps that reflect a nation's cultural heritage, such as issues featuring traditional art, notable leaders, or local landmarks.
- **Scarcity and Exclusivity:** Limited editions, rare errors, and unique variations are particularly attractive to investors, as their inherent rarity ensures long-term value.

B. Rising Popularity of Thematic Collecting

Themes are gaining prominence among both seasoned collectors and newcomers. By focusing on topics like wildlife, science, or cultural heritage, thematic collections offer a unique blend of personal interest and investment potential.

- **Modern Trends:** Themes such as space exploration, environmental conservation, and famous artworks resonate with younger collectors, creating fresh market demand.
- **Special Editions:** Postal services worldwide are issuing thematic series, like lunar exploration or world heritage sites, to cater to niche markets and encourage new investors.
- **Cross-Generational Appeal:** Thematic collecting draws interest from diverse age groups, fostering sustained demand across generations.

C. Digital Innovations

Technology is revolutionizing the stamp market, offering both new investment avenues and tools for collectors.

- **Blockchain and NFTs:** Digital stamps and blockchain-backed certificates of authenticity are emerging as innovative investment options, ensuring provenance and security.
- **Online Marketplaces:** Platforms like eBay, Delcampe, and HipStamp have made trading and investing in stamps more accessible and transparent, attracting a global audience.
- **Data Analytics:** Investors now use online tools and analytics to track market trends, evaluate historical price trajectories, and make informed decisions.

Reflection: Staying informed about current trends equips you to capitalize on emerging opportunities and adapt to the ever-evolving philatelic landscape.

15.2 How to Build a Strong and Profitable Portfolio

A well-planned portfolio is the cornerstone of successful stamp investing. By diversifying your holdings and conducting thorough research, you can create a collection that balances passion and profit.

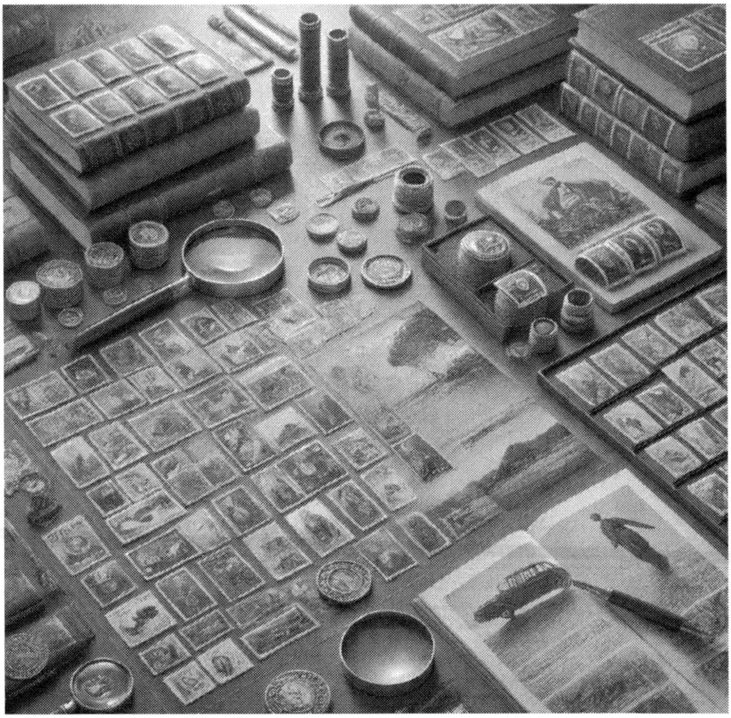

Build a portfolio that balances passion and profit.

A. Diversify Across Categories

Diversification helps reduce risk while increasing your collection's appeal and potential for growth.

- **Thematic Diversity:** Include stamps from a variety of themes, such as historical events, wildlife, or technological milestones, to appeal to different markets.
- **Geographical Range:** Build a global portfolio by collecting stamps from various countries, focusing on regions with strong collector bases like Europe, Asia, and North America.
- **Era Variety:** Mix classic stamps from the 19th and early 20th centuries with modern limited editions to capture a broader market and hedge against fluctuations.

B. Focus on Quality and Condition

The quality and condition of stamps directly impact their value and desirability.

- **Grading Standards:** Invest in stamps graded by reputable certification bodies like the Philatelic Foundation or Professional Stamp Experts (PSE). High-grade stamps maintain better appeal over time.
- **Condition Matters:** Prioritize stamps in mint or excellent condition, as imperfections like creases, tears, or discoloration significantly impact value.
- **Protective Measures:** Use archival-quality materials, such as acid-free albums and glassine envelopes, to preserve stamps and prevent environmental deterioration.

C. Research Before Purchasing

Conducting thorough research helps ensure your investments are well-informed and strategically sound.

- **Market Trends:** Study auction results, dealer listings, and catalog updates to identify stamps with strong appreciation potential.
- **Provenance:** Ensure that stamps have clear and trustworthy provenance, especially for high-value pieces. Certification and historical documentation add credibility.
- **Expert Opinions:** Consult philatelic experts, attend webinars, or join collector forums to gain insights into potential investments.

Reflection: A diversified and well-researched portfolio minimizes risk and increases the potential for long-term financial growth, while also showcasing your passion for philately.

15.3 Avoiding Costly Mistakes in the Stamp Market

Even experienced investors can make mistakes that reduce returns or damage their collections. Awareness of common pitfalls can help you protect your investment.

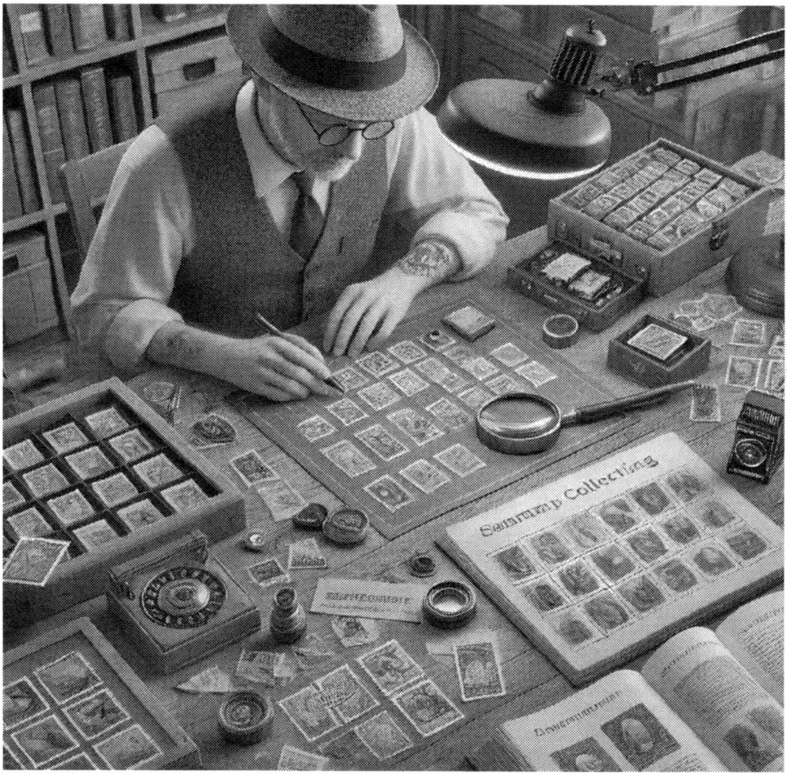

Learn to avoid costly errors and protect your investments.

A. Overpaying for Common Stamps

Paying too much for readily available stamps can erode your investment potential.

- **Research is Key:** Verify market prices using catalogs, auction results, and online listings to avoid overpaying.
- **Beware of Hype:** Avoid falling for marketing tactics that exaggerate the rarity or value of a stamp. Stick to factual evidence and expert evaluations.

B. Failing to Authenticate

Authentication is critical for protecting your collection from counterfeits.

- **Risk of Counterfeits:** Counterfeit stamps can be convincing. Always seek certification for high-value purchases from reputable organizations.
- **Avoid Questionable Sellers:** Work only with trusted dealers and auction houses to minimize the risk of buying fakes or altered stamps.

C. Neglecting Proper Storage

Improper storage can lead to environmental damage and a significant loss in value.

- **Environmental Damage:** Exposure to light, humidity, or improper handling can degrade your stamps and diminish their value.
- **Use Archival Materials:** Invest in acid-free albums, glassine envelopes, and climate-controlled storage solutions to maintain your stamps' integrity.

D. Ignoring Market Trends

Failing to adapt to market trends can result in missed opportunities or stagnant investments.

- **Adaptability:** The stamp market is dynamic; failing to adjust your strategy to current trends can result in missed opportunities.
- **Stay Informed:** Regularly review price guides, participate in forums, and attend stamp exhibitions to keep up with evolving values and collector interests.

Reflection: Avoiding these common mistakes ensures your investment remains secure, allowing you to focus on building a collection with lasting value and appeal.

15.4 Balancing Short-Term and Long-Term Investment Goals

Balancing immediate gains with future growth is essential for creating a sustainable stamp investment strategy. Each approach has its advantages and requires careful planning.

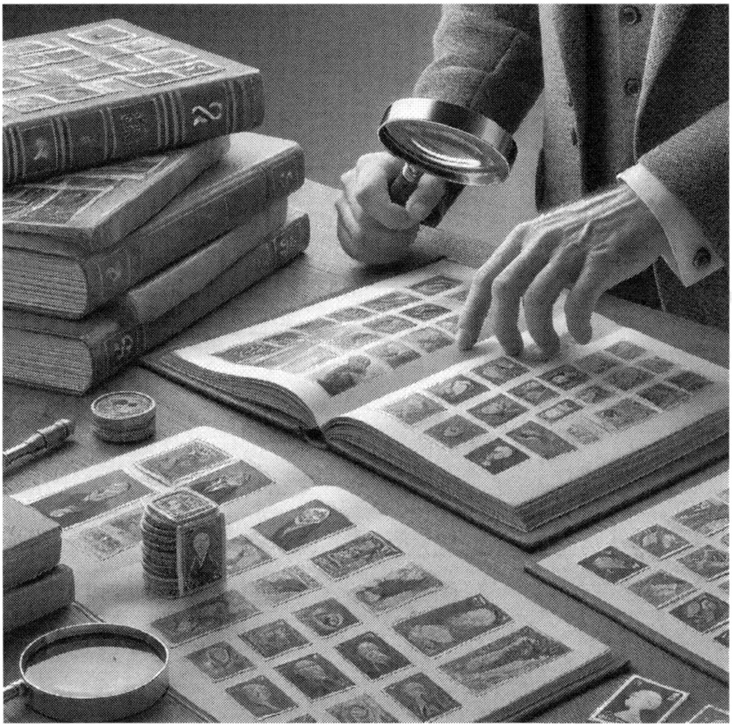

Combine short- and long-term strategies for a dynamic investment approach.

A. Short-Term Strategies

Short-term strategies focus on quick gains through market opportunities.

- **Flipping Stamps:** Purchase undervalued stamps or collections, then resell them at a profit through online platforms or auctions.
- **Trend Exploitation:** Capitalize on sudden spikes in demand for specific themes or events, such as anniversary-related stamps or limited-edition releases.

- **Quick Turnover:** Focus on liquid assets that can be easily sold, such as popular commemoratives or highly sought-after thematic issues.

B. Long-Term Strategies

Long-term strategies prioritize consistent growth and legacy building.

- **Building a Legacy Collection:** Focus on acquiring rare, historically significant stamps that appreciate steadily over decades.
- **Patience Pays Off:** Hold onto valuable items until market conditions are optimal, ensuring maximum returns when demand peaks.
- **Generational Investment:** Preserve stamps as heirlooms to pass down or sell in the future when values have matured and markets have evolved.

C. Achieving Balance

Achieving balance allows you to enjoy immediate rewards while building long-term value.

- **Portfolio Mix:** Combine short-term and long-term assets to ensure liquidity while building wealth over time. For instance, balance rare 19th-century issues with modern commemoratives.
- **Regular Evaluation:** Periodically reassess your goals and adjust your portfolio to align with market conditions and personal objectives.
- **Financial Planning:** Use profits from short-term sales to reinvest in high-quality, long-term pieces that have enduring value.

Reflection: Balancing short- and long-term strategies allows you to enjoy the immediate rewards of investing while building a collection with lasting value. By maintaining this equilibrium, you can create a dynamic portfolio that evolves with the market.

Stamp investing combines passion, knowledge, and strategy into a pursuit that is both personally fulfilling and financially rewarding. By exploring the rich history and artistry of philately, collectors can secure assets with lasting value while uncovering endless opportunities for growth. With thoughtful planning and a balanced approach, your journey can preserve history, inspire future generations, and yield meaningful financial rewards.

Chapter 15 Review: Investing in Stamps

Chapter 15 explores the potential of stamp collecting as a rewarding financial venture. It provides insights into current market trends, strategies for building a profitable portfolio, avoiding common pitfalls, and balancing short- and long-term investment goals. This chapter is essential for collectors seeking to turn their passion for philately into a viable investment opportunity.

15.1 Current Trends in Stamp Investing

- **Rare and Historical Stamps:** Stamps tied to iconic events, cultural heritage, or rare production errors continue to command high prices. Their scarcity ensures long-term demand.
- **Thematic Collecting:** Popular themes like space exploration, wildlife, and cultural heritage attract younger generations, fostering sustained market interest.
- **Digital Innovations:** Blockchain-backed certificates, online marketplaces, and analytics tools are reshaping the stamp market, offering transparency and new investment avenues.

15.2 How to Build a Strong and Profitable Portfolio

- **Diversification:** Collect across themes, regions, and eras to hedge against market fluctuations and appeal to diverse buyers.
- **Quality and Condition:** High-grade, mint-condition stamps retain value better. Invest in proper storage to preserve condition.

- **Research:** Analyze market trends, provenance, and expert opinions to make informed purchases that align with growth potential.

15.3 Avoiding Costly Mistakes in the Stamp Market

- **Overpaying for Common Stamps:** Use catalogs and auction data to verify market prices and avoid overhyped items.
- **Authentication:** Protect investments by purchasing from trusted dealers and obtaining certification for high-value stamps.
- **Improper Storage:** Environmental damage can significantly reduce value. Use archival-quality materials and climate-controlled storage to safeguard your collection.
- **Ignoring Trends:** Stay informed about evolving collector interests to capitalize on emerging opportunities.

15.4 Balancing Short-Term and Long-Term Investment Goals

- **Short-Term Strategies:** Flip undervalued stamps or capitalize on trend-driven spikes for quick returns.
- **Long-Term Strategies:** Acquire rare, historically significant pieces that appreciate steadily over decades.
- **Achieving Balance:** Maintain a mix of short-term and long-term assets, periodically reevaluating your portfolio to align with market conditions.

Chapter 15 highlights the dynamic nature of stamp investing, combining historical significance, artistic beauty, and financial growth. By staying informed, diversifying your portfolio, and balancing immediate and future goals, you can create a meaningful collection that yields both personal and financial rewards. Let stamp investing transform your passion into a valuable legacy!

Part 6: Advanced Techniques and the Future of Stamp Collecting

Stamp collecting has evolved over the years, blending traditional practices with innovative techniques and forward-thinking trends. Part 6 explores the cutting-edge tools, advanced methods, and exciting developments shaping the future of philately. From mastering the art of stamp identification to leveraging digital tools and blockchain technology, this section equips collectors with the knowledge and strategies needed to thrive in a modern, interconnected world. Whether you're a seasoned collector or just beginning to explore, these insights will ensure your collection remains relevant, valuable, and meaningful in the years to come.

Chapter 16: Mastering Stamp Identification

Identifying stamps with precision is a cornerstone of advanced philately. Whether you're authenticating a rare find, determining its value, or preserving its condition, mastering identification techniques and utilizing modern tools is essential. Chapter 16 provides a comprehensive guide to the tools, methods, and systems that enhance your expertise and ensure your collection's authenticity and organization.

16.1 Tools of the Trade: UV Lights, Watermark Detectors, and More

Modern tools have revolutionized the way collectors analyze and identify stamps. These devices provide clarity and accuracy, helping to reveal hidden features and ensure authenticity.

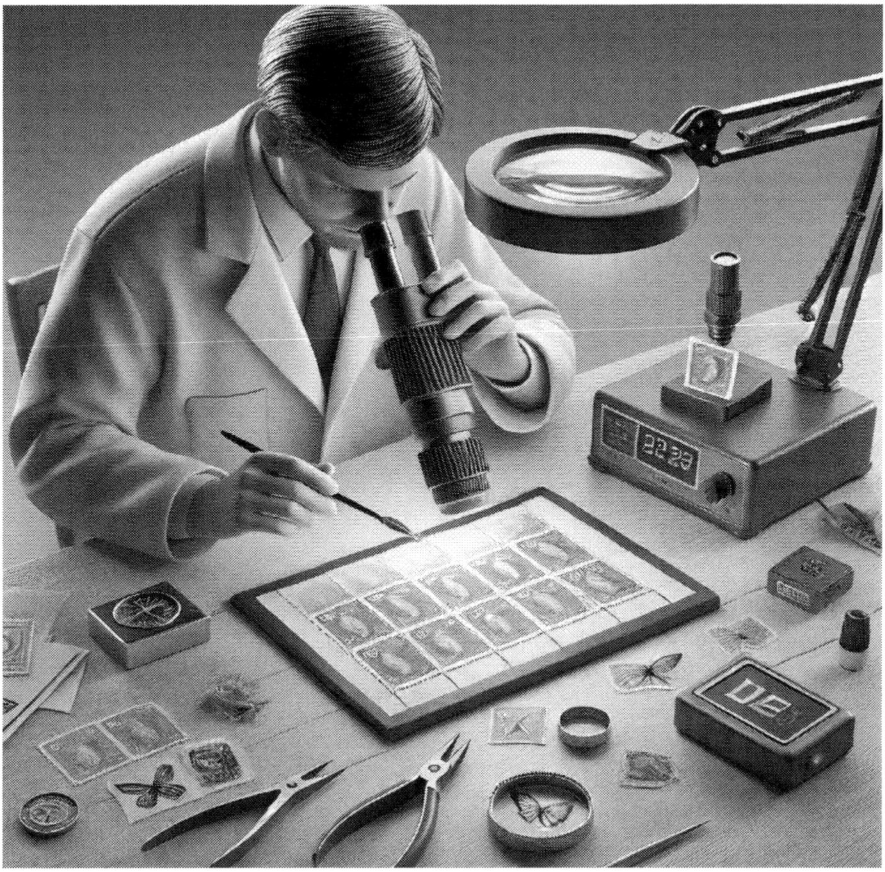

Enhance your identification skills with advanced tools of the trade.

A. UV Lights:

- **Purpose:** UV lights expose phosphorescent and fluorescent markings on stamps, which are often invisible under normal light. These markings are used by postal authorities for security purposes.
- **Application:** Essential for identifying modern issues or verifying stamps with unique luminescent features.
- **Tip:** Invest in a high-quality UV lamp designed specifically for philatelic use to ensure consistent results.

B. Watermark Detectors:

- **Purpose:** Watermarks are subtle patterns embedded into stamp paper to prevent counterfeiting. Detecting them can confirm a stamp's authenticity and identify its issue.
- **Application:** Use tools like watermark trays, detection fluid, or specialized watermark detectors.
- **Tip:** Handle stamps carefully during this process to avoid damage from liquids or pressure.

C. Magnifying Glasses and Microscopes:

- **Purpose:** High-power magnification helps analyze perforations, printing details, and surface texture.
- **Application:** Use a loupe with at least 10x magnification for general inspection or a digital microscope for detailed analysis.
- **Tip:** A microscope with lighting options can highlight fine details and reveal imperfections.

D. Perforation Gauges:

- **Purpose:** Perforation patterns are critical for identifying specific stamp varieties. A gauge measures the number of perforations per two centimeters.
- **Application:** Compare perforation measurements with catalog specifications to confirm a stamp's identity.
- **Tip:** Opt for a transparent, durable gauge for accurate and easy readings.

E. Color Grading Tools:

- **Purpose:** Subtle color variations can distinguish rare issues or identify fading.
- **Application:** Use color comparators or daylight lamps to assess shades accurately.

- **Tip:** Keep reference samples of known authentic stamps for direct comparisons.

Reflection: Utilizing these tools ensures precise identification and helps uncover the unique characteristics that make stamps valuable and fascinating. Investing in quality equipment enhances your ability to identify, preserve, and showcase your collection effectively.

16.2 How to Spot Forgeries, Reprints, and Altered Stamps

The stamp market's value has attracted counterfeiters, making it crucial for collectors to recognize fakes, reprints, and altered stamps. By honing your detection skills, you can protect your collection from fraudulent items.

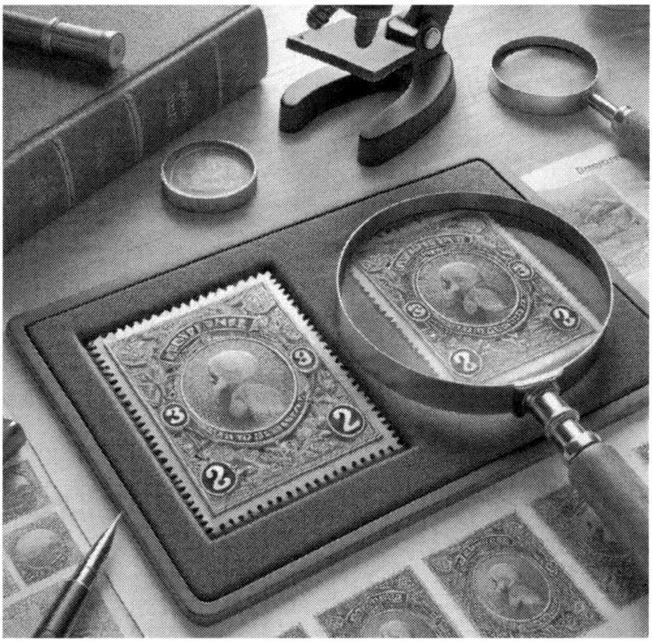

Protect your collection by learning to detect forgeries and alterations.

A. Common Signs of Forgeries:

- **Inconsistent Printing:** Blurred designs, uneven ink, or off-center images can indicate a fake.
- **Incorrect Paper:** Genuine stamps are often printed on specific paper types. Compare the texture and weight against known authentic examples.
- **Watermark Discrepancies:** Missing or incorrect watermarks are red flags for counterfeit stamps.
- **Tip:** Always compare the suspected stamp to a certified reference or catalog image.

B. Identifying Reprints:

- **What to Look For:** Reprints are legitimate reproductions made after the original issue date but often lack the value of originals.
- **Differences in Design:** Subtle changes in color, perforation, or inscriptions can distinguish reprints from originals.
- **Tip:** Check catalogs for documented reprints and their distinguishing features.

C. Detecting Altered Stamps:

- **Types of Alterations:** Alterations include adding fake overprints, repairing tears, or trimming perforations.
- **Signs to Watch:** Look for mismatched ink, uneven edges, or signs of tampering under magnification.
- **Tip:** Professional certification services can confirm a stamp's authenticity and condition.

D. Using Certification Services:

- **Purpose:** Certification provides a trusted evaluation of a stamp's authenticity and condition.
- **Reputable Organizations:** Use services from the American Philatelic Society (APS) or Philatelic Foundation.

- **Tip:** Certification increases buyer confidence and adds value to your stamps.

Reflection: Developing your expertise in spotting forgeries and alterations protects your investments and enhances your confidence as a collector. Staying vigilant and informed helps you maintain the integrity and value of your collection.

16.3 Measuring Perforations and Analyzing Colors Like a Pro

Understanding the intricacies of perforations and colors is vital for differentiating stamp varieties. Mastering these techniques enhances your ability to identify rare or valuable stamps accurately.

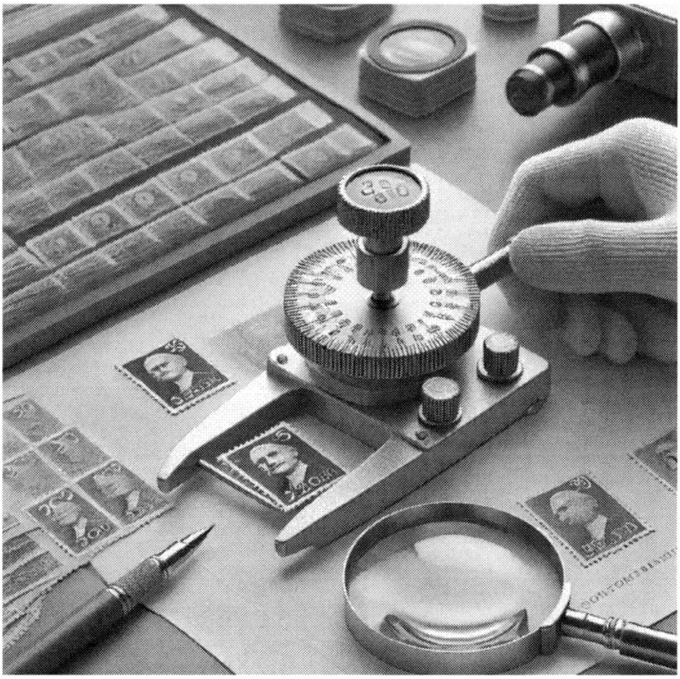

Master the art of measuring perforations and analyzing colors accurately.

A. Measuring Perforations:

- **Why It Matters:** Perforation differences can distinguish similar-looking stamps or identify rare variations.
- **Using a Gauge:** Align the perforations on your stamp with the markings on a perforation gauge to measure accurately.
- **Tip:** Handle stamps gently during this process to prevent tears or bends.

B. Analyzing Colors:

- **Color Variations:** Subtle differences in shade or hue can indicate different printings or issues.
- **Tools for Analysis:** Use daylight-balanced lighting or a color comparator to assess shades accurately.
- **Tip:** Refer to catalogs for documented color variations and their associated values.

C. Identifying Fading or Alterations:

- **Natural Fading:** Exposure to light or poor storage conditions can alter a stamp's original color.
- **Artificial Alterations:** Counterfeiters may bleach or dye stamps to mimic rare varieties.
- **Tip:** Study multiple examples of the same issue to build familiarity with authentic color ranges.

D. Understanding Printing Techniques:

- **Engraving vs. Lithography:** Recognize the differences in texture and detail between these common techniques.
- **Photogravure:** Understand the unique qualities of this method, often used for high-quality stamps.
- **Tip:** Catalog descriptions often specify the printing technique, aiding identification.

Reflection: Precise measurement and color analysis unlock deeper insights into your stamps, revealing their true identity and value. These skills set advanced collectors apart and ensure accurate classification.

16.4 Keeping a Digital Inventory for Easy Management

A well-maintained digital inventory streamlines your collection management and provides valuable records for organization, valuation, and insurance purposes.

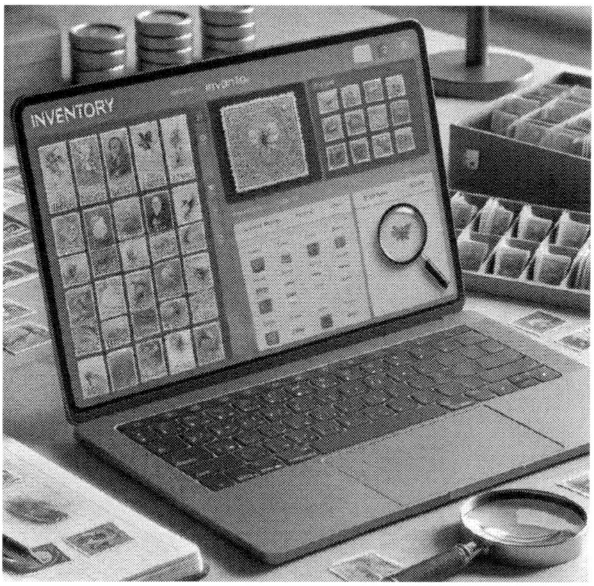

Simplify collection management with a detailed digital inventory.

A. Choosing the Right Software:

- **Popular Tools:** Programs like Stamp Mate, EzStamp, and Colnect offer features tailored to philatelists, including cataloging, valuation, and search functions.
- **Custom Features:** Look for options that allow high-resolution image uploads, notes, and cross-referencing.

- **Tip:** Opt for software that syncs with cloud storage to ensure your data is backed up.

B. Creating Detailed Records:

- **What to Include:** Document catalog numbers, condition, purchase history, and current market value for each stamp.
- **High-Quality Images:** Upload clear, detailed photos to accompany each entry for reference and verification.
- **Tip:** Regularly update your inventory to reflect changes in value or new additions.

C. Benefits of Digital Management:

- **Organization:** Easily sort and filter your collection by theme, country, or value.
- **Insurance and Valuation:** A detailed inventory simplifies insurance claims and appraisals in case of loss or damage.
- **Sharing:** Share your collection digitally with fellow collectors or display it online.

D. Backup and Security:

- **Cloud Solutions:** Use platforms with secure cloud storage to prevent data loss.
- **Encryption:** Ensure sensitive information is protected with encryption.
- **Tip:** Periodically download backups for offline access.

Reflection: A digital inventory enhances the efficiency and enjoyment of managing your collection while safeguarding its long-term value. It's an indispensable tool for modern philatelists.

Mastering stamp identification combines traditional expertise with modern tools, ensuring your collection remains authentic, valuable, and well-organized. By leveraging advanced techniques and staying vigilant against fraud, you'll build confidence in your abilities and deepen your appreciation for the intricate details that make stamp collecting a truly rewarding pursuit.

Chapter 16 Review: Mastering Stamp Identification

Chapter 16 delves into the essential skills and tools needed to accurately identify stamps, ensuring authenticity, preserving value, and enhancing organization. With insights into modern tools, techniques for detecting forgeries, and advanced methods for analyzing details, this chapter equips collectors to elevate their philatelic expertise.

16.1 Tools of the Trade: UV Lights, Watermark Detectors, and More

- **UV Lights:** Reveal phosphorescent markings that authenticate modern issues, making them invaluable for security verification.
- **Watermark Detectors:** Detect subtle patterns in stamp paper to confirm authenticity and identify issues.
- **Magnifying Glasses and Microscopes:** Provide detailed views of printing, perforations, and surface textures, essential for analyzing condition.
- **Perforation Gauges:** Accurately measure perforation patterns to differentiate between similar stamp varieties.
- **Color Grading Tools:** Highlight subtle color variations to identify rare issues or signs of tampering.

16.2 How to Spot Forgeries, Reprints, and Altered Stamps

- **Forgeries:** Look for inconsistent printing, incorrect paper types, and missing watermarks to identify fakes.
- **Reprints:** Subtle differences in design or inscriptions can distinguish reprints from original issues.

- **Alterations:** Detect tampering, such as fake overprints or trimmed perforations, with tools like microscopes.
- **Certification Services:** Use trusted organizations like the American Philatelic Society to authenticate high-value stamps.

16.3 Measuring Perforations and Analyzing Colors Like a Pro

- **Perforations:** Use gauges to measure and compare against catalog specifications, ensuring accuracy.
- **Colors:** Analyze shades under balanced lighting or with comparators to detect variations or fading.
- **Alterations:** Identify natural fading versus artificial alterations, such as bleaching or dyeing, often used by counterfeiters.
- **Printing Techniques:** Recognize engraving, lithography, and photogravure methods to further validate authenticity.

16.4 Keeping a Digital Inventory for Easy Management

- **Software:** Use tools like Stamp Mate or Colnect for cataloging, valuation, and detailed records.
- **Records:** Document catalog numbers, condition, purchase history, and market value, along with high-quality images.
- **Benefits:** Simplify organization, enable insurance claims, and easily share your collection digitally.
- **Backup:** Utilize secure cloud storage and offline backups to protect data from loss or breaches.

Chapter 16 empowers collectors with the knowledge and techniques to identify, authenticate, and manage stamps with precision. By mastering these skills, you'll protect the integrity of your collection and gain a deeper appreciation for the artistry and history of philately. Let these tools and strategies guide you toward becoming a confident and informed philatelist!

Chapter 17: The Future of Stamp Collecting

The world of stamp collecting is entering an exciting new era, where traditional practices blend seamlessly with technological advancements and emerging trends. Chapter 17 explores how digital stamps, blockchain technology, personalized designs, and shifting collector interests are shaping the future of philately. Whether you're a seasoned collector or new to the hobby, understanding these trends will help you navigate and thrive in a rapidly evolving landscape.

17.1 Digital Stamps and NFTs: The New Frontier

The advent of digital stamps and non-fungible tokens (NFTs) is transforming the way collectors interact with philatelic assets. These innovations offer new opportunities for ownership, trading, and showcasing collections.

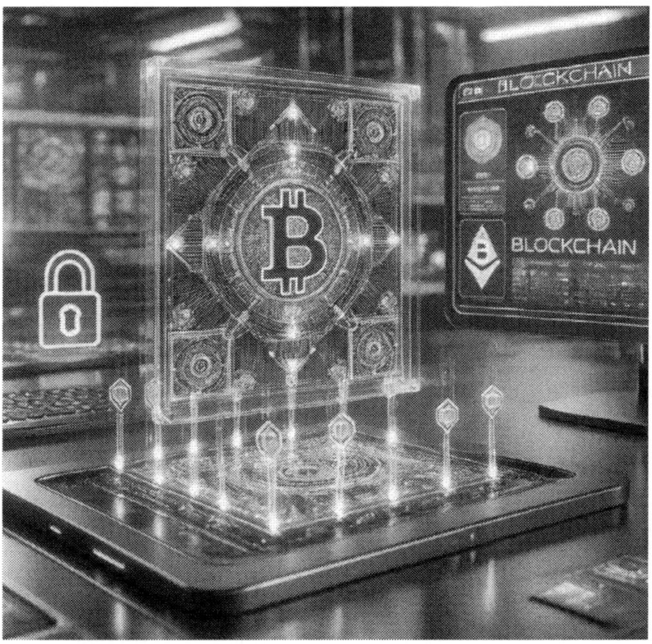

Discover how digital stamps and NFTs are reshaping philately.

A. What Are Digital Stamps?

- **Definition:** Digital stamps are virtual collectibles issued by postal authorities, representing designs or commemorative themes in a digital format.
- **Examples:** Countries like Austria, Switzerland, and the Netherlands have already issued official digital stamps that are traded and collected online.
- **Advantages:** These stamps are tamper-proof, environmentally friendly, and accessible to a global audience.

B. NFTs and Their Role in Philately:

- **What Are NFTs?** Non-fungible tokens are unique digital assets secured on a blockchain, ensuring authenticity and exclusivity.
- **Application in Stamps:** NFTs allow collectors to own and trade rare digital stamps, complete with metadata detailing their origin and ownership history.
- **Popularity:** High-profile NFT stamp releases, such as the United Nations' blockchain-powered stamps, have gained attention for their innovative approach.

C. Opportunities and Challenges:

- **Opportunities:** Digital stamps and NFTs provide access to a younger, tech-savvy audience, enhancing the hobby's appeal.
- **Challenges:** Concerns about long-term value, security, and market volatility remain key considerations for collectors.

Reflection: Digital stamps and NFTs represent a bold step forward for philately, merging traditional collecting with cutting-edge technology. Embracing these changes can open new doors for collectors and redefine the boundaries of the hobby.

17.2 Using Blockchain for Authentication and Ownership

Blockchain technology is revolutionizing the way collectors verify and manage their stamps, ensuring authenticity and transparency.

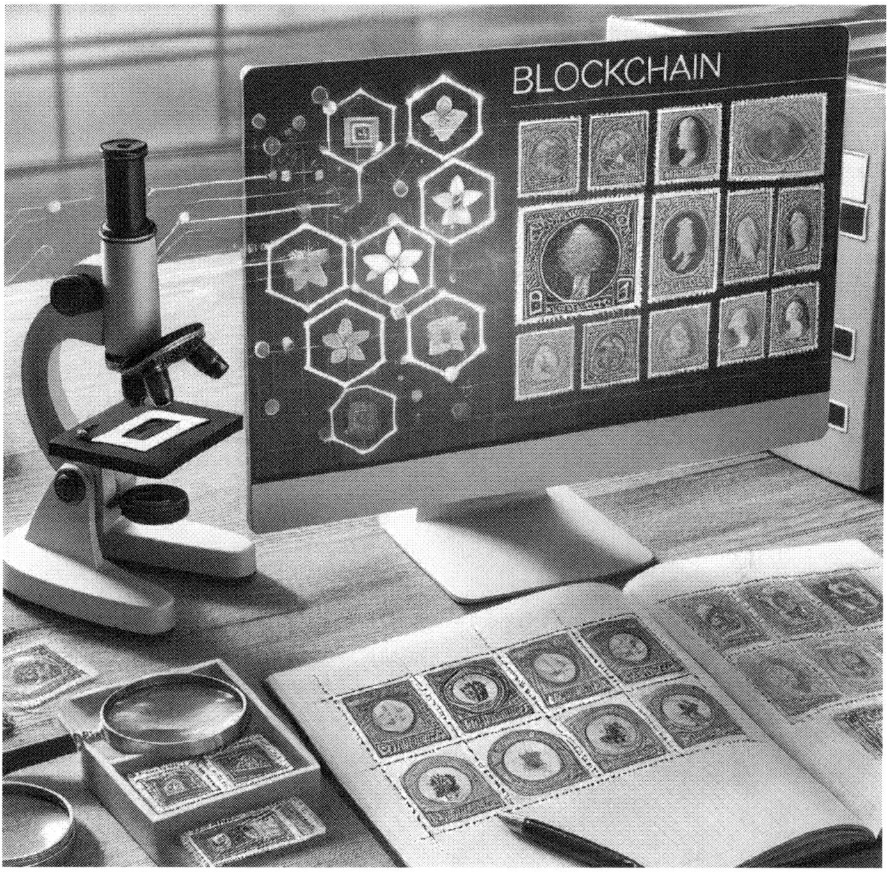

Leverage blockchain technology for secure authentication and trading.

A. How Blockchain Works in Philately:

- **Immutable Records:** Blockchain creates permanent, tamper-proof records of stamp ownership, provenance, and certification.
- **Digital Certificates:** Stamps linked to blockchain records come with verifiable digital certificates of authenticity.

- **Global Accessibility:** Blockchain enables cross-border verification and trading with ease.

B. Benefits for Collectors:

- **Fraud Prevention:** Blockchain minimizes the risk of forgery and misrepresentation, a persistent challenge in the stamp market.
- **Enhanced Trust:** Collectors and investors gain confidence knowing that their assets are securely verified.
- **Ease of Transactions:** Blockchain simplifies the buying, selling, and transferring of stamps between parties.

C. Current Applications:

- **Examples:** Platforms like StampX and PhilatelyChain offer blockchain-based solutions for authenticating and managing philatelic assets.
- **Integration with NFTs:** Blockchain also underpins NFT stamps, ensuring the uniqueness and provenance of digital collectibles.

Reflection: Blockchain technology brings a new level of trust and efficiency to stamp collecting. By adopting these innovations, collectors can safeguard their investments and participate in a more transparent market.

17.3 Personalized and Limited-Edition Stamps: What's Next?

The demand for personalized and exclusive stamps is reshaping how postal authorities and collectors approach philately. This trend emphasizes creativity, individuality, and rarity.

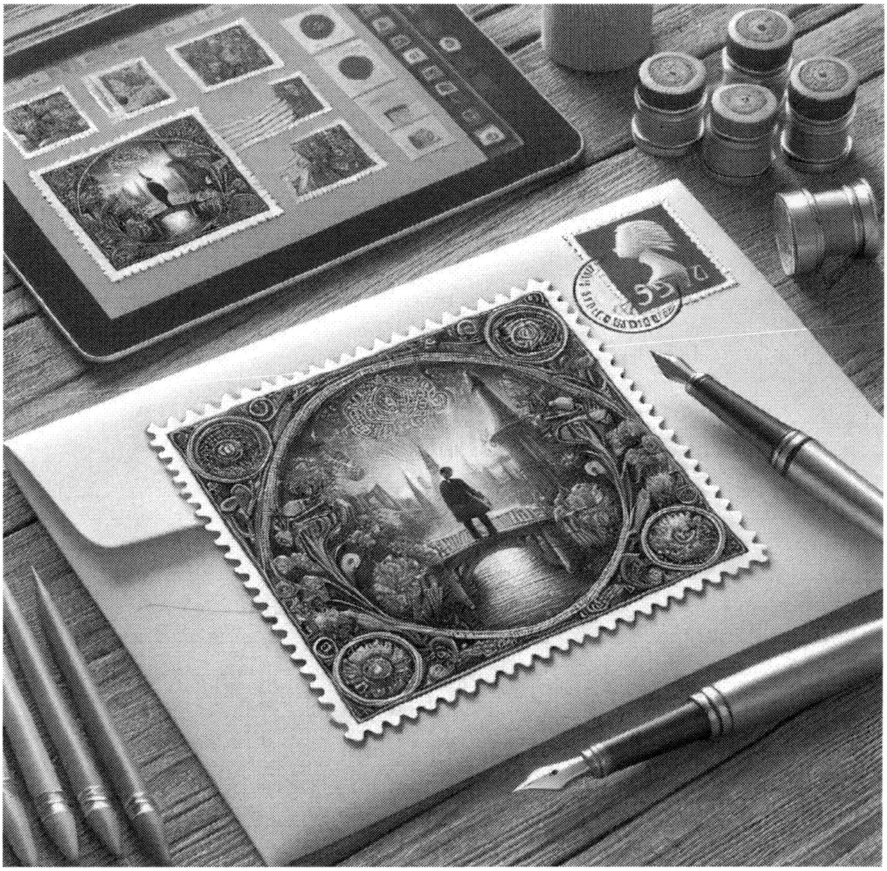

Explore the creative possibilities of personalized and limited-edition stamps.

A. Personalized Stamps:

- **Definition:** Personalized stamps allow individuals or organizations to create custom designs featuring photos, logos, or special messages.
- **Global Trends:** Countries like the United States, Canada, and Australia offer services to design personalized stamps for events such as weddings, anniversaries, and corporate branding.
- **Appeal:** Personalized stamps add a unique touch to collections, making them meaningful and memorable.

B. Limited-Edition Releases:

- **Scarcity as a Selling Point:** Limited print runs of commemorative or thematic stamps drive demand and value.
- **Special Features:** Innovations such as holograms, QR codes, and interactive elements enhance the appeal of limited editions.
- **Collector Engagement:** Postal services increasingly collaborate with artists, designers, and cultural institutions to create exclusive series.

C. Collaborative and Thematic Projects:

- **Collaborations:** Joint issues between countries or partnerships with popular franchises bring fresh interest to stamp collecting.
- **Themes for the Future:** Sustainability, technological advancements, and global unity are emerging as popular motifs for modern stamps.

Reflection: Personalized and limited-edition stamps offer a creative and exclusive avenue for collectors to express their individuality and stay engaged with contemporary trends. These innovations breathe new life into the hobby.

17.4 Trends to Watch: What's Driving the Hobby Forward

The philatelic world continues to evolve, driven by cultural shifts, technological advances, and changing collector interests. Keeping an eye on these trends ensures collectors remain ahead of the curve.

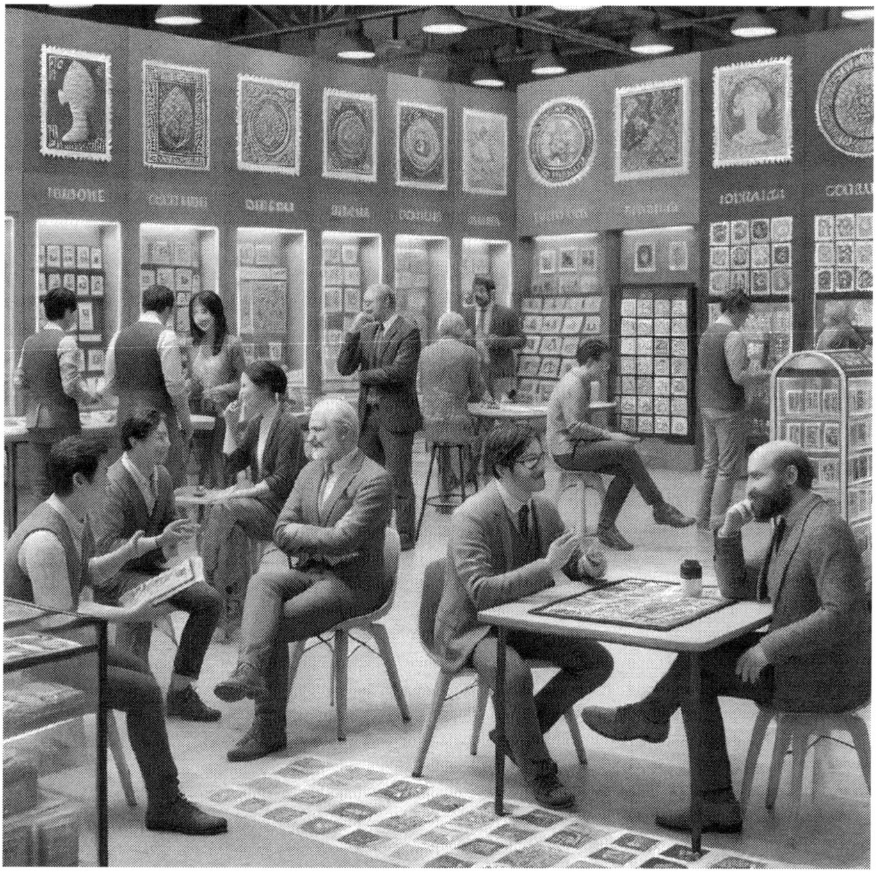

Stay informed on trends that are shaping the future of stamp collecting.

A. Growing Popularity Among Younger Collectors:

- **Digital Engagement:** Social media platforms and online forums introduce stamp collecting to a younger, tech-savvy audience.
- **Interactive Elements:** Features like augmented reality (AR) stamps attract new generations by combining tradition with technology.
- **Education Initiatives:** Schools and cultural organizations are incorporating philately into educational programs to spark early interest.

B. Sustainability and Eco-Friendly Practices:

- **Eco-Conscious Designs:** Stamps featuring environmental themes, endangered species, or renewable energy are gaining popularity.
- **Sustainable Production:** Many postal services are adopting eco-friendly materials and processes for stamp production.
- **Green Collecting:** Collectors are increasingly prioritizing sustainable storage and display options.

C. The Role of Technology:

- **AI-Powered Tools:** Artificial intelligence is revolutionizing stamp identification, grading, and valuation.
- **Virtual Stamp Shows:** Online exhibitions and marketplaces are expanding access to global philatelic communities.
- **Smart Displays:** Digital frames and interactive displays bring collections to life, appealing to modern sensibilities.

D. Global Expansion of the Hobby:

- **Emerging Markets:** Countries in Asia, Africa, and South America are seeing a rise in philatelic interest, bringing fresh perspectives and designs to the global stage.
- **Cross-Cultural Connections:** International collaborations and cultural themes are fostering greater inclusivity in the hobby.
- **Philatelic Tourism:** Stamp expos and exhibitions are becoming popular travel destinations for collectors worldwide.

Reflection: The future of stamp collecting is shaped by innovation, inclusivity, and environmental consciousness. By embracing these trends, collectors can ensure the hobby remains vibrant and relevant for generations to come.

The future of stamp collecting is bright, offering endless possibilities for exploration and creativity. From digital innovations to personalized designs, the hobby continues to evolve while staying rooted in its rich history. By understanding and adapting to these trends, you can not only enhance your collection but also play a part in shaping the next chapter of philately.

Chapter 17 Review: The Future of Stamp Collecting

Chapter 17 delves into the dynamic evolution of stamp collecting, where tradition meets innovation. This chapter highlights how digital advancements, blockchain technology, personalized stamps, and global trends are redefining the philatelic experience. By exploring these cutting-edge developments, collectors can embrace new opportunities while preserving the timeless essence of the hobby.

17.1 Digital Stamps and NFTs: The New Frontier

- **Digital Stamps:** Virtual stamps issued by postal authorities offer an environmentally friendly, globally accessible option for collectors.
- **NFTs in Philately:** Non-fungible tokens (NFTs) secure authenticity and ownership of rare digital stamps, combining blockchain technology with modern collecting.
- **Opportunities and Challenges:** While digital stamps attract younger, tech-savvy audiences, concerns about long-term value and market volatility remain.

17.2 Using Blockchain for Authentication and Ownership

- **Immutable Records:** Blockchain creates tamper-proof records of stamp provenance and ownership, enhancing trust in the market.
- **Fraud Prevention:** Collectors benefit from secure transactions and reduced risks of counterfeiting.
- **Current Applications:** Platforms like StampX and PhilatelyChain leverage blockchain to authenticate and manage stamps seamlessly.

17.3 Personalized and Limited-Edition Stamps: What's Next?

- **Personalized Stamps:** Custom designs allow collectors to create unique stamps for personal or corporate use, enhancing emotional and artistic value.
- **Limited Editions:** Scarcity drives demand for commemorative and thematic issues, often featuring holograms, QR codes, or collaborations with artists.
- **Collaborative Projects:** Joint issues and cultural themes bring innovation and broader appeal to philately.

17.4 Trends to Watch: What's Driving the Hobby Forward

- **Youth Engagement:** Social media, augmented reality stamps, and educational initiatives introduce younger generations to philately.
- **Sustainability:** Eco-conscious themes and green production practices resonate with modern values.
- **Technological Advancements:** AI tools, virtual exhibitions, and interactive displays make collecting more accessible and engaging.
- **Global Growth:** Emerging markets and international collaborations foster inclusivity and new design perspectives in the hobby.

Chapter 17 offers an inspiring glimpse into the future of stamp collecting, showcasing its ability to adapt and thrive in a rapidly changing world. By embracing digital innovations, personalized creations, and sustainable practices, collectors can ensure the hobby remains vibrant and relevant. The future of philately is a celebration of tradition and innovation, inviting collectors to explore limitless possibilities.

Chapter 18: Innovative Technology for Modern Collectors

As technology continues to shape the way we interact with and collect stamps, it's essential for modern collectors to embrace the tools and trends that are reshaping the hobby. From AI tools for identification to virtual stamp shows and augmented reality, technology is revolutionizing the way collectors manage, buy, and sell stamps. Chapter 18 explores cutting-edge tools and trends that will help you stay ahead in the world of stamp collecting.

18.1 AI Tools for Identifying and Valuing Stamps

AI-powered tools are quickly becoming indispensable for collectors who want to streamline the process of identifying stamps and evaluating their worth. These tools offer enhanced accuracy and efficiency, making it easier to catalog and assess your collection.

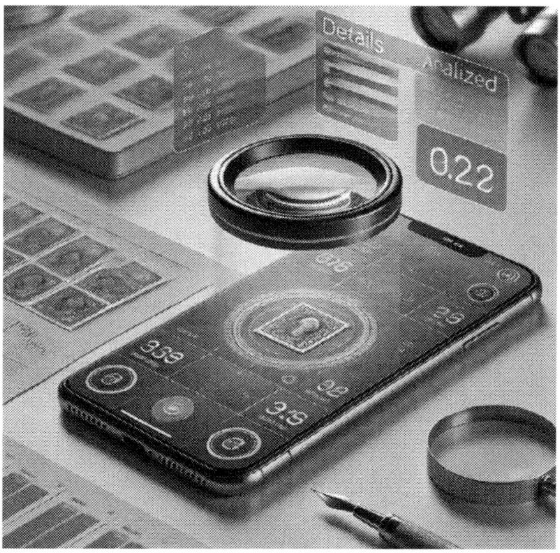

Use AI tools to streamline stamp identification and valuation.

A. How AI is Used in Stamp Identification:

AI tools can analyze images of stamps and compare them to vast databases, identifying their origins, historical context, and value.

- **Image Recognition:** AI algorithms can scan stamp images to recognize features such as designs, watermarks, and perforations. This helps identify stamps quickly and accurately.
- **Comparison with Databases:** By comparing scanned images to extensive stamp databases, AI tools can provide instant identification of rare stamps.
- **Historical Context:** AI can also offer insights into the history and significance of a stamp, helping collectors understand its place within philatelic history.

B. Valuation Tools:

AI also assists with assessing the value of stamps by analyzing past auction prices, current market trends, and condition data.

- **Price Prediction:** Some AI tools offer price predictions based on trends and the condition of a stamp, providing an estimate of its current market value.
- **Dynamic Valuations:** As the market fluctuates, AI tools update valuations to reflect real-time data, ensuring you always have the most accurate information.

C. Advantages of AI Tools:

- **Efficiency:** AI tools dramatically speed up the identification and valuation process.
- **Accuracy:** With access to vast datasets and machine learning capabilities, AI tools offer high accuracy in both identification and pricing.
- **Convenience:** Many AI tools are available via mobile apps, making them accessible to collectors on the go.

Reflection: AI tools are transforming the world of stamp collecting, offering collectors a smarter, more efficient way to identify, value, and track their collections.

18.2 Best Apps for Organizing and Cataloging Your Collection

In today's digital world, keeping track of your stamp collection has never been easier. A variety of mobile apps and software solutions are available to help collectors organize and catalog their stamps, ensuring that no piece is ever lost or forgotten.

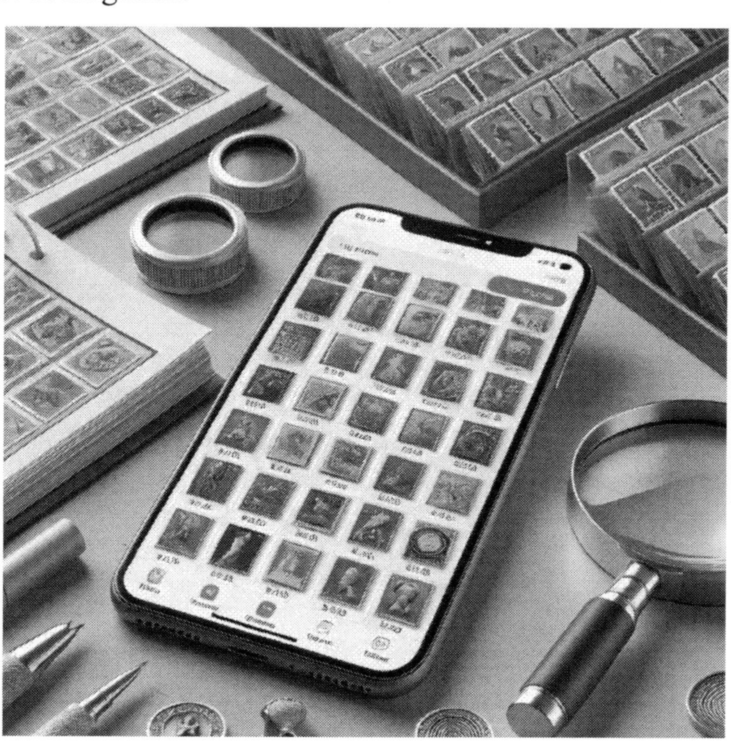

Simplify organization with cutting-edge stamp cataloging apps.

A. Key Features of Top Apps:

The best stamp cataloging apps offer features tailored to philatelic needs, including detailed stamp entries, condition tracking, and search functions.

- **Barcode Scanning:** Some apps allow you to scan barcodes or QR codes on stamps to quickly add them to your collection.
- **Customizable Fields:** Create personalized categories to track details like stamp condition, rarity, provenance, and purchase price.
- **Search and Sort:** Easily find stamps based on various criteria, such as country, theme, or date of issue, with advanced search filters.

B. Popular Apps for Collectors:

- **Stamp Mate:** This app allows collectors to catalog their stamps, providing access to detailed information about each stamp and its current market value.
- **Colnect:** Colnect offers an extensive stamp catalog and database, allowing collectors to manage their collections, exchange stamps, and keep track of their inventory.
- **My Stamp Collection:** My Stamp Collection offers an easy-to-use platform for organizing stamps, with customizable fields and the ability to track sales and acquisitions.

C. Benefits of Digital Organization:

- **Portability:** Access your collection from anywhere, whether you're at home or attending a stamp show.
- **Cloud Storage:** Many apps offer cloud-based storage, ensuring your collection is safe and accessible at all times.
- **Synchronization:** Sync your collection across multiple devices to keep your inventory up to date.

Reflection: Using an app to catalog and organize your collection helps maintain order and provides a quick way to track your stamps' details, making your collecting experience more efficient and enjoyable.

18.3 Virtual Stamp Shows and Augmented Reality

Virtual stamp shows and augmented reality (AR) are revolutionizing how collectors experience stamp exhibitions and interact with rare stamps. These technologies provide new ways to explore and engage with stamps from around the world.

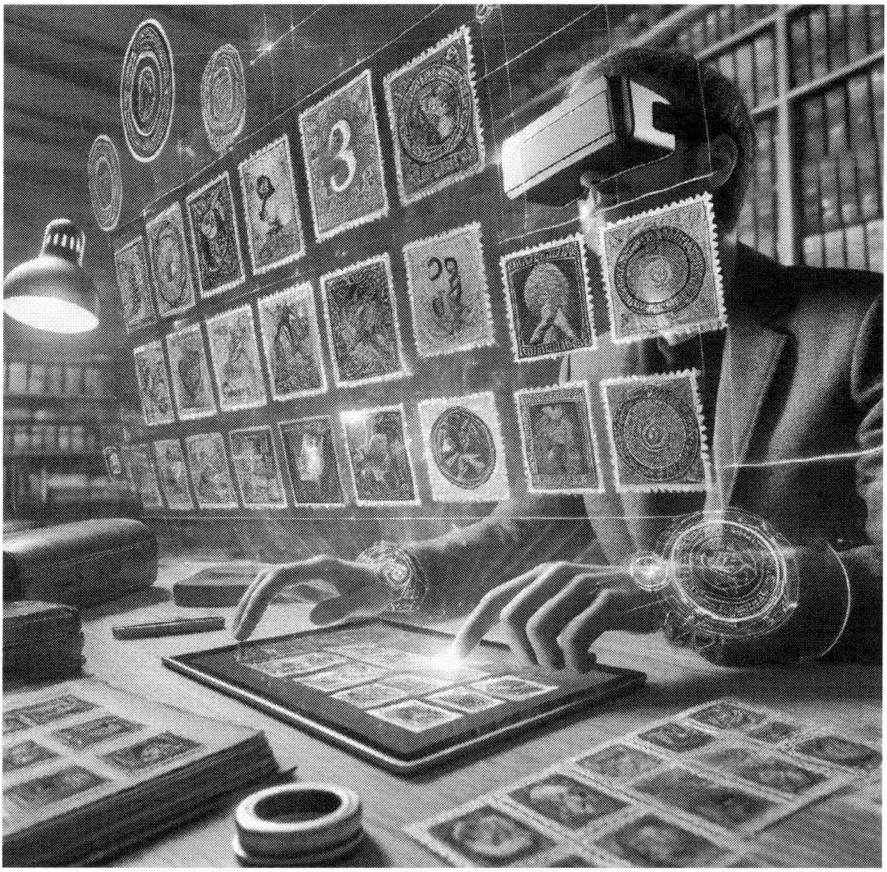

Experience virtual stamp shows and AR-enhanced collections.

A. Virtual Stamp Shows:

With the rise of virtual platforms, collectors no longer need to travel to in-person events to experience stamp shows. Online stamp exhibitions bring theworld of philately to your home, offering access to a wider range of stamps and exhibitors.

- **Global Access:** Virtual shows allow collectors from all over the world to participate, expanding the audience for rare stamps and collections.
- **Interactive Exhibits:** Many virtual shows offer interactive elements, such as live presentations, Q&A sessions, and virtual booth tours.
- **Auction Opportunities:** Some virtual shows incorporate live auctions, allowing collectors to bid on rare stamps from the comfort of their own homes.

B. Augmented Reality for Stamp Collecting:

Augmented reality is enhancing the way collectors experience stamps by blending the physical and digital worlds.

- **Interactive Viewing:** With AR apps, collectors can view stamps through their smartphone or tablet, providing additional information such as the stamp's history and significance.
- **Virtual Displays:** AR allows collectors to create virtual displays of their collections, sharing them with others through social media or stamp exhibitions.
- **Enhanced Learning:** AR can be used to show magnified views of stamps, highlighting intricate details such as printing errors or watermarks.

C. Advantages of Virtual and AR Technologies:

- **Accessibility:** Virtual shows and AR tools make it easier for collectors to access exhibitions and interact with stamps.
- **Educational Value:** Virtual and AR experiences can deepen a collector's understanding of stamp history, production, and value.

- **Convenience:** Attend shows and interact with stamps without the need to travel, making the hobby more accessible to collectors with time or mobility limitations.

Reflection: Virtual stamp shows and augmented reality are expanding the possibilities for collectors, offering new ways to learn, engage, and connect with the world of philately.

18.4 Staying Ahead of the Curve with New Tools

As technology continues to evolve, it's essential for collectors to stay informed about the latest tools and innovations that can enhance their collecting experience.

A. Emerging Technologies:

New technologies are constantly being developed to meet the needs of modern collectors.

- **Blockchain for Authentication:** Blockchain is becoming a key tool in verifying the authenticity and provenance of stamps, offering collectors a secure way to track ownership and ensure their investments are protected.
- **3D Printing for Stamp Preservation:** 3D printing technology is being explored for creating replicas of rare stamps, allowing collectors to display high-value items without risk.
- **Artificial Intelligence for Valuation:** AI is increasingly being used to predict the value of stamps, analyzing historical pricing data and current market trends to help collectors make informed buying and selling decisions.

B. Staying Informed:

It's important for collectors to stay updated on the latest tools and trends in the hobby.

- **Join Online Communities:** Participate in forums, online groups, and social media to exchange knowledge and discover new tools.

- **Read Industry Publications:** Subscribe to philatelic magazines, blogs, and newsletters to stay informed about emerging technologies and innovations in stamp collecting.
- **Attend Workshops and Webinars:** Many philatelic organizations offer educational resources and online workshops to help collectors learn about new tools and trends.

C. Embracing Change:

The world of stamp collecting is evolving, and embracing new technologies will help you stay ahead of the curve. Whether it's adopting new tools for organization, using AI for valuations, or exploring the possibilities of blockchain, staying informed will keep you at the forefront of this exciting hobby.

Reflection: By embracing new tools and technologies, collectors can enhance their collecting experience and ensure that they are always up to date with the latest trends and innovations in the hobby.

Innovative technology is shaping the future of stamp collecting, offering exciting new tools for collectors to enhance their collections, track market trends, and connect with others. By staying informed about the latest advancements, collectors can keep their passion for philately alive and thriving in the digital age.

Chapter 18 Review: Innovative Technology for Modern Collectors

Chapter 18 introduces modern technologies that are transforming the world of stamp collecting. From AI tools to augmented reality and blockchain, this chapter explores how innovation is helping collectors streamline processes, enhance collection management, and stay ahead in an ever-evolving field.

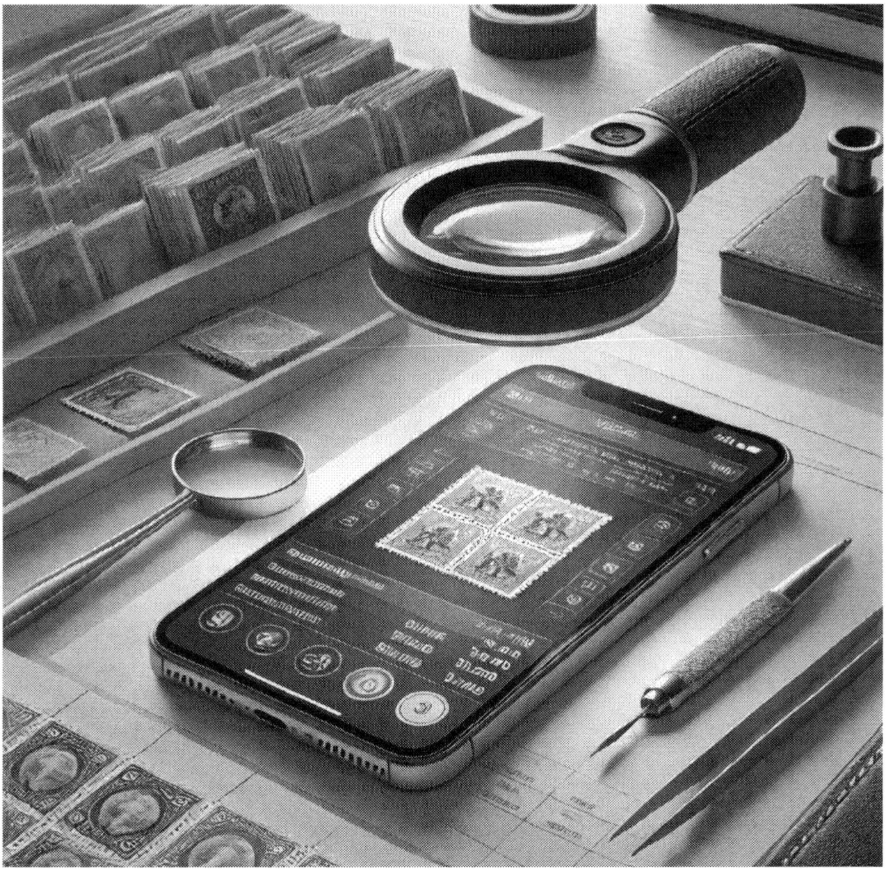

Stay ahead with innovative tools that redefine philately.

18.1 AI Tools for Identifying and Valuing Stamps

- **AI Identification:** AI-powered apps can quickly identify stamps and assess their value by matching them with vast databases. This helps collectors save time and avoid errors when identifying and evaluating stamps.
- **Valuation Assistance:** AI tools estimate stamp values based on trends, rarity, and condition, offering a more efficient way to gauge worth before buying or selling.

18.2 Best Apps for Organizing and Cataloging Your Collection

- **Mobile Cataloging:** Cataloging apps allow collectors to track their stamps from anywhere. These apps store key details, such as country of origin and condition, keeping your collection organized.
- **Cloud Syncing:** Many apps offer cloud storage, making your collection accessible across devices and ensuring your data is safe and up-to-date.

18.3 Virtual Stamp Shows and Augmented Reality

- **Virtual Experiences:** Virtual stamp shows break geographic barriers and enable collectors to explore exhibits worldwide. These events also foster global connections within the philatelic community.
- **Augmented Reality (AR):** AR lets collectors view stamps in 3D, enhancing detail inspection and engagement. Virtual platforms offer a deeper, more interactive experience.

18.4 Staying Ahead of the Curve with New Tools

- **Blockchain and Digital Stamps:** Blockchain ensures secure ownership records and authentication, while digital stamps and NFTs provide innovative ways to trade and collect.
- **Continuous Innovation:** The rapid development of new technologies, such as digital tools for cataloging and blockchain for provenance, ensures collectors can stay competitive and informed.

Chapter 18 offers an exciting look at how technology is reshaping the stamp-collecting world. By embracing AI tools, virtual experiences, and emerging tech like blockchain, collectors can streamline their collections and keep up with the latest trends. Stay ahead of the curve and let innovation enhance your collecting journey!

Conclusion: Leaving Your Mark in Philately

Congratulations on completing **HowExpert Guide to Stamp Collecting**! As you reach the final pages of this guide, it's time to reflect on your journey as a collector and envision the legacy you'll leave behind. Stamp collecting is more than a hobby; it's a bridge to history, a celebration of art, and a deeply personal expression of curiosity and passion. Whether you're just starting out or are a seasoned philatelist, there's always room to grow, learn, and inspire others. This chapter focuses on how you can preserve the significance of your collection, maintain your enthusiasm, and inspire future generations to embrace the joy of philately.

I. Reflecting on Your Growth as a Collector

Every collector's journey is unique, shaped by the stamps they choose and the stories they uncover. Reflecting on your progress is a powerful way to appreciate how far you've come and recognize the impact your collection has made.

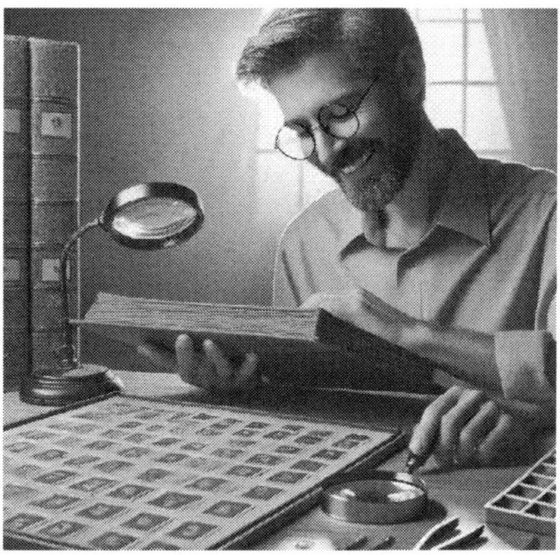

Reflect on your journey and celebrate your achievements in philately.

A. Milestones in Your Collection:

- **First Stamp:** Think back to the excitement of acquiring your very first stamp. Was it a local issue, a family heirloom, or a serendipitous find?
- **Special Finds:** Recall the rare or meaningful stamps that stand out in your collection. Perhaps it was a limited-edition commemorative or a beautifully designed thematic piece.
- **Skills Gained:** Acknowledge the expertise you've developed over time, such as identifying forgeries, grading stamps, or mastering cataloging systems.

B. Personal Impact:

- **Knowledge Enrichment:** Consider the historical events, artistic styles, and cultural insights you've encountered through philately.
- **Community Connections:** Reflect on the friendships, mentorships, and shared experiences you've had with other collectors.
- **A Living Legacy:** Recognize how your collection serves as a tangible reflection of your interests, values, and the moments that have inspired you.

Reflection: Taking the time to celebrate your journey not only reinforces your passion but also sets the stage for what lies ahead in your philatelic pursuits.

II. How to Stay Passionate About Your Hobby

Maintaining enthusiasm for stamp collecting requires exploration, creativity, and connection. Here are strategies to ensure your love for the hobby endures.

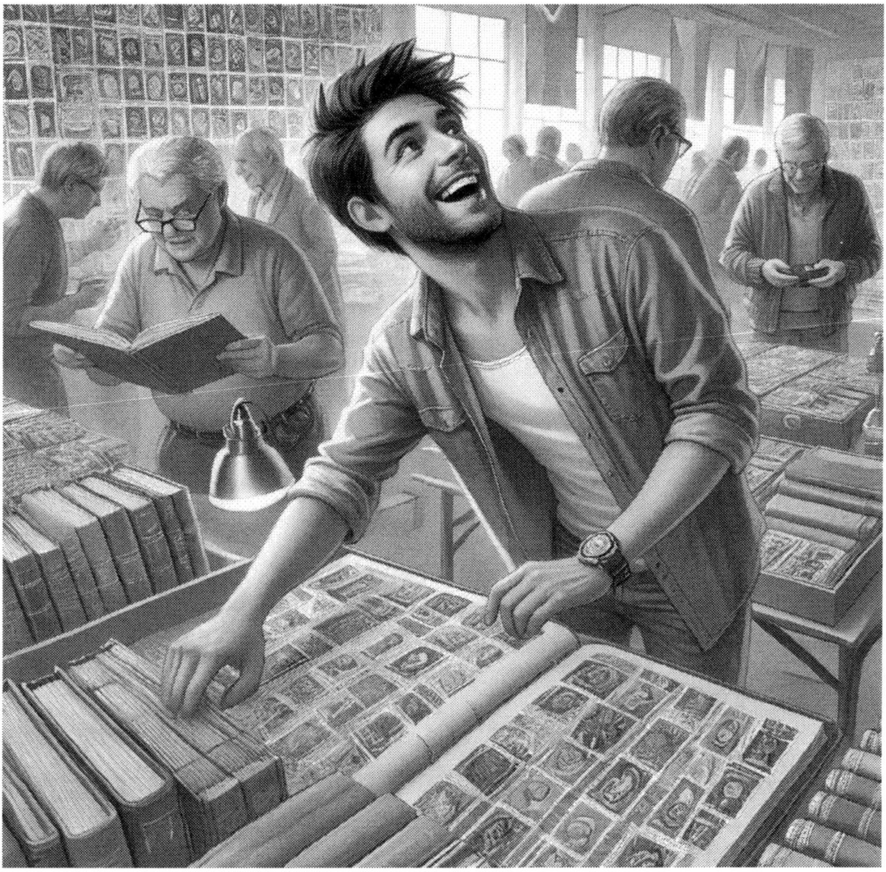

Reignite your passion by exploring and connecting with others.

A. Explore New Horizons:

- **Expand Themes:** Venture into new categories, such as stamps featuring wildlife, space exploration, or global festivals. Diversity keeps your collection fresh and exciting.
- **Discover the Unusual:** Seek out stamps made from unique materials like silk or wood, or explore interactive designs with holograms or QR codes.
- **Set Challenges:** Create goals for your collection, such as completing a country-specific set or acquiring stamps from every continent.

B. Engage with the Philatelic Community:

- **Attend Events:** Participate in local or international stamp shows, exhibitions, and competitions to stay inspired and discover new opportunities.
- **Join Clubs:** Become a member of a philatelic society or online group where you can exchange ideas, tips, and stories.
- **Collaborate:** Partner with other collectors on joint projects or trades to broaden your horizons.

C. Share Your Passion:

- **Educate Others:** Host workshops or talks to introduce newcomers to the joy of stamp collecting.
- **Showcase Your Collection:** Use social media platforms or blogs to share images, stories, and insights about your stamps.
- **Inspire Young Collectors:** Encourage children and teens to start their own collections by gifting starter kits or leading hands-on activities.

Reflection: Staying passionate is about embracing the limitless potential of philately, always finding new ways to connect with the hobby and its community.

III. Preserving and Passing Down Your Collection

A well-preserved collection is a timeless treasure, offering future generations a glimpse into history and your personal legacy. Proper planning ensures your stamps' stories endure.

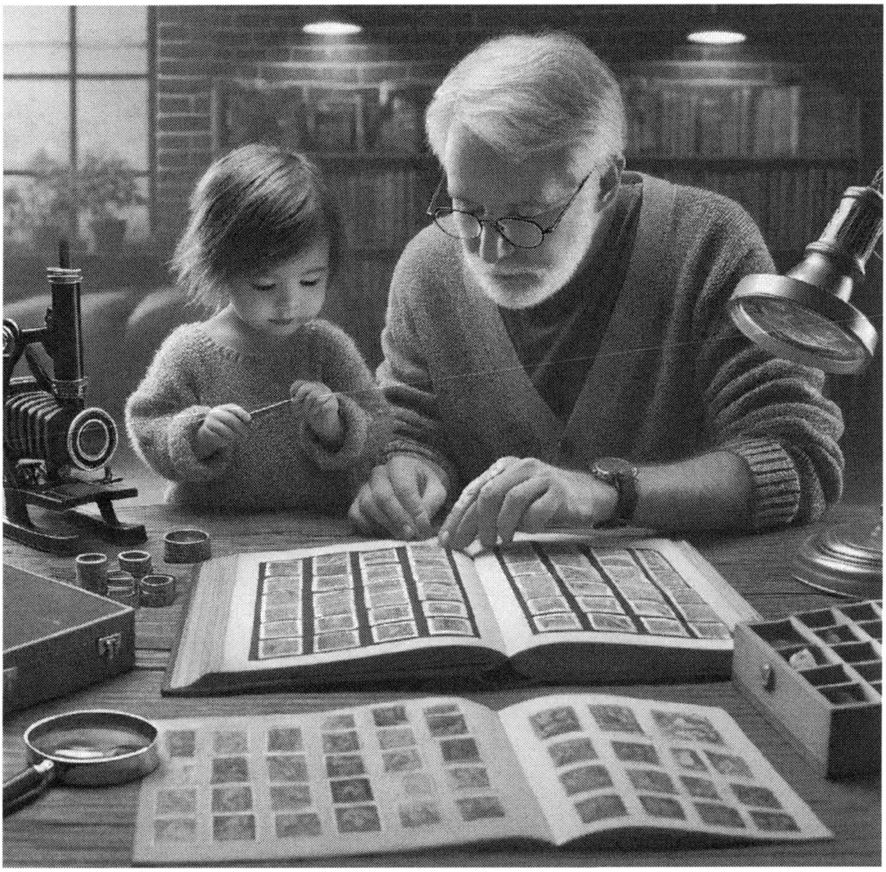

Preserve your collection and inspire the next generation.

A. Creating a Comprehensive Inventory:

- **Digital Records:** Use cataloging software to document details such as catalog numbers, acquisition dates, and estimated values.
- **Photographic Documentation:** Take high-resolution images of each stamp, noting any unique features or backstory.
- **Backup Systems:** Store your inventory digitally with cloud-based backups for added security.

B. Ensuring Long-Term Protection:

- **Storage Solutions:** Invest in archival-quality albums, stock books, and protective mounts to prevent damage from light, humidity, and pests.
- **Environmental Control:** Store your collection in a temperature-controlled environment to avoid deterioration.
- **Secure Displays:** Use locking cases or UV-protective frames for stamps on display.

C. Planning for the Future:

- **Family Heirloom:** Pass your collection to a loved one with clear instructions for its care and significance.
- **Charitable Donations:** Consider donating to museums, libraries, or philatelic organizations to preserve your collection's historical value.
- **Appraisal and Insurance:** Have your collection professionally appraised and insured to protect its financial worth.

Reflection: Preserving your collection ensures that its beauty, history, and value remain intact for years to come, offering inspiration and joy to future generations.

IV. Inspiring Future Collectors to Join the Journey

The future of philately depends on fostering curiosity and enthusiasm in new generations. By sharing your passion, you can play a vital role in ensuring the hobby's longevity.

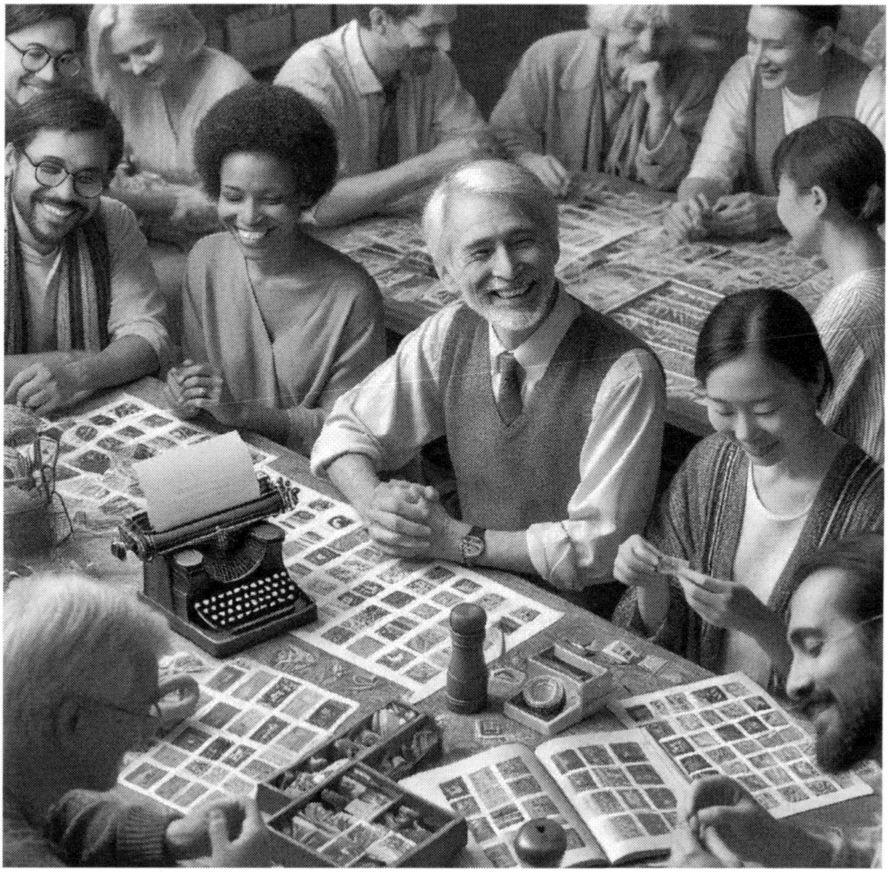

Share your love for stamps to inspire future collectors.

A. Engaging with Youth:

- **Interactive Experiences:** Organize school visits, workshops, or stamp-themed activities to introduce children to the world of philately.
- **Starter Kits:** Create beginner-friendly kits with stamps, tweezers, and simple guides to help young collectors get started.
- **Storytelling:** Share the fascinating stories behind your stamps to spark interest and wonder.

B. Showcasing Philately's Relevance:

- **Connecting to Modern Issues:** Highlight how stamps reflect current events, environmental efforts, or global achievements.
- **Artistic Value:** Emphasize the creativity and craftsmanship involved in stamp design.
- **Personalized Stamps:** Introduce newcomers to the appeal of creating custom designs for special occasions or milestones.

C. Building a Supportive Community:

- **Local Clubs:** Organize meetups or stamp swaps to create opportunities for connection and collaboration.
- **Online Platforms:** Use social media and forums to foster engagement with collectors around the world.
- **Mentorship:** Offer guidance to beginners, sharing your expertise and encouraging their growth.

Reflection: By inspiring others to embrace philately, you contribute to a thriving, inclusive community that celebrates the joy of collecting and preserves its legacy.

Stamp collecting is a lifelong journey filled with discovery, creativity, and connection. By reflecting on your growth, staying engaged, preserving your collection, and inspiring others, you contribute to a vibrant and enduring legacy. As you close this chapter, remember that every stamp tells a story—and your collection is a testament to the stories you've chosen to preserve and share. Together, let's ensure that **HowExpert Guide to Stamp Collecting** continues to inspire collectors worldwide and that philately thrives for generations to come.

Conclusion Chapter Review: Leaving Your Mark in Philately

The concluding chapter of *HowExpert Guide to Stamp Collecting* invites readers to reflect on their journey as collectors while emphasizing the importance of preserving, sharing, and inspiring future generations. It provides thoughtful insights on personal growth, sustained passion, and the legacy that stamp collecting can create.

I. Reflecting on Your Growth as a Collector

- **Milestones:** Recall the first stamp you acquired, the rare finds you've added, and the skills you've honed, such as identifying forgeries or mastering cataloging techniques.
- **Personal Impact:** Stamp collecting enriches knowledge, fosters community connections, and serves as a tangible reflection of your values and interests.
- **Living Legacy:** Your collection is a testament to your passion and a bridge to history, culture, and art.

II. How to Stay Passionate About Your Hobby

- **Exploration:** Expand into new themes or materials, challenge yourself with goals, or venture into unusual collectibles like holographic or wooden stamps.
- **Community Engagement:** Join clubs, attend events, and collaborate with fellow collectors for shared inspiration.
- **Sharing Passion:** Host workshops, create social media content, or encourage young collectors to explore the joys of philately.

III. Preserving and Passing Down Your Collection

- **Digital Documentation:** Maintain an organized inventory with high-quality images, detailed records, and cloud backups.

- **Protective Measures:** Use archival-quality materials, climate-controlled storage, and secure displays to safeguard your collection.
- **Legacy Planning:** Pass your collection to loved ones, donate it to institutions, or have it appraised and insured for future protection.

IV. Inspiring Future Collectors

- **Youth Engagement:** Create starter kits, host stamp-themed activities, and share the compelling stories behind your stamps.
- **Modern Relevance:** Highlight how stamps connect to current events, artistic value, and cultural milestones.
- **Community Building:** Encourage connections through local meetups, online platforms, and mentorship programs.

This chapter beautifully underscores that philately is more than a personal pastime—it is a gateway to history, a form of storytelling, and a source of inspiration for others. By reflecting on your journey, staying curious, and fostering connections, you not only enhance your experience but also contribute to the enduring legacy of stamp collecting.

Your collection is a unique narrative that celebrates history, art, and passion—keep sharing it, and let it inspire others for years to come.

Appendices

The appendices serve as a practical toolkit for stamp collectors, offering valuable resources, templates, and guidance to enhance their philatelic journey. Whether you're a beginner or an advanced collector, these appendices provide actionable insights and tools to take your collection to the next level.

Appendix A: Glossary of Essential Stamp Terms from A to Z

This comprehensive glossary is your ultimate reference for philatelic terminology. Understanding these terms will help you navigate catalogs, auctions, and collector communities with confidence. Whether you're a beginner or an experienced philatelist, mastering these definitions will elevate your collecting experience.

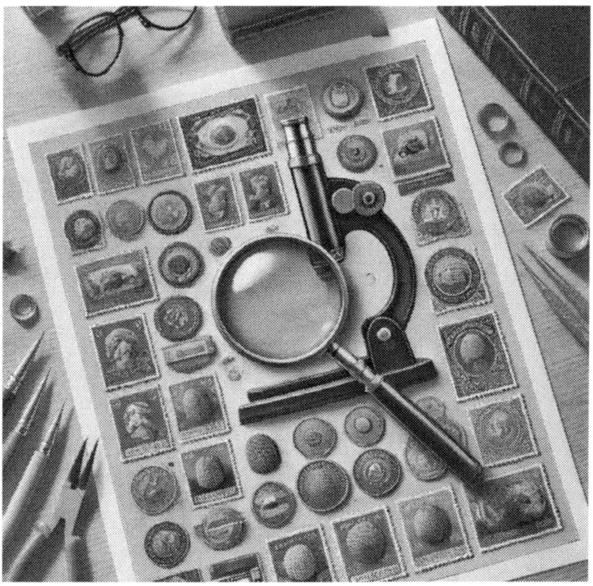

Master essential terms to navigate the world of philately with confidence.

A

- **Adhesive Stamp**: A stamp with a sticky backing, typically activated by moisture, used for affixing to mail.
- **Album**: A book or binder specifically designed for organizing and displaying a stamp collection.
- **Aerogram**: A lightweight, pre-stamped sheet of paper folded to form an envelope, used for international air mail.
- **Appraisal**: The process of professionally evaluating a stamp's market value or condition.

B

- **Block**: A group of four or more unseparated stamps from the same sheet, collected for their aesthetic or monetary value.
- **Booklet**: A small booklet containing a set number of stamps, often enclosed in a cardboard cover for protection.
- **Brilliant Gum**: A shiny gum finish applied to the back of a mint stamp, adding a distinct gloss.
- **Broken Set**: A partial set of stamps missing one or more items from a complete series.

C

- **Cancel**: The postmark or marking applied to a stamp to show it has been used.
- **Catalogue**: A detailed publication listing stamps by country, with descriptions, images, and estimated values (e.g., Scott, Stanley Gibbons).
- **Centenary Issue**: A commemorative stamp issued to celebrate the 100th anniversary of an event or institution.

- **Cinderella Stamp**: A non-postage stamp-like label, such as advertising labels, charity seals, or revenue stamps.

D

- **Definitive Stamp**: A standard postage stamp issued for regular use, typically featuring long-term designs.
- **Die**: A metal plate used in engraving the design of a stamp during the printing process.
- **Dull Gum**: A matte gum finish applied to some stamps, differing from glossy finishes.
- **Dummy Stamp**: A non-postal stamp created for training purposes or promotional materials, often marked "SPECIMEN."

E

- **Engraving**: A printing method that produces raised designs on stamps by etching a design onto a metal plate.
- **Error**: A stamp with a printing mistake, such as missing colors, inverted images, or design misalignments, often highly collectible.
- **Essay**: A preliminary design for a stamp that was not approved for issuance.

F

- **Face Value**: The monetary value printed on a stamp, indicating its postage worth at the time of issue.
- **First-Day Cover (FDC)**: An envelope with a stamp canceled on its official first day of issue, often accompanied by decorative designs.
- **Flaw**: A minor defect or irregularity in the design or printing of a stamp.

- **Forerunner**: A stamp used in a region before the establishment of a formal postal system.

G

- **Gum**: The adhesive coating on the back of a stamp, which can be original (mint) or disturbed due to handling.
- **Grading**: The assessment of a stamp's condition based on factors like centering, color, gum, and perforations.
- **Grill**: A pattern of tiny indentations applied to some U.S. stamps in the 19th century to prevent reuse.
- **Gutter Pair**: Two stamps separated by the blank space (gutter) between panes of a sheet, collected for their unique format.

H

- **Hinge**: A small, folded piece of paper used to affix stamps to an album page, often leaving a mark on the gum.
- **Holed Stamp**: A stamp with intentional perforations forming initials or designs, often used by companies to prevent theft.
- **Hybrid Stamp**: A stamp that combines multiple printing techniques, such as engraving and lithography.

I

- **Imperf (Imperforate)**: A stamp without perforations, requiring cutting or tearing to separate.
- **Inscription**: Text on a stamp, such as country names, dates, or denominations, that provides identifying information.
- **Invert**: A stamp with part of its design, such as the vignette, printed upside down, creating a valuable error.

J

- **Joint Issue**: A stamp issued collaboratively by two or more countries, often commemorating shared events or themes.
- **Jubilee Line**: A border line printed around a stamp pane, serving as a visual aid during the printing process.

K

- **Kiloware**: A bulk lot of used stamps sold by weight, often on clipped envelope corners.
- **Key Plate**: The primary printing plate used to produce a stamp, often combined with additional plates for multi-color designs.

L

- **Label**: A stamp-like item with no postal value, often included in stamp panes for advertising or decoration.
- **Local Post**: A private or municipal postal service operating within a limited area, often issuing unique stamps.
- **Luster**: The glossiness or sheen of a stamp's surface, indicative of its condition and preservation.

M

- **Margin**: The blank area around the design of a stamp, which can be wide (selvage) or narrow.
- **Mint Condition**: A stamp in its original, unused state, with intact gum on the back.
- **Mulready**: Pre-stamped letter sheets issued by Great Britain in 1840, considered a precursor to modern stamps.

N

- **New Issue**: A recently released stamp available for purchase from postal authorities.
- **Non-Denominated Stamp**: A stamp without a printed monetary value, often marked with a service level (e.g., “Forever”).
- **Number Cancel**: A cancellation mark in the form of a number, used to identify specific postal offices.

O

- **Overprint**: Additional text or design printed over a stamp, often to change its purpose or value.
- **Obliteration**: A heavy cancel or marking applied to render a stamp’s design or value unreadable.

P

- **Perforations**: The small holes or cuts along the edges of a stamp that allow for easy separation from a sheet.
- **Philately**: The study and collection of postage stamps, postal history, and related materials.
- **Plate Number**: A number printed in the margin of a stamp pane, identifying the printing plate used.

Q

- **Quadruple Cancel**: A stamp with four overlapping cancellation marks, often found on high-value mail.
- **Quickset Ink**: A type of ink that dries rapidly, often used in modern stamp printing to enhance clarity.

R

- **Revenue Stamp**: A stamp used to indicate tax payment rather than for postal purposes.
- **Reissue**: A stamp design reprinted after its original issuance, often with minor modifications.
- **Rouletting**: A separation method using small slits instead of perforations, creating a jagged edge.

S

- **Selvage**: The border surrounding a stamp sheet, often containing plate numbers or inscriptions.
- **Souvenir Sheet**: A small sheet containing one or more stamps, issued for collectors and often commemorative.
- **Specimen Stamp**: A stamp overprinted with the word "SPECIMEN," used as a sample or demonstration.

T

- **Thematic Collecting**: Collecting stamps based on a specific theme, such as animals, sports, or historical events.
- **Tongs**: Specialized tweezers used to handle stamps without damaging them.
- **Tête-Bêche**: A pair of stamps printed upside-down relative to each other, often a collectible curiosity.

U

- **Unused**: A stamp that has not been postally used but may not retain its original gum.
- **Ultraviolet Light**: A tool used to detect phosphorescent or fluorescent features on stamps.

V

- **Variety**: A difference in a stamp's design, perforation, or color, often the result of a production anomaly.
- **Vignette**: The central design of a stamp, usually surrounded by a border or inscription.

W

- **Watermark**: A faint design embedded in stamp paper to prevent counterfeiting, visible when held up to light.
- **Wilding Stamps**: A series of British stamps featuring Queen Elizabeth II's portrait, issued between 1952 and 1967.

X

- **Xeproof**: A rare type of proof made for experimental purposes, often by postal authorities testing new designs or printing techniques.

Y

- **Year Set**: A collection of all the stamps issued by a country during a specific year, often sold as a complete package by postal services.
- **Youth Philately**: Programs or initiatives aimed at encouraging stamp collecting among young people, fostering the next generation of collectors.

Z

- **Zeppelin Stamp**: A stamp issued to pay for mail carried by airships, particularly during the early 20th century. These stamps are iconic and highly sought after by thematic collectors

Reflection: This glossary provides an in-depth look at essential stamp terms, offering clarity and guidance for collectors at all levels. From the basics to advanced terminology, it ensures you have the knowledge to explore philately with confidence and expertise. Keep this reference handy as you continue your journey into the fascinating world of stamps!

Appendix B: Trusted Resources: Books, Websites, and Tools

Expand your philatelic knowledge and skills with these trusted resources. Whether you're looking to deepen your understanding, find stamps, or organize your collection, these resources will enhance your journey.

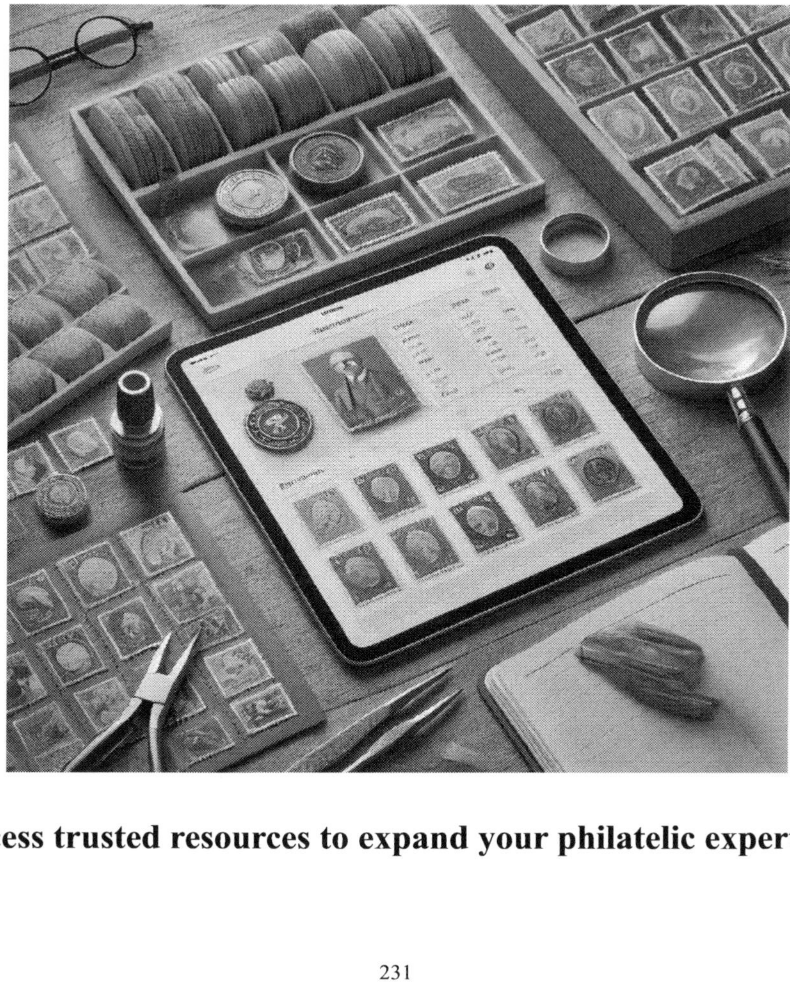

Access trusted resources to expand your philatelic expertise.

A. Books: Your Comprehensive Philatelic Library

Books are indispensable for collectors, offering in-depth insights, detailed catalogs, and expert advice:

1. **Scott Specialized Catalogue of Stamps & Covers**
   - A cornerstone for U.S. collectors, covering stamps and covers with detailed descriptions and valuations.
   - Includes special sections on postal history, varieties, and errors.
2. **Stanley Gibbons Catalogue**
   - A leading reference for British and Commonwealth stamps.
   - Offers thorough coverage of historical issues and modern releases.
3. **The American Philatelist**
   - A monthly magazine by the American Philatelic Society.
   - Features articles on philatelic research, auction trends, and collector stories.
4. **Linn's Stamp News Almanac**
   - A practical reference with market trends, auction highlights, and philatelic tips.
   - Includes annual updates on top-selling stamps and market insights.
5. **Postage Stamps of the World by John Easton**
   - A classic guide for global collectors, delving into designs, history, and cultural significance.

B. Websites: Online Hubs for Collectors

Harness the power of the internet to explore global resources and connect with fellow enthusiasts:

1. **StampWorld (www.stampworld.com)**
   - A free, comprehensive online catalog for identifying and valuing stamps from around the world.
   - Features a user-friendly search function and a collector marketplace.
2. **Delcampe (www.delcampe.net)**
   - A trusted marketplace for buying and selling stamps, with filters for themes, regions, and rarity.
   - Active forums for discussions and expert advice.
3. **The British Library's Philatelic Collections**
   - Explore one of the largest stamp archives in the world online.
   - Access detailed descriptions of rare stamps, postal artifacts, and thematic collections.
4. **HipStamp (www.hipstamp.com)**
   - A platform tailored for philatelists, offering a vast selection of stamps with buyer protection.
   - Tools for tracking auctions and setting up notifications for desired items.
5. **The American Philatelic Society (www.stamps.org)**
   - A hub for U.S. collectors, offering membership perks like digital libraries, expertizing services, and event listings.

C. Tools: Essential Equipment for Every Collector

Equip yourself with the right tools to preserve, analyze, and showcase your stamps:

1. **Stamp Mate**

    - A robust app for cataloging and organizing your collection digitally.
    - Includes features for valuation tracking, photo uploads, and wish lists.
2. **Perforation Gauges**
    - A must-have tool for measuring the perforation differences between stamp varieties.
    - Transparent models ensure accuracy and ease of use.
3. **UV Lights**
    - Essential for detecting phosphorescent or fluorescent markings, often invisible to the naked eye.
    - Also helpful for spotting repairs, alterations, or forgeries.
4. **Watermark Detectors**
    - Devices or trays paired with fluid to reveal hidden watermarks embedded in stamp paper.
5. **Digital Magnifiers**
    - High-powered magnification with LED lighting to inspect details like engravings and printing techniques.
    - Some models connect to your computer for easy viewing and analysis.

Tip: Bookmark these resources and keep your tools organized for quick access. With these trusted books, websites, and tools, you'll have everything you need to enhance your philatelic journey and refine your collection.

Appendix C: Templates for Organizing, Grading, and Tracking

Streamline your stamp collection management with these versatile templates. Whether you prefer printable forms or digital solutions, these tools will help you stay organized, evaluate your collection effectively, and track your progress over time.

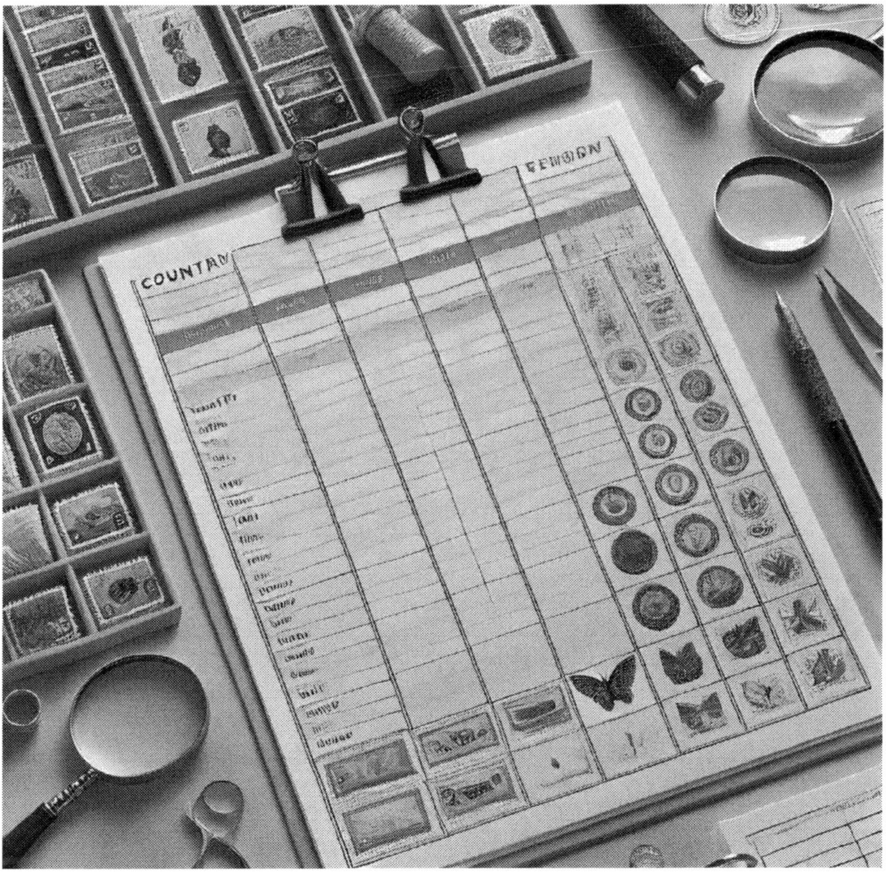

Streamline your collection with customizable templates.

A. Inventory Template: Documenting Your Collection

An inventory template is essential for maintaining a detailed record of your stamps. Keeping accurate data helps you monitor value, plan acquisitions, and provide documentation for insurance or appraisals.

Suggested Fields for Your Inventory Template:

1. **Stamp Name**: The common or official name of the stamp.
2. **Country of Origin**: The issuing country or postal authority.
3. **Issue Year**: The year the stamp was released.
4. **Condition**: Mark as Mint, Used, or specify details (e.g., lightly canceled, hinged).
5. **Catalog Number**: Include Scott, Stanley Gibbons, Michel, or relevant catalog references.
6. **Design Theme**: Add themes like wildlife, sports, or historical events.
7. **Estimated Value**: Track the current market value or appraisal price.
8. **Purchase Information**: Record the date, source, and price paid for the stamp.
9. **Notes**: Include any unique features, such as watermarks, errors, or provenance.

Tip: Use spreadsheet software (like Excel, Google Sheets, or Stamp Mate) to digitize your inventory for easy sorting, searching, and backup.

B. Grading Checklist: Evaluating Stamp Condition

A grading checklist helps ensure consistency and accuracy when assessing stamp quality. This is especially useful for high-value items or when preparing for sales or exhibitions.

Categories to Evaluate:

1. **Centering**: Determine how well the design is aligned within the stamp margins (e.g., Perfectly Centered, Off-Center).
2. **Perforations**: Inspect perforations for uniformity, completeness, and alignment.
3. **Gum Condition**: For mint stamps, check if the original adhesive is intact and unaltered (e.g., pristine, slightly disturbed, or regummed).
4. **Surface Wear**: Look for creases, folds, smudges, or stains on the stamp's face.
5. **Color Vibrancy**: Assess whether the colors are bright and true to the original design or faded over time.
6. **Postmark Quality**: For used stamps, evaluate the clarity, placement, and aesthetic appeal of the cancellation mark.
7. **Damage Assessment**: Note any tears, thinning, or missing sections.

Tip: Create a numeric scoring system for each category (e.g., 1–10) to calculate an overall grade for your stamps.

C. Organizational Guides: Structuring Your Collection

Templates for organizing your collection provide a framework for displaying your stamps in a logical and visually appealing manner.

1. **Thematic Layout Template**:
   - Organize stamps by themes, such as flora, fauna, space exploration, or cultural heritage.
   - Include subcategories for better structure (e.g., "Birds" under "Wildlife" or "Olympics" under "Sports").
2. **Chronological Layout Template**:
   - Arrange stamps by issue year or significant historical eras.

        - Add explanatory notes for historical context, highlighting events tied to each stamp.
3. **Geographical Layout Template**:
    - Group stamps by continent, country, or region.
    - Include maps or visuals to enhance understanding and interest.
4. **Custom Display Layout Template**:
    - Design templates for unique arrangements, such as favorite acquisitions, high-value items, or rare errors.

Tip: Use acid-free sheets, labeled dividers, or digital organizing tools to keep your layouts neat and safe.

Practical Applications:

- **Personal Use:** Adapt these templates to reflect your collection's size, focus, and goals.
- **Sharing:** Share organized layouts with fellow collectors or at exhibitions for a polished presentation.
- **Efficiency:** Save time by standardizing how you record, grade, and organize your stamps.

By leveraging these templates, you can enhance both the enjoyment and management of your stamp collection while ensuring its value and significance are well-documented.

Appendix D: Auction Preparation Checklist

Participating in stamp auctions can be both exciting and rewarding, offering access to rare and valuable items that can elevate your collection. To ensure success and avoid common pitfalls, follow this comprehensive step-by-step guide to prepare effectively for auctions.

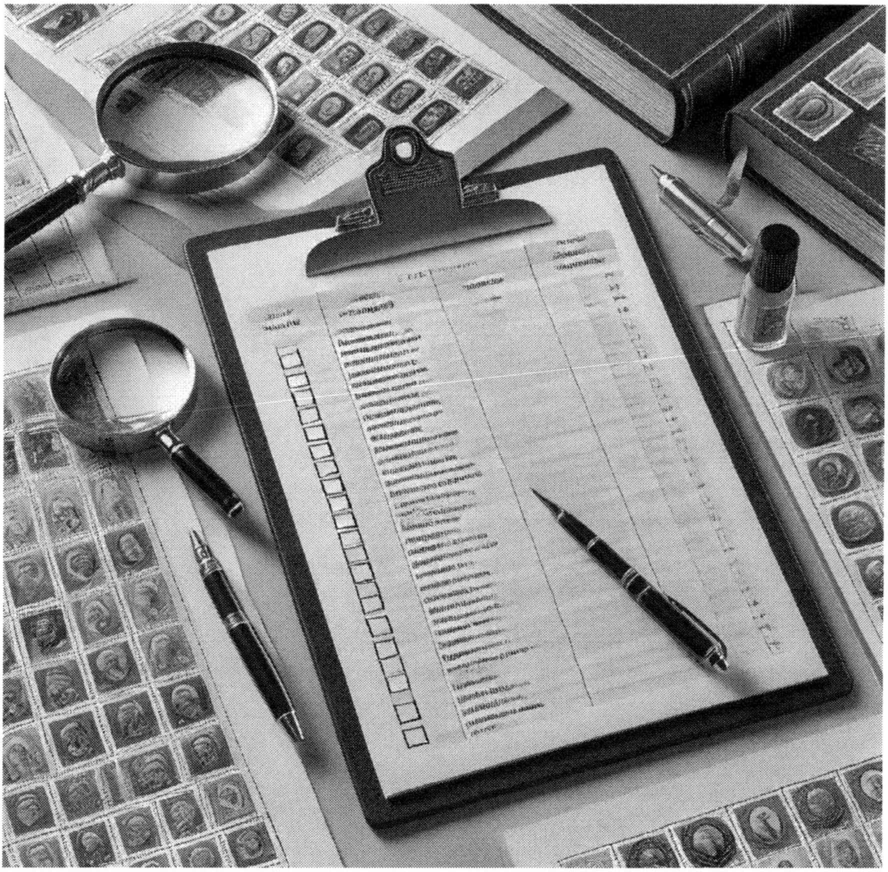

Prepare for auctions with a step-by-step guide to success.

A. Before the Auction: Laying the Groundwork

Preparation is key to making informed decisions and maximizing your success.

1. **Research the Auction House**:
   - Verify the auction house's reputation by checking reviews, collector forums, or past performance.
   - Ensure the house specializes in philatelic items and has a track record of authenticity and transparency.

2. **Set a Clear Budget**:
    - Define your overall spending limit to avoid overspending.
    - Break down your budget by lot, prioritizing high-interest items.
3. **Review the Auction Catalog**:
    - Study the catalog thoroughly, noting detailed descriptions, estimated prices, and condition reports.
    - Shortlist items of interest based on your collection goals, themes, or investment strategies.
4. **Verify Authenticity and Condition**:
    - Examine provided images for details like centering, perforations, and postmarks.
    - Contact the auction house for additional information or images if necessary.
5. **Research Market Prices**:
    - Compare listed items with current market values in catalogs, online platforms, or previous auction results.
    - Identify potential bargains or overpriced lots.

Tip: Prepare a list of maximum bids for your shortlisted items to maintain focus during the auction.

B. During the Auction: Navigating the Process

Staying composed and strategic during the auction ensures you make the most of the experience.

1. **Arrive Early (for In-Person Auctions)**:
    - Preview items in person to assess their condition and authenticity firsthand.

- Take notes on your shortlisted items for quick reference during bidding.

2. **Follow Bidding Strategies**:
   - Start with a moderate opening bid to gauge competition without overcommitting.
   - Avoid emotional bidding by sticking to your pre-determined limits.
3. **Monitor Trends**:
   - Pay attention to the bidding patterns of competitors to identify when interest in an item is waning.
   - Be prepared to adjust your strategy for highly competitive lots.
4. **Stay Alert for Opportunities**:
   - Keep an eye on overlooked or undervalued lots that may present unexpected bargains.
   - Consider smaller, less popular lots for hidden gems.

Tip: If attending an online auction, ensure a stable internet connection and test the bidding platform beforehand.

C. After the Auction: Post-Sale Success

Securing your winnings is just the beginning—proper follow-up ensures your purchases add value to your collection.

1. **Verify Your Purchases**:
   - Inspect acquired items for accuracy against their descriptions and images.
   - Report any discrepancies to the auction house immediately.
2. **Request Certificates of Authenticity**:

    - For high-value items, obtain certification from a trusted philatelic organization if not already provided.
    - Retain all documentation for future reference and resale potential.

3. **Update Your Inventory**:
    - Record your new acquisitions with details such as lot numbers, purchase prices, and catalog references.
    - Photograph each item to maintain a complete and organized record.

4. **Reflect and Refine**:
    - Assess your performance and results to identify areas for improvement.
    - Note bidding trends, successful strategies, and lessons learned for future auctions.

Tip: Practice at smaller or local auctions to build confidence and refine your strategies before participating in larger events.

Practical Applications:

- **Beginners:** Use this checklist to gain confidence and navigate the auction process effectively.
- **Advanced Collectors:** Enhance your strategy and streamline your participation in competitive auctions.
- **Investors:** Maximize returns by carefully selecting and authenticating high-value items.

By following this auction preparation checklist, you can approach every auction with confidence, ensuring a rewarding and successful experience while building a collection that reflects your passion and expertise.

Appendix E: Collection Tracking Spreadsheet

A well-maintained tracking spreadsheet is an invaluable tool for managing your stamp collection, providing easy access to important details, monitoring your collection's value, and ensuring organized documentation. This appendix outlines how to create a comprehensive and user-friendly spreadsheet tailored to your philatelic needs.

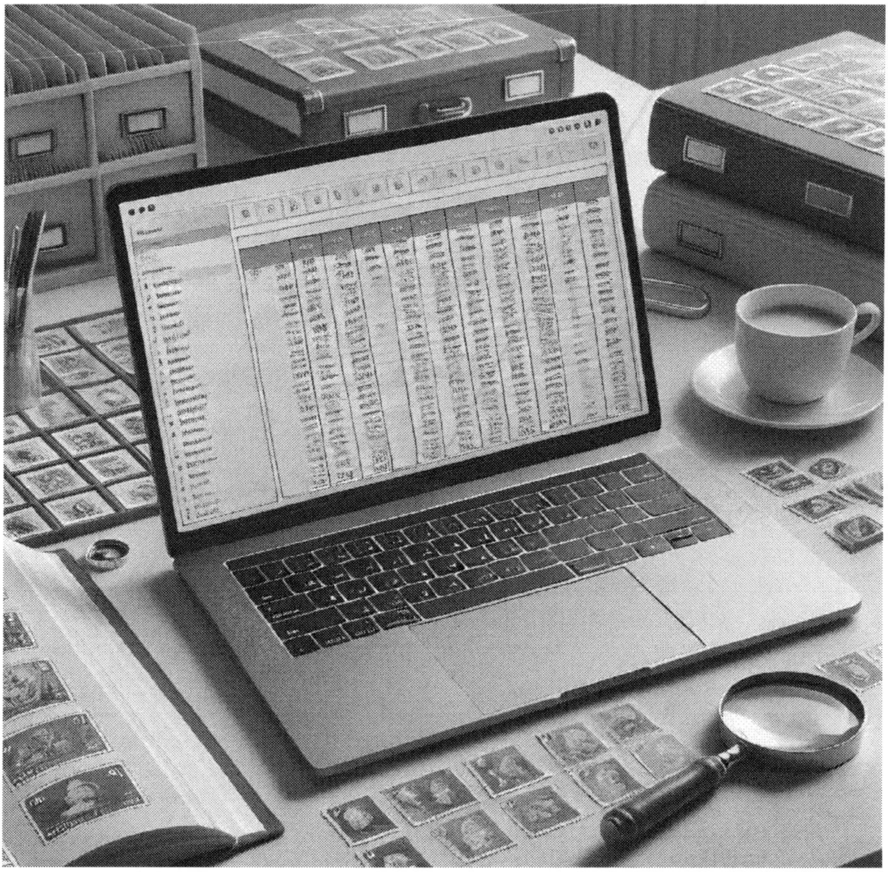

Keep your collection organized with a detailed tracking spreadsheet.

A. Key Columns to Include

Design your spreadsheet with these essential columns to capture all relevant information about your stamps:

1. **Stamp Name**:
    - Example: "Penny Black" or "1935 Silver Jubilee Issue."
    - Use this column to specify the name or title of each stamp or series.
2. **Country of Origin**:
    - Record the issuing country or territory, e.g., "United Kingdom" or "India."
    - Helps you group stamps geographically or by origin themes.
3. **Issue Date**:
    - Note the year or exact date of the stamp's release.
    - Useful for chronological organization and historical reference.
4. **Denomination**:
    - Enter the face value of the stamp, e.g., "1 Cent" or "5 Francs."
    - Critical for identifying stamps in series or distinguishing similar designs.
5. **Condition**:
    - Options: Mint, Used, Hinged, or Damaged.
    - Helps evaluate the overall value and appeal of each stamp.
6. **Catalog Number**:
    - Include references from catalogs like Scott, Stanley Gibbons, or Michel.

- Enables easy cross-referencing during research or appraisal.

7. **Purchase Price**:
   - Record the amount you paid for each stamp.
   - Useful for tracking investments and calculating profit margins.
8. **Current Value**:
   - Update regularly based on market trends, auction results, or appraisals.
   - Provides insight into your collection's financial growth.
9. **Notes**:
   - Add details about provenance, rarity, or historical significance.
   - Example: "First-day issue with original envelope" or "Limited-edition commemorative."

B. Features to Enhance Your Spreadsheet

1. **Color Coding**:
   - Assign colors to highlight specific themes, eras, or regions.
   - Example: Green for modern issues, blue for classic stamps, or red for rare finds.
2. **Dropdown Menus**:
   - Use dropdown menus for consistent data entry in fields like condition or country.
   - Simplifies input and reduces errors.
3. **Summary Section**:
   - Create a separate section to calculate:

        - **Total Stamps**: Count the total entries in your collection.
        - **Total Purchase Cost**: Sum of all purchase prices.
        - **Total Value**: Sum of all current values for a snapshot of your collection's worth.
        - **Profit/Loss**: Subtract total purchase cost from total value to track your investment performance.

4. **Filters and Sorting**:
    - Add filters to sort stamps by date, country, or condition.
    - Quickly locate specific entries based on your criteria.
5. **Image Attachments**:
    - If using advanced software, link high-resolution images to each entry.
    - Visual references make identification and sharing easier.

C. Storing and Securing Your Spreadsheet

1. **Cloud-Based Platforms**:
    - Use services like Google Sheets, Excel Online, or Dropbox for remote access and real-time updates.
    - Cloud storage provides automatic backups and allows collaboration with other collectors.
2. **Regular Updates**:
    - Schedule periodic reviews to update values, add new acquisitions, or refine data.
    - Keeping your spreadsheet current ensures accurate records for insurance, sales, or appraisals.
3. **Backup Copies**:

    - Create offline backups on external drives or local storage for added security.
    - Protect your data from accidental deletions or internet issues.

Practical Applications

- **Beginners**: Start with basic fields like name, origin, and condition, and expand your tracking system as your collection grows.
- **Advanced Collectors**: Use the spreadsheet to analyze trends, identify gaps in your collection, or prepare for auctions and sales.
- **Investors**: Track market values to monitor returns on investment and make data-driven decisions.

By customizing your tracking spreadsheet to suit your collection's needs, you'll have a powerful tool for organizing, evaluating, and enjoying your stamps. With accurate records and accessible data, you can take your philatelic journey to the next level and make informed decisions about your collection's future.

Appendix F: The Best Stamp Shows and Events Worldwide

Stamp shows and events provide unparalleled opportunities to network, learn, and expand your collection. This appendix highlights premier philatelic gatherings in the U.S. and beyond, offering something for every collector.

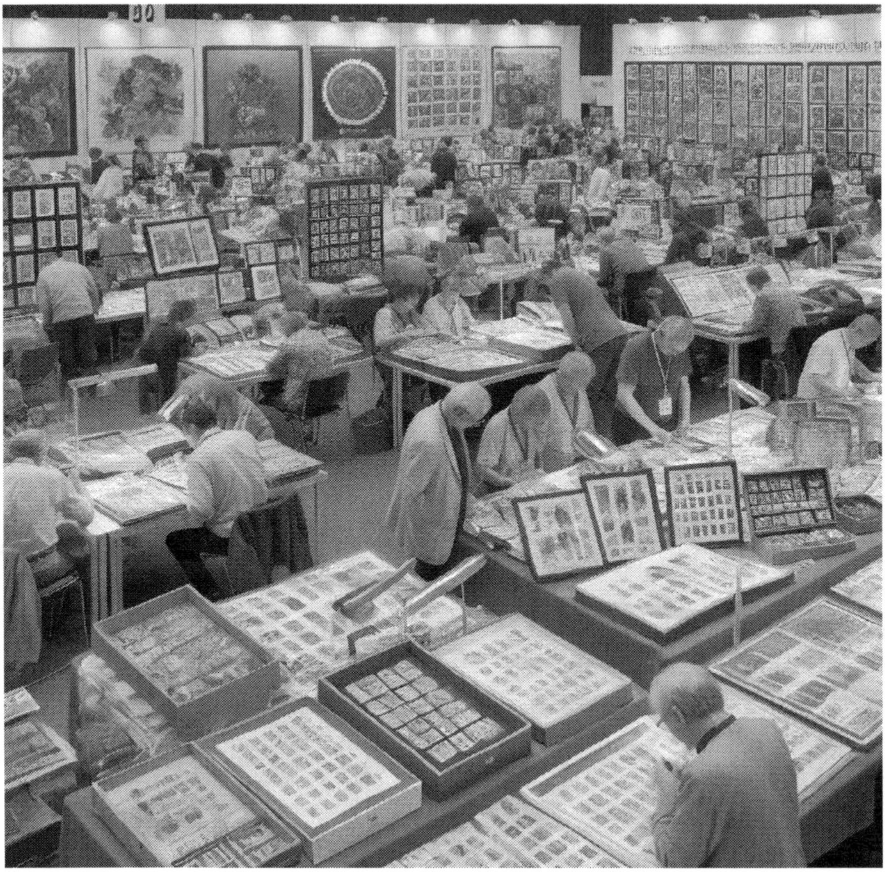

Discover the world's premier stamp shows and connect with collectors.

A. World Stamp Show (USA)

- **Overview**: Held every decade, this is the largest stamp exhibition in the U.S., attracting global attention.
- **Highlights**:
    - Rare and iconic exhibits like the Penny Black and Inverted Jenny.
    - Live auctions, educational workshops, and interactive displays.

    - Opportunities to meet top dealers and collectors.
- **Website**: www.ny2016.org (Check for the next World Stamp Show updates)
- **Why Attend**: The ultimate philatelic event for both beginners and seasoned collectors.

B. Great American Stamp Show (USA)

- **Overview**: The largest annual stamp show in the U.S., hosted by the American Philatelic Society (APS).
- **Highlights**:
    - Features over 100 dealers, live auctions, and thematic exhibits.
    - APS members showcase award-winning collections.
    - Educational seminars for collectors of all levels.
- **Website**: www.stamps.org/great-american-stamp-show
- **Why Attend**: A must-attend for U.S. collectors, offering extensive buying, selling, and networking opportunities.

C. WESTPEX Stamp Show (USA)

- **Overview**: A prestigious annual stamp show held in the San Francisco Bay Area.
- **Highlights**:
    - Known for its high-quality exhibits and rare material from around the world.
    - Features specialty societies and thematic displays.
    - A well-curated bourse with reputable dealers.
- **Website**: www.westpex.org

- **Why Attend**: A premier event on the West Coast, perfect for exploring unique collections and networking with top-tier dealers.

D. Chicagopex Stamp Show (USA)

- **Overview**: One of the oldest philatelic events in the Midwest, showcasing both modern and historical stamps.
- **Highlights**:
    - Competitive exhibits judged by accredited philatelists.
    - Access to regional and national dealers specializing in U.S. and worldwide stamps.
    - Workshops and youth activities to engage new collectors.
- **Website**: www.chicagopex.com
- **Why Attend**: A Midwest favorite for collectors seeking a mix of traditional and contemporary philatelic materials.

E. London International Stamp Exhibition (UK)

- **Overview**: A world-class event held every decade, attracting collectors from all over the globe.
- **Highlights**:
    - Renowned for its prestigious exhibits and auctions.
    - A gathering of international dealers and thematic displays.
    - Educational talks and expert panel discussions.
- **Website**: www.london2022.co
- **Why Attend**: A deep dive into global philately, offering insights into rare British and international issues.

F. ARIPEX Stamp Show (USA)

- **Overview**: An annual show in Arizona that focuses on both competitive exhibits and a dealer-friendly bourse.
- **Highlights**:
  - Competitive exhibits recognized by the APS.
  - Access to Western U.S. dealers and rare finds.
  - A welcoming environment for collectors of all experience levels.
- **Website**: www.aripex.org
- **Why Attend**: Perfect for collectors looking to explore unique regional offerings.

G. China International Collection Expo (China)

- **Overview**: A leading event in Asia showcasing the philatelic richness of the region.
- **Highlights**:
  - Exhibitions featuring ancient and modern Asian stamps.
  - Auctions of regional rarities and themed collections.
  - Insights into Asia's growing philatelic market.
- **Website**: www.chinaexhibition.com (Search for "stamp expos")
- **Why Attend**: Discover the unique artistry and history of Asian stamps in a global context.

H. Essen Stamp Fair (Germany)

- **Overview**: A European hub for philatelists, with a focus on historical and thematic collections.
- **Highlights**:

- Extensive dealer offerings and live auctions.
- Access to European philatelic tools and resources.
- A showcase of European philatelic artistry and history.

- **Website**: www.briefmarkenmesse-essen.de
- **Why Attend**: Ideal for collectors interested in European issues and historical pieces.

I. Practical Tips for Attending Stamp Shows

1. **Plan Ahead**:
   - Research event schedules and participating dealers.
   - Book accommodations early, especially for international events.
2. **Prepare Your Collection**:
   - Bring a list of stamps or themes you're seeking.
   - Pack essential tools like magnifiers, catalogs, and protective sleeves.
3. **Engage with Exhibitors**:
   - Ask questions and share your collecting goals.
   - Learn about trends and values from industry experts.
4. **Combine Philately with Travel**:
   - Explore local attractions and museums during your visit.
   - Make your trip memorable by immersing yourself in the culture of the host city.

Attending stamp shows not only enhances your collection but also provides valuable experiences to connect with the philatelic community. With more U.S. events included, this appendix ensures collectors have access to opportunities close to home and abroad, offering endless possibilities to grow their passion for stamps.

Appendix G: Quick-Reference Guides

Quick-reference guides are an indispensable tool for stamp collectors, providing essential information at a glance. Whether you're identifying a new addition, preserving your collection, or evaluating its worth, these guides serve as your go-to resource. Designed for ease of use, they ensure you can make informed decisions on the spot, whether at home, a show, or an auction. Below are detailed, practical guides covering identification, preservation, and valuation.

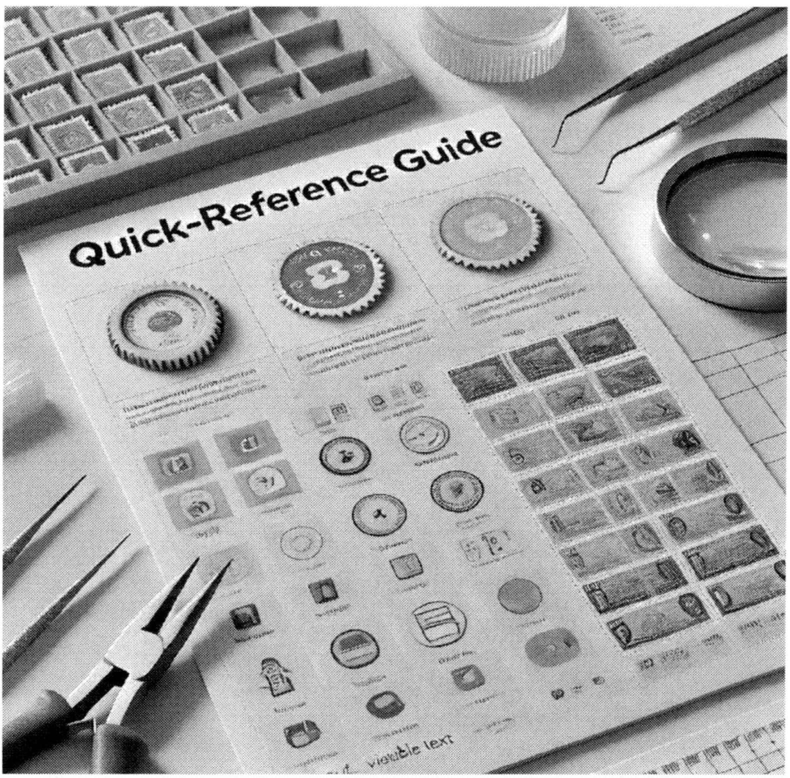

Keep essential philatelic tips at your fingertips.

A. Stamp Identification Guide

Accurate identification is the cornerstone of philately. This guide highlights key features and techniques to help you confidently identify stamps by their origin, era, and production details.

Key Tips for Identification:

1. **Country of Origin:**
    - Look for inscriptions: Many stamps clearly display the issuing country's name. For instance, U.S. stamps often feature "USA," while British stamps may include the monarch's image instead of a country name.
    - Learn international symbols: Some countries use unique scripts or symbols, like Japan's kanji or Cyrillic on Russian stamps.
2. **Era and Time Period:**
    - Check for issue dates: Many modern stamps include visible years of issuance, while older stamps require referencing cataloged designs.
    - Stylistic indicators: Recognize era-specific designs, such as the ornate frames on Victorian-era stamps versus the minimalist aesthetics of modern stamps.
3. **Printing Techniques:**
    - Examine the surface: Use a magnifying glass to distinguish between engraved (raised lines) and lithographed (smooth surface) stamps.
    - Check for microprinting: Modern security features often include tiny text or details visible only under magnification.

Notable Features to Analyze:

- **Watermarks:** Hold stamps up to light or use watermark detectors to reveal hidden patterns that verify authenticity.

- **Perforations:** Use a perforation gauge to measure holes along the edges, as these can distinguish between similar issues.
- **Cancellations:** Study postmarks for historical or geographical context, which can enhance a stamp's story and value.

B. Preservation Best Practices

Proper preservation is essential for maintaining a stamp collection's value, aesthetics, and longevity. This guide outlines best practices to protect your stamps from environmental damage and improper handling.

What to Do:

1. **Storage Materials:**
    - Invest in archival-quality, acid-free albums, stock books, and mounts to prevent yellowing and deterioration.
    - Use glassine envelopes or clear mounts to protect individual stamps from direct contact.
2. **Handling Stamps:**
    - Always use tweezers or tongs with soft, rounded tips to avoid transferring oils or dirt from your hands.
    - Handle with clean, dry hands when necessary, and hold stamps by their edges to prevent creases or smudges.
3. **Climate Control:**
    - Store stamps in a cool, dry environment, maintaining humidity levels between 30% and 50%. Extreme humidity can cause mold or adhesive degradation.
    - Avoid direct sunlight or fluorescent lighting, which can fade ink and damage paper over time.
4. **Regular Inspections:**

    - Periodically review your collection for signs of mold, fading, or pest damage. Early detection can prevent widespread issues.

What Not to Do:

- **Avoid Adhesives:** Never use glue, tape, or any sticky substances to mount or display stamps, as these can cause irreversible damage.
- **Don't Stack Unprotected Stamps:** Overlapping stamps can lead to scratches, tears, or gum transfer.
- **Limit Exposure:** Avoid leaving stamps in high-temperature areas like attics or near heat sources.

C. Valuation Overview

Determining a stamp's value involves evaluating several factors, from its rarity to its condition. This guide provides a quick framework for assessing worth.

Key Factors Influencing Value:

1. **Rarity:**
    - Stamps issued in limited quantities, discontinued designs, or with printing errors are highly sought after.
    - Examples: The British Guiana 1c Magenta and the Inverted Jenny are prized for their extreme rarity.
2. **Condition:**
    - Stamps in mint condition, with intact gum and no flaws, command the highest prices.
    - Common flaws like tears, creases, or discoloration can reduce value significantly.
3. **Demand:**

    - Themes like space exploration, famous personalities, or wildlife attract broad interest and often hold strong market demand.
    - Limited-edition thematic issues frequently gain popularity over time.
4. **Provenance:**
    - A well-documented history or certification enhances a stamp's credibility and value.
    - Certificates of authenticity from recognized organizations like the American Philatelic Society (APS) add buyer confidence.

Practical Steps for Valuation:

- **Consult Catalogs:** Use resources like Scott, Stanley Gibbons, or Michel catalogs to compare catalog numbers, descriptions, and values.
- **Auction Research:** Study recent auction results to gauge real-world pricing trends for similar stamps.
- **Seek Expert Opinions:** Professional appraisals or dealer consultations can provide precise evaluations, especially for high-value items.

Practical Tip:

Print and laminate these guides for portability or save digital copies to your smartphone or tablet. Having quick access to these resources ensures you're prepared for auctions, shows, or on-the-spot evaluations.

By integrating these quick-reference guides into your philatelic toolkit, you can enhance your expertise and confidence in every aspect of stamp collecting. Whether you're identifying a rare find, ensuring proper preservation, or evaluating value, these tools are essential companions for any collector.

These appendices are your gateway to mastering the art of philately, equipping you with the practical tools, trusted resources, and essential knowledge to thrive in this fascinating hobby. Whether you're organizing your collection, enhancing your expertise, or exploring the vibrant community of collectors, let these guides serve as your trusted companions. With **HowExpert Guide to Stamp Collecting** as your resource, you're now prepared to refine your skills, expand your collection, and leave your unique mark in the ever-evolving world of stamp collecting.

About HowExpert

HowExpert publishes quick 'how to' guides on all topics from A to Z. Visit HowExpert.com to learn more.

About the Publisher

Byungjoon "BJ" Min (민병준) is an author, publisher, entrepreneur, and the founder of HowExpert. He started off as a once broke convenience store clerk to eventually becoming a fulltime internet marketer and finding his niche in publishing. He is the founder and publisher of HowExpert where the mission is to make a positive impact in the world for all topics from A to Z. Visit BJMin.com and HowExpert.com to learn more. John 14:6

Recommended Resources

- HowExpert.com – How To Guides on All Topics from A to Z.
- HowExpert.com/free – Free HowExpert Email Newsletter.
- HowExpert.com/books – HowExpert Books
- HowExpert.com/courses – HowExpert Courses
- HowExpert.com/clothing – HowExpert Clothing
- HowExpert.com/membership – HowExpert Membership Site
- HowExpert.com/affiliates – HowExpert Affiliate Program
- HowExpert.com/jobs – HowExpert Jobs
- HowExpert.com/writers – Write About Your #1 Passion/Knowledge/Expertise & Become a HowExpert Author.
- HowExpert.com/resources – Additional HowExpert Recommended Resources
- YouTube.com/HowExpert – Subscribe to HowExpert YouTube.
- Instagram.com/HowExpert – Follow HowExpert on Instagram.
- Facebook.com/HowExpert – Follow HowExpert on Facebook.
- TikTok.com/@HowExpert – Follow HowExpert on TikTok.

Printed in Great Britain
by Amazon

fb26237d-3b8f-48a0-b12c-85da5a23463cR01